COMPUTER SUPPORTED COOPERATIVE WORK

Also in this series

CSCW in Practice: An Introduction and Case Studies
(ISBN 3-540-19784-2)
Dan Diaper and Colston Sanger (Eds.)

Computer Supported Collaborative Writing
(ISBN 3-540-19782-6)
Mike Sharples (Ed.)

CSCW: Cooperation or Conflict?
(ISBN 3-540-19755-9)
Steve Easterbrook (Ed.)

Design Issues in CSCW
(ISBN 3-540-19810-5)
Duska Rosenberg and Chris Hutchison (Eds.)

and Tyler (1991), Gray et al. (1993). So far, however, in the CSCW literature only scant attention has been paid to the use of AI techniques. Thus, it is opportune to offer the present book as the first to be devoted to the task of exploring in detail the ways in which AI may contribute to CSCW.

One of the key features of this book is its multidisciplinary nature, with technological, organizational, psychological, linguistic and semiotic perspectives all being represented. This multidisciplinarity is inherent in the subject matter of the book, and is therefore entirely appropriate.

A concept that has emerged as central in discussion of AI in relation to HCI is that of the "agent". This notion features in every one of the eleven chapters of this book. The reader should note, however, that not all authors use the term "agent" in exactly the same way. Some apply the term to any entity, human or automatic, that is capable of taking an initiative, whereas others restrict its use to computer-based processes that act on behalf of human users or other software processes. (The sense in which each author in the present volume employs the term is made clear in the relevant chapters.) Despite this terminological variation, however, the core notion of an intelligent system possessed of the ability to carry out useful tasks without slavish prompting by another is common to most concepts of "agent", and will be seen to recur throughout the book.

Intercommunication among agents, too, is an important theme, which is addressed by several authors. Its relevance stems from the fact that CSCW is a field in which the application of Distributed Artificial Intelligence (DAI) readily suggests itself.

The chapters that follow are all revised versions of papers presented at a seminar organized by the UK Department of Trade and Industry CSCW Special Interest Group at Kingsgate House, London, on 30 June 1992. The eleven contributions will now be briefly introduced.

Since the concept of the agent is of such significance in the present book, we have chosen to introduce the book with a chapter by Michael Smyth, entitled "Towards a Cooperative Software Agent", which begins with an outline history of the term "agent" and its usage in both AI and HCI. Smyth then proceeds to examine another crucial concept in CSCW, namely "cooperation", and discusses how this relates to the behaviour of agents. Finally, he describes an implemented system in which both key concepts (agents and cooperation) have been realized.

John H. Connolly and
Ernest A. Edmonds (Eds.)

CSCW and Artificial Intelligence

Springer-Verlag
London Berlin Heidelberg New York
Paris Tokyo Hong Kong
Barcelona Budapest

John H. Connolly, PhD
Department of Computer Studies
University of Technology
Loughborough
Leicestershire LE11 3TU, UK

Ernest A. Edmonds, PhD
Department of Computer Studies
University of Technology
Loughborough
Leicestershire LE11 3TU, UK

Series Editors

Dan Diaper, PhD
Department of Computer Science
University of Liverpool
PO Box 147, Liverpool L69 3BX, UK

Colston Sanger
GID Ltd
69 King's Road
Haslemere, Surrey GU27 2QG, UK

ISBN-13: 978-3-540-19816-1 e-ISBN-13: 978-1-4471-2035-3
DOI: 10.1007/978-1-4471-2035-3

British Library Cataloguing in Publication Data
A catalogue record for this book is available from the British Library

Library of Congress Cataloging-in-Publication Data
A catalog record for this book is available from the Library of Congress

Typeset from authors' disks by The Electronic Book Factory, Fife, Scotland.

34/3830–543210 Printed on acid-free paper

Preface

Computing, despite the relative brevity of its history, already evolved into a subject in which a fairly large nun of subdisciplines can be identified. Moreover, there has l a noticeable tendency for the different branches of the sul each to develop its own intellectual culture, tradition momentum. This is not, of course, to suggest that any indi ual subdiscipline has become a watertight compartment or developments in one branch of the subject have tended to place in total isolation from developments in other related a Nevertheless, it does mean that a deliberate effort is require order to bring different subdisciplines together in a fruitful beneficial manner.

Artificial Intelligence (AI) and Computer Supported Coop tive Work (CSCW) jointly constitute a good example of branches of computing that have emerged separately and g rise to largely distinct research communities and initiatives the one hand, the history of AI can be traced back to the 1 the term "Artificial Intelligence" being generally attribute John McCarthy, who first used it in print in 1956. "Comp Supported Cooperative Work", on the other hand, is a ter more recent coinage, having been devised by Irene Greif Paul Cashman in 1984.

CSCW is generally associated with, or included within, broader area of Human–Computer Interaction (HCI). Thi right and proper, since CSCW involves communicating v user interface with a process mediated by that interface CSCW, of course, the process concerned is not the operatio a computer program but the communicative activity of ano human being in cooperating towards the achievement of s common goal; hence the distinctive nature and characte CSCW in comparison with other branches of computing.

In recent years, AI has come to play an increasingly impor role within conventional HCI, with the notion of intelligent u interfaces coming into prominence; see, for example, Sulli

Both agents and their intercommunication are discussed in Chapter 2, by Rachel Jones and Ernest Edmonds, "A Framework for Negotiation". This contribution deals with the issue of designing knowledge-based CSCW systems aimed at supporting a geographically distributed group of users engaged in negotiating solutions to problems. The CSCW system makes available to the group computer-based tools that support the decision making activity. The authors offer a theoretical framework to assist in the design of this kind of system. The framework involves the recognition of several different types of agent, in addition to other knowledge-based components, and the provision of the necessary communication channels to sustain their interaction.

Interaction among agents is also a central issue in the chapter by Alan Dix, Janet Finlay and Jonathan Hassell, "Environments for Cooperating Agents: Designing the Interface as Medium". The main thrust of this contribution is that the user interface should be seen as the medium via which agents can communicate with one another and act upon the passive elements (or objects) within the system. This view has the interesting consequence of providing a means of reconciling consistency with adaptivity in the interface: adaptivity is made the remit of agents, while the interface itself is made to offer a stable environment for human–computer interaction. The application of such ideas to CSCW areas such as conferencing is also discussed.

Providing for interaction among agents within a system inevitably raises the question of appropriate architectures. This issue is addressed by Douglas McGregor, Craig Renfrew and Iain MacLeod in their chapter, "Domain Knowledge Agents for Information Retrieval". Taking as their field of application the problems experienced by engineers in finding the information they require in documents such as journals or compendia of standards, the authors identify three different types of agent which together may assist users in the task of retrieving relevant information. Moreover, the agent architecture proposed in this chapter has the advantage not only of providing for the retrieval of such information but also enabling it to be shared among different users.

The next chapter, "Autonomous Agents in the Support of Cooperative Authorship" by Geof Staniford and Paul Dunne, again deals with system architecture, but this time in relation to the writing rather than the reading of documents. A vital aspect of the contribution of these authors is the presentation of a graph-based formalism for specifying architectural design of systems which, like the one described in this chapter, incorporate intercommunicating agents.

The following chapter, by Gregory O'Hare, Paul Dongha, Linda Macaulay and Steve Viller, is entitled "Agency within CSCW: Towards the Development of Active Cooperating Working Environments", and is concerned with the cooperative capture of system requirements by geographically distributed, multidisciplinary teams of people. The authors propose an agent-based system to support this cooperative requirements capture process. Once again, system architecture figures among the topics discussed. Another important consideration is the social dynamics of the team members during the cooperative process, and the system is designed to help manage these.

Team problem solving and its support by means of a computing system is also the concern of John Gammack and Robert Stephens in their chapter, "A Model for Supporting Interacting Knowledge Sources". They offer a formal model, both for representing expert knowledge relevant to the solution of problems in a domain such as metallurgical quality control and for describing the interactions among team members during the problem solving process.

The description of interactions is also a central issue in David Benyon's chapter, "A Functional Model of Interacting Systems: A Semiotic Approach", in which a model of interaction that provides a basis for understanding the prerequisites for and the process of communication among agents is proposed. This model, being semiotically founded, embodies a view of communication as the exchange of meaningful and structured signals, which have to be interpreted in relation to their context.

Context is also a vital consideration in Stefan Kirn's contribution, entitled "Supporting Human Experts' Collaborative Work: Modelling Organizational Context Knowledge in Cooperative Information Systems". In this chapter, the author demonstrates why a knowledge of the organizational context of tasks is required for an effective computer-based system that supports collaborative work among human users. The application domain around which discussion revolves is that of cooperative expert systems in banking.

A further dimension to the treatment of communication in the present volume is provided by John Connolly's chapter, "Artificial Intelligence and Computer Supported Cooperative Working in International Contexts". Drawing where appropriate on concepts from linguistics, the author outlines various kinds of problems that can arise when geographically distributed users with different national/cultural backgrounds attempt to

engage in CSCW. He then suggests ways in which AI may be employed in order to reduce the difficulties involved.

The book ends with a somewhat cautionary chapter by David Jennings, "On the Definition and Desirability of Autonomous User Agents in CSCW". The author points out that practitioners of different academic disciplines may have rather different ideas of what an "agent" is, and that this fact represents an obstacle to the idea of taking agents as the basis for user interface design. Instead, he argues, the task and other aspects of the context in which the group work is to be carried out should determine whether agents should be incorporated and what intelligence they should manifest.

It will thus be evident that the application of AI to CSCW is an area in which a multiplicity of approaches exist and controversy is to be expected. Many questions are unanswered, and even unasked. However, it is clear from this volume that a number of central issues remain. Understanding the human users' tasks, capabilities and preferences must be high on any research agenda. Of particular concern is the scope that can be offered to autonomous system agents while generating real benefit to users. The resolution of an agreed set of underlying architectural concepts is also important for the enabling and encouraging of research in the application of AI to CSCW. It is hoped that the present volume will serve as a stimulus to further investigation of the field and to further enlightening debate.

Loughborough
1993

John Connolly
Ernest Edmonds

John H. Connolly and
Ernest A. Edmonds (Eds.)

CSCW and Artificial Intelligence

Springer-Verlag
London Berlin Heidelberg New York
Paris Tokyo Hong Kong
Barcelona Budapest

John H. Connolly, PhD
Department of Computer Studies
University of Technology
Loughborough
Leicestershire LE11 3TU, UK

Ernest A. Edmonds, PhD
Department of Computer Studies
University of Technology
Loughborough
Leicestershire LE11 3TU, UK

Series Editors

Dan Diaper, PhD
Department of Computer Science
University of Liverpool
PO Box 147, Liverpool L69 3BX, UK

Colston Sanger
GID Ltd
69 King's Road
Haslemere, Surrey GU27 2QG, UK

ISBN-13: 978-3-540-19816-1 e-ISBN-13: 978-1-4471-2035-3
DOI: 10.1007/978-1-4471-2035-3

British Library Cataloguing in Publication Data
A catalogue record for this book is available from the British Library

Library of Congress Cataloging-in-Publication Data
A catalog record for this book is available from the Library of Congress

Typeset from authors' disks by The Electronic Book Factory, Fife, Scotland.

34/3830–543210 Printed on acid-free paper

Preface

Computing, despite the relative brevity of its history, has already evolved into a subject in which a fairly large number of subdisciplines can be identified. Moreover, there has been a noticeable tendency for the different branches of the subject each to develop its own intellectual culture, tradition and momentum. This is not, of course, to suggest that any individual subdiscipline has become a watertight compartment or that developments in one branch of the subject have tended to take place in total isolation from developments in other related areas. Nevertheless, it does mean that a deliberate effort is required in order to bring different subdisciplines together in a fruitful and beneficial manner.

Artificial Intelligence (AI) and Computer Supported Cooperative Work (CSCW) jointly constitute a good example of two branches of computing that have emerged separately and given rise to largely distinct research communities and initiatives. On the one hand, the history of AI can be traced back to the 1950s, the term "Artificial Intelligence" being generally attributed to John McCarthy, who first used it in print in 1956. "Computer Supported Cooperative Work", on the other hand, is a term of more recent coinage, having been devised by Irene Greif and Paul Cashman in 1984.

CSCW is generally associated with, or included within, the broader area of Human–Computer Interaction (HCI). This is right and proper, since CSCW involves communicating via a user interface with a process mediated by that interface. In CSCW, of course, the process concerned is not the operation of a computer program but the communicative activity of another human being in cooperating towards the achievement of some common goal; hence the distinctive nature and character of CSCW in comparison with other branches of computing.

In recent years, AI has come to play an increasingly important role within conventional HCI, with the notion of intelligent user interfaces coming into prominence; see, for example, Sullivan and Tyler (1991), Gray et al. (1993). So far, however, in the CSCW literature only scant attention has been paid to the use of AI techniques. Thus, it is opportune to offer the present book as the first to be devoted to the task of exploring in detail the ways in which AI may contribute to CSCW.

One of the key features of this book is its multidisciplinary nature, with technological, organizational, psychological, linguistic and semiotic perspectives all being represented. This multidisciplinarity is inherent in the subject matter of the book, and is therefore entirely appropriate.

A concept that has emerged as central in discussion of AI in relation to HCI is that of the "agent". This notion features in every one of the eleven chapters of this book. The reader should note, however, that not all authors use the term "agent" in exactly the same way. Some apply the term to any entity, human or automatic, that is capable of taking an initiative, whereas others restrict its use to computer-based processes that act on behalf of human users or other software processes. (The sense in which each author in the present volume employs the term is made clear in the relevant chapters.) Despite this terminological variation, however, the core notion of an intelligent system possessed of the ability to carry out useful tasks without slavish prompting by another is common to most concepts of "agent", and will be seen to recur throughout the book.

Intercommunication among agents, too, is an important theme, which is addressed by several authors. Its relevance stems from the fact that CSCW is a field in which the application of Distributed Artificial Intelligence (DAI) readily suggests itself.

The chapters that follow are all revised versions of papers presented at a seminar organized by the UK Department of Trade and Industry CSCW Special Interest Group at Kingsgate House, London, on 30 June 1992. The eleven contributions will now be briefly introduced.

Since the concept of the agent is of such significance in the present book, we have chosen to introduce the book with a chapter by Michael Smyth, entitled "Towards a Cooperative Software Agent", which begins with an outline history of the term "agent" and its usage in both AI and HCI. Smyth then proceeds to examine another crucial concept in CSCW, namely "cooperation", and discusses how this relates to the behaviour of agents. Finally, he describes an implemented system in which both key concepts (agents and cooperation) have been realized.

Contents

Contents

Contributors

David Benyon

Computing Department, The Open University, Walton Hall, Milton Keynes MK7 6AA, UK

John H. Connolly

LUTCHI Research Centre, Department of Computer Studies, Loughborough University of Technology, Loughborough LE11 3TU, UK

Alan Dix

Department of Computer Science, University of York, Heslington, York YO1 5DD, UK

Paul Dongha

Department of Computation, UMIST, PO Box 88, Manchester M60 1QD, UK

Paul E.S. Dunne

Department of Computer Science, University of Liverpool, Chadwick Building, PO Box 147, Liverpool L69 3BX, UK

Ernest A. Edmonds

LUTCHI Research Centre, Department of Computer Studies, Loughborough University of Technology, Loughborough LE11 3TU, UK

Janet Finlay

Department of Computing and Mathematics, University of Huddersfield, Queensgate, Huddersfield HD1 3DH, UK

John G. Gammack

Department of Computing and Information Systems, University of Paisley, High Street, Paisley PA1 2BE, UK

Jonathan Hassell

Department of Computer Science, University of York, Heslington, York YO1 5DD, UK

David Jennings
Occupational Psychology Branch, Employment Service, B3 Porterbrook House, Pear Street, Sheffield S11 8JF, UK

Rachel Jones
LUTCHI Research Centre, Department of Computer Studies, Loughborough University of Technology, Loughborough LE11 3TU, UK

Stefan Kirn
Westfaelische Wilhelms-Universität Münster, Institut für Wirtschaftsinformatik, Grevener Strasse 91, D-4400 Münster, Germany

Linda A. Macaulay
Department of Computation, UMIST, PO Box 88, Manchester M60 1QD, UK

Iain A. MacLeod
Department of Civil Engineering, University of Strathclyde, 26 Richmond Street, Glasgow G1 1XH, UK

Douglas R. McGregor
Department of Computer Science, University of Strathclyde, 26 Richmond Street, Glasgow G1 1XH, UK

Gregory M.P. O'Hare
Department of Computation, UMIST, PO Box 88, Manchester M60 1QD, UK

Craig R. Renfrew
Department of Computer Science, University of Strathclyde, 26 Richmond Street, Glasgow G1 1XH, UK

Michael Smyth
LUTCHI Research Centre, Department of Computer Studies, Loughborough University of Technology, Loughborough LE11 3TU, UK

Geof Staniford
Department of Computer Science, University of Liverpool, Chadwick Building, PO Box 147, Liverpool L69 3BX, UK

Robert A. Stephens
Faculty of Computer Studies and Mathematics, University of the West of England, Bristol BS16 1QY, UK

Steve Viller
Department of Computation, UMIST, PO Box 88, Manchester M60 1QD, UK

Chapter 1

Towards a Cooperative Software Agent

M. Smyth

1.1 Introduction

This chapter introduces the concept of software agents and focuses on their impact at the level of the user interface, particularly the relationship between the level of task action undertaken by agents and their corresponding representation to the user. It is proposed that this relationship is central to the widespread acceptance of software agents because it will shape the dynamics of current and future interactions. Existing interaction strategies adopted by human problem solving groups are reviewed, and cooperation is proposed as a behavioural metaphor on which to base software agents. The chapter concludes with a description of a prototype cooperative partner agent, developed as part of the Human Computer Cooperation Project (Alvey MMI/062), undertaken at the LUTCHI Research Centre.

1.1.1 The Concept of Software Agents

The study of software agents has blossomed during the past six years, most notably in the fields of Artificial Intelligence (AI) and Human–Computer Interaction (HCI). While attempts to implement agents are still relatively new, some of the concepts that underpin the work date back to the 1950s. The idea of an agent can be attributed to the work of both John McCarthy ("The Advice Taker"; McCarthy 1959) and Oliver Selfridge ("The Pandemonium Paradigm for Learning"; Selfridge 1959). Their idea was deceptively simple. Systems were conceived as being goal directed entities that communicated in human terms and undertook various tasks on behalf of the user. An agent would be a "soft robot" living and doing its business within the computer's world (Kay 1984).

1.1.2 A Description of Software Agents

Today, software agents are studied from two complementary perspectives. The first, which can be characterized as the AI approach, views software agents as entities within a larger community of agents. The inspiration for much of this work can be attributed to Marvin Minsky and in particular to his book *The Society of the Mind* (Minsky 1987). In the prologue of this book, Minsky described how he would show that you can build a mind from many little parts, each mindless by itself. It was this that Minsky referred to as the Society of the Mind, an idea where each mind is made up of many small processes: "These [processes] we'll call agents. Each mental agent by itself can only do some simple thing that needs no mind or thought at all. Yet when we join these agents in societies – in certain very special ways – this leads to true intelligence" (Minsky 1987). This position forms the basis of Distributed Artificial Intelligence (DAI), where agents are viewed as entities with different skills and knowledge, but essentially part of a community or society. Through a process of communication, agents collaborate in order to solve a shared problem. A wider perspective on distributed agents is claimed by Decentralized Artificial Intelligence (DzAI), which focuses on the activities of essentially autonomous agents in a multi-agent world (Demazeau and Muller 1990). In DzAI, agents are viewed as independent or autonomous, in that each agent has its own existence which is not justified by the existence of other agents. Each agent may accomplish its own tasks or cooperate with other agents to perform a personal or global task. Critically, DAI and DzAI share a common interest in the problem solving behaviour of distributed entities. (For further discussion of DAI, see Chapters 6, 8 and 9. The subject of cooperation is addressed in Chapters 3, 5, 6, 9, 10 and 11.)

The second approach to the study of software agents concentrates on the necessity for agents to interact with users at the level of the interface. How agents behave, and how this behaviour is perceived by the user via the interface, will be critical to widespread acceptance of agent technology (see Chapter 11 for further discussion). Agents provide expertise, skill and labour. They must of necessity be capable of understanding the needs and goals of the user and how they will impact upon the agents' task performance. User goals can be derived either implicitly, by monitoring the current activity state and its associated history, or explicitly, based on specific instruction by the user. Agents will be required to translate those goals into an appropriate set of actions, which will be undertaken independently of the user. Finally, agents must be able to deliver results in a form that is both amenable to the user and pertinent to the current task. Throughout the whole process the agent must be able to determine when further information is required and appropriate sources of that information (Laurel 1990).

1.1.3 Agents as Processes

Users will interact with agents, which will manage and perform processes on their behalf in order to achieve the users' goals. The study of software agents forms part of the vanguard in the move to encompass the study of processes within the traditionally tool-based approach to computing. Just such a shift of emphasis was predicted by Alan Kay when he stated that tool-based "manipulation is still vibrantly alive, not exhausted. But it is now time to consider management of intelligent computer processes as an inevitable partner to tool-based work and play" (Kay 1990). The creation of autonomous processes that can be successfully communicated with and managed will be a qualitative jump from the tool, yet one that must be made. A successful transition will be mediated by the user interface.

1.1.4 An Analogy Based on Human Agents

In order to identify some of the characteristics associated with agency, it is proposed to draw an analogy with human interaction. If one's goal is to paint a door, or more literally to have the door in a painted state, the first action might be to select an appropriate tool from the available tool set; in this case, a paintbrush. The next state would be to interact or operate the tool in such a way as to perform the process of painting the door. If successful, the action of performing this process will achieve the original goal. Alternatively, one could employ the services of an agent – in this analogy, a painter – to perform the process on your behalf in order to achieve the original goal. The act of employing an agent highlights a number of issues pertinent to the design of software agents which aspire to such a role at this level of the interface. Employing the services of an agent involves the requirement to communicate the goal such that a sufficient level of agreed understanding is achieved. Implicit within the user–agent relationship is the assumption that the agent has sufficient task knowledge to perform the process successfully. Agents are employed to achieve goals for us either when we do not possess sufficient knowledge or when we cannot spare the necessary time to undertake them. Finally, in terms of the analogy, it is conceivable that the painter might subcontract various processes to more specialized agents. Software agents can be thought of in a similar way to the human "painter agent", in that they perform processes on behalf of the user or, indeed, other processes (Pankoke-Babatz 1989). In terms of the distinction between the manipulation of tools and the management of processes, software agents are indeed tools but, as with human agents, they are characterized by the processes that they perform.

1.1.5 Characteristics of an Interface Agent

Critical to the acceptance and widespread usage of software agents will be the level of sophistication in terms of the processes they can undertake on behalf of the user. Coupled with this will be the level of representation of action exhibited by the agents.

The initiation of dialogue with a software agent will centre on the communication of goals. If agents are to evolve from a highly task-specific nature to the position of being able to perform complex tasks, they must provide a mechanism whereby users can adequately express their goals. These goals will, in the majority of cases, be ill formed and vague. In order to interpret such requests, agents will require a high level of task-specific knowledge, i.e. a task model. The level of detail to express a goal will be directly related to the degree of task knowledge contained in the agent. Agents will be required to know when and how to present results to the user, and the timing of when information should be presented with respect to what the user is currently doing. Also, the form of representation of information should be such that it will be immediately accessible to the user. In short, software agents will be required to incorporate a user model (see also Chapters 10 and 11). Finally, agents must be aware of the available information sources and how to access supplementary data appropriate to the current task.

Laurel (1990) has identified three characteristics central to the development of software agents: responsiveness, competence and accessibility. What is clear is that the degree to which each of these requirements will have to be met will be determined by the nature of the task that the agent is designed to undertake. This is not underestimating the difficulty. Ultimately complex task participation will require sophisticated software agents.

Currently, agents perform routine background tasks, for example sorting new mail into folders as it arrives or automatically reminding the user of deadlines (e.g. OBJECT LENS, Crowston and Malone 1988), facilitate interaction with databases (e.g. GUIDES, Laurel et al. 1990) or attempt active participation during problem solving (e.g. EAGER, Cypher 1991). As software agents become more sophisticated in terms of their task actions, a corresponding development must occur with respect to their interaction with the user (Laurel 1991). The representation of agent behaviour, as perceived by the user, will shape the dynamics of current and future interaction. The acceptance of software agents by users will be determined by a combination of the tasks they undertake and their representation to the user. Their behaviour must be both recognizable and predictable by the user. The challenge to software designers is how best to incorporate the characteristics of agents into a coherent representation. It is proposed that interaction with software agents should be based on existing models of human interaction. In particular, the study of the dynamics of small, task-orientated, human groups could reveal both behavioural and task characteristics critical to the acceptance of software agents as active participants in this problem solving relationship.

1.2 Cooperation: A Behavioural Metaphor for Software Agents

If software agents are to move successfully from the performance of routine, background tasks to the point where they will actively participate during problem solving, then their behaviour must be based on a consistent model. The study of interpersonal behaviour among human groups could provide a rich source of data for the design of computer systems. Tasks requiring joint or dependent actions from human participants can lead to either cooperative or competitive behaviour (Marwell and Schmitt 1975). Several factors have been identified which affect this choice of behavioural strategy. These include the nature of the task, the expectations of the participants and the personal goals of either party. If cooperation, and not competition, is to be the model of interaction between the agent and the user, it is essential to identify the task-related and social factors that induce such behaviour among humans.

1.2.1 Factors that Induce and Maintain Human Cooperation

Central to the maintenance of cooperative behaviour among humans is the existence of superordinate goals. These are goals that are compelling for the individuals involved, but that cannot be achieved by one individual by his or her own efforts. Such work was initially reported by Sherif and Sherif (1953), and later replicated by Blake and Mouton (1962) and Blake et al. (1964), for a variety of tasks. The existence of superordinate goals would appear to be one of the strongest factors in the development and maintenance of cooperation, among both individuals and groups.

Cooperation is not a fixed pattern of behaviour but is a changing, adaptive process directed to future results. The representation (and understanding) of intent by every participant is essential to cooperation. Cooperation places a special burden on communication between participants. For example, Grice's "cooperative principle" has identified quality, quantity, relevance and manner as guidelines to communication during cooperation (Grice 1975). The style, as well as the content, of communication facilitates cooperation, but does not create cooperation (Shure et al. 1965). Communication that can be identified by the other party as reducing potential threat is best suited to increasing cooperative behaviour (Deutsch and Krauss 1960).

Cooperative behaviour among human groups is maintained by a combination of such factors as clarity of communication, exchange of information and the existence of superordinate goals.

1.2.2 Task Factors that Support Cooperation

Not all tasks enable the potential of cooperation to be realized. Tasks that require a single correct answer (e.g. mathematical problems) tend to provide little scope for cooperation, whereas situations where more than one possible answer is sought provide a problem solving environment that favours cooperation. Empirical support was provided by Husband (1940), who found that pairs were superior to individuals when working on problems requiring some originality or insight, but not on more routine arithmetic problems.

1.2.3 Advantages of Cooperation During Problem Solving

Empirical studies of cooperative behaviour between humans appear to support the contention that joint effort during complex problem solving tasks is reflected in both the process of achievement and the quality of solution (Deutsch 1949a, 1949b, 1968; Laughlin et al. 1968). Dynamic social interaction during complex problem solving may reinforce or negate existing beliefs and support the formation of new attitudes between and within the participants. It is the potential for mutual growth that makes cooperative behaviour so important in human problem solving.

1.2.4 Human–Computer Interaction

Cooperation is an active process. The aim of software agents is to evolve into active participants with the human user during problem solving. It therefore seems a natural progression that software agents could employ some of the techniques of cooperation in order to present the human user with a coherent model of interaction. In order to facilitate the human user, software agents should aspire to exhibit cooperative behaviour. Consequently, a cooperative agent, while remaining focused on an expressible goal, could prompt the human user to adopt a more divergent style of thinking during problem solving. It is suggested that such interaction will foster a greater interdependency between the human and the agent and, as a consequence, increase the quality of solution and encourage greater user satisfaction.

A principal element of cooperative behaviour during problem solving is the creation of an environment where solutions can be refined by logical argument and the resolution of different perspectives. Through these discussions the very essence of the problem is revealed. Essential to this view is the ability of either party to generate and communicate alternative solutions, as it is these that spark the iterative process of solution implicit in cooperation (Broadbent 1973). In short, different but sympathetic beliefs are vital to a successful and productive cooperative relationship. Although it is recognized as being only one facet of the complex relationships involved in human cooperation, the generation of alternative solutions is felt to provide a starting point for representing the cooperative relationship between a human and a machine.

1.3 The Cooperative Machine

The remainder of this chapter describes work undertaken at Loughborough University of Technology between 1986 and 1989, as part of the Alvey Initiatives Human–Computer Cooperation (HCC) Project (MMI/062). A more detailed description of the work can be found in Smyth and Clarke (1990) and Clarke and Smyth (1993).

The goal of this work was to develop a single-user cooperative mechanism where the generation of a satisfactory solution could be enhanced by a machine having the ability to generate alternative and supplementary information based on a solution proposed by the user. It was never the project's intention to build a software agent. In fact, the term "agent" was not common currency at the outset of the work. It is only in retrospect that the mechanisms developed within the HCC project appear to have relevance to software agents. Thus it is from the rather fortunate position of hindsight that the work will be reviewed and the findings related to the current trend toward agent technology.

The cooperative machine was based on a design reflecting three processes identified as being central to cooperation: (i) the existence of superordinate goals, referred to as goal-orientated working; (ii) a model that contained knowledge about the specific task domain and would thereby represent the computer-based partner, referred to as a Partner Model; and (iii) a language common to both the cooperating parties, referred to as the Agreed Definition Knowledge Base (ADKB).

1.3.1 The Underlying Mechanisms of a Cooperative Machine

1.3.1.1 Goal-Orientated Working

If the cooperative relationship is to succeed, there must be agreement at the outset of the goal to be accomplished. A goal may be defined as the intended state of an object or the intended relationship between two or more objects. The action of achieving the goal is directed toward goal objects, which may be physical or virtual, and can result in their creation, elimination or modification. Goal objects have an associated number of attributes which may be altered in the act of achieving a goal (Smyth and Clarke 1990). For example, in the analogy of painting the door, successfully achieving the goal will result in a change in the colour attribute associated with the door object.

1.3.1.2 The Partner Model

In order to generate alternative solutions it was necessary to construct a model, consisting of domain-specific rules which had access to a knowledge base common to both machine and user, the ADKB. The application of the model's rule set to the ADKB and the communication of the result represented the process of alternative solution generation.

The partner model's functions were to generate alternatives and to facilitate interaction with the user. To reflect the divergence of thinking, characteristic of cooperation, the partner model was autonomous from the user.

1.3.1.3 The Agreed Definition Knowledge Base

Clarity of communication is vital to successful cooperation. Consequently, it is important that all participants share the same object definitions. Definitions may be updated during the lifetime of the task as long as changes are agreed by both parties.

1.3.2 An Exemplar of Human–Computer Cooperation

1.3.2.1 The Task Domain

If a task is to benefit from cooperative working, it must be one where solutions are reached through logical debate. Appropriate domains are those in which there exist no right or wrong answers, only better or worse ones. Typically, such domains are characterized by a balance of requirements and constraints. The problem domain of room layout design was chosen to illustrate this process of cooperation.

At the outset of implementation two design decisions were made: (i) to place, when possible, control of the interaction in the hands of the user; and (ii) to minimize the requirement for explicit broadband communication by adopting the technique of graphically based interaction. The exemplar was implemented in C-Prolog on a Hewlett-Packard workstation and used a general purpose environment developed as part of the HCC project.

1.3.2.2 The Interface

In order to present alternative solutions, while not distracting the user, the decision was made to implement two dedicated graphical windows which represented views of the floorplans of the user and the partner. Other user-initiated actions, such as the construction of goals, were catered for by software buttons. Two modes of interaction were available: solve and interactive. In the solve mode, the partner model generated solutions based on the current active goals and the location of objects in the user's solution. In the interactive mode, the partner model was controlled by the user's choice of object locations, and it updated its solution after each user action.

1.3.2.3 The Agreed Definition Knowledge Base

The exemplar contained a deliberately constrained, hand crafted object set which was presented visually throughout the interaction. The object set included items of furniture typically found in offices. Selection of an object generated an instance, which could then be used as part of a goal expression or placed directly on the floorplan. Based on this data, the partner model generated an alternative solution, which it displayed in its window. Throughout this process parallel knowledge bases were continually updated, reflecting the user and partner solutions. At all times transfer of data from the databases was at the discretion of the user, who could either freeze objects in the user's window, thereby disabling the effect of the partner model, or transfer object configurations generated by the partner model to be incorporated in the user solution.

1.3.2.4 Goal-Orientated Working

A software technique developed as part of the HCC project provided the enabling technology for the representation of goal-orientated working. Using a graphically based method of interaction, users were able to construct spatial relationships between objects, which were then translated into a Prolog rule base, enabling manipulation by the partner model. A representative number of spatial relationships were available and users were able to construct and delete goals as required during the interaction. The mechanism also included simple error checking, which alerted the user to possible goal conflict. Once the goal list had been created, the appropriate order of object placement was calculated. For example, if the following goals were created:

(i) phone1 ON desk2
(ii) desk2 NEAR wall3

the desk would have to be located first prior to satisfying the initial goal.

1.3.2.5 The Partner Model

Central to the performance of the partner model was a representative rule base concerned with the proportionality of objects within a finite space; in this case, the location of furniture within a room. Example rules included symmetry, golden section and safety. At any stage in the development of the user's solution the partner model could interrogate the appropriate rule base and, via the application of its rules, generate an alternative solution within the user defined goals. The user also had the ability to alter the priority of the partner model's rules. This enabled the user to view a number of alternative object configurations, each generated by the partner model, but each reflecting a different emphasis on style.

1.4 Conclusions

The results of the HCC project's initial attempt to build a machine based on the principles of cooperation have a number of implications for the design of future software based agents, particularly if it is envisaged that agents will successfully evolve from the role of assistants to that of active partners in the problem solving relationship. The study of the techniques employed within human interaction, in particular cooperation, have provided valuable insights into the requirements of such a relationship.

Cooperation is a dynamic blend of cognitive and behavioural characteristics aimed at future events. The challenge facing software design is how to represent such an interaction within a machine. The degree of cooperation achieved by an agent will be determined by the interaction of the underlying mechanisms, not by their individual actions. How the resulting agent behaviour will be manifest to the user will be dependent on the interface. If agents are to be perceived as cooperative then their behaviour must reflect the dynamic nature of the relationship. To this extent the partner model failed because it was static, resulting in predictable alternatives which soon failed to act as a spur to the user's imagination. The perception of cooperation changes over time, and if agents are to be cooperative they must reflect this ability to adapt. Mechanisms should be provided that enable the agent to change with respect to the human partner and also with respect to the task. Changes can be achieved either by enabling end user manipulation of the knowledge bases or by the incorporation of task related data from alternative sources. For instance, the technique of programming by example has been adopted as a method for creating the task-specific agents available in Hewlett-Packard's New Wave 4.0 environment (Linderholm 1992). The experience of building a machine based on cooperative principles has led to the conclusion that two distinct functionalities should be incorporated in a cooperative agent: (i) a user model which manages the representation and presentation of information tailored to the needs of the particular user; and (ii) a task model which is independent of the user and forms the basis of agent generated alternative solutions. It is critical that part of this knowledge remains autonomous from the user if the agent is to avoid the pitfall of simply mimicking the solutions generated by the human partner.

A number of general conclusions can be drawn from the work. Firstly, the depth of task knowledge required to support cooperative working suggests that the technique is domain-specific. Secondly, what constitutes cooperation varies between tasks. Consequently, the existing problem solving process adopted by human partners must be clearly identified before attempting to build a cooperative agent. Finally, it will be the interaction of the underlying mechanisms represented in the agent and how the resulting behaviour is manifest to the user, via the interface, that will determine the extent of cooperative participation perceived by the user.

If software based agents are to interact fully with their human counterparts at a meaningful level during complex problem solving, then their behaviour should be based on existing models used during human interaction. Cooperation is one such model.

Acknowledgements The work described was funded by the Alvey programme (MMI), Human–Computer Cooperation (MMI/062). Thanks are due to my colleagues at the LUTCHI Research Centre, in particular Ernest Edmonds and Tony Clarke.

Chapter 2

A Framework for Negotiation

R. Jones and E. Edmonds

2.1 Introduction

This chapter presents a framework to assist in the construction of applications which support group working, in particular, the activity of negotiation. The framework is intended to provide knowledge-based support for individuals within the group and for the group itself, rather than replace, or partially replace, some of the actors by automatic systems. The concern, therefore, is with the organization and support of negotiation between the human actors in the system, between the humans and the knowledge-based components and between the knowledge-based components themselves.

The chapter outlines the context of the work and describes the three types of negotiation supported by the framework. It identifies three interrelated categories of support in order to convey the concepts incorporated in the framework: communications support, task support and group support. It outlines the software components within the scope of these categories, with particular emphasis on describing the intelligent agents.

The term "agent", as it is used in this chapter, means a software-based module that assumes responsibility for carrying out particular activities, and, at times, might act on behalf of users. Agents vary in their degree of autonomy and might need to communicate with actors (human agents) and other agents.

2.2 Context

The aim of the work reported here was to support the human activity of negotiation. To explain what is meant by this, consider a problem which requires the knowledge and expertise of a group of people to arrive at a satisfactory solution (Branki et al. 1993). The group discusses the problem and comes to a shared understanding of the issues. Several solutions are explored and tools are often used to answer "what if" questions. There are technical implications to consider, in addition to political issues concerned with the power positions of the various roles that the participants assume. Participants have stakes in the outcome of the discussion which may lead to conflicts, and highly confrontational situations are expected still to require conventional meetings to resolve them. Finally, the group arrives at a solution.

To put this activity in context, the spatial planning domain can be used as an example (Branki et al. 1994). Consider the siting of a major supermarket in a town. The main issue regarding where the supermarket is to be located is assumed to have been agreed. This might have involved a confrontational meeting between urban planners, the developer and representatives of the local community, such as councillors. However, there will be more detailed issues to resolve, such as where the entrance and exit to the supermarket will be located, and details of its architectural form. An urban planner may take the lead role in such a meeting. In addition, there might be representatives of the developers, the supermarket owner and traffic planners. Issues raised might include consideration of traffic congestion, ease of access to the supermarket, expected usage of the supermarket and car-parking provision. Tools that are required might include a site plan, a road map of the area, a map of the local population, a map showing local car-parking facilities, a map showing the location of nearby buildings and sophisticated traffic flow modelling tools. There are the technical implications to consider, and, in addition, there could well be some conflict between the developers and traffic planners, whose interests may differ at certain points.

It may be difficult for the interested parties to meet at appropriate times when the problem needs further discussion. In addition, it may not be possible to bring the necessary tools to the meeting that would inform the discussion. Thus, there is a requirement for remotely supporting this type of activity. Participants located at different places may wish to participate in what is termed a "conference", that is, a technology assisted discussion.

The central question that this chapter addresses is: what type of support needs to be provided by the software system to enable the activity of negotiation to take place? Whenever a software system is built, the issue of human–machine allocation of "function" is raised. In other words, decisions are made regarding the functions that are performed by the machine and those performed by the users. The decision depends partly on whether it is feasible for the machine to perform a particular function.

However, the levels of automation can be dynamic. That is, it is possible to construct a software system that enables users, if they wish, to perform the functions, and if not, for the software to handle them. Hence, it is possible to have a form of negotiation between the software and users. In summary, decisions have to be made regarding what parts of the activity the machine will support, what should be left to the users and what should be negotiated between the machine and the users.

The user or group negotiation with the machine is related to an important issue in Computer Supported Cooperative Work (CSCW) concerned with tailorability. This involves identifying parts of the activity that need to be tailored by individuals and by the group. Many systems that have been built to support group working have failed. Grudin (1990) outlines reasons for these failures, including "Groupware may fail if it does not allow for the wide range of exception handling and improvisation that characterizes much group activity". It can be argued that users should always be given the choice, but that the added burden of being aware of the meta-communication may distract users from the task at hand. Thus, sensible defaults are required for parts of the activity.

The software system presented in this chapter consists of a number of components, some of which incorporate knowledge-based support. Hence, the support for the activity is distributed among a number of knowledge bases. Edmonds and Ghazikhanian (1991) develop a strategy for how this distribution might take place. It has been proposed that negotiation is an appropriate metaphor for the cooperation between distributed knowledge bases. (For further discussion of cooperation, see Chapters 1, 3, 5, 6, 9, 10 and 11.)

Thus, the system can be viewed as supporting three levels of negotiation: negotiation between users, negotiation between the user or group

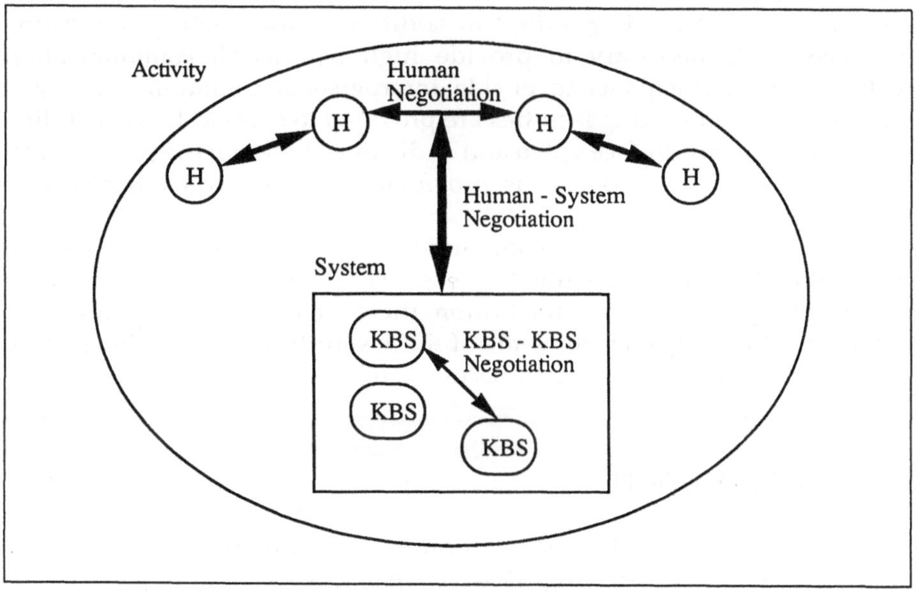

Fig. 2.1.

and the system, and negotiation between distributed knowledge bases. Figure 2.1 illustrates this point.

2.3 The Framework

This chapter presents a framework which assists developers in building groupware applications. The framework is composed of reusable components that can be modified by developers in the construction of applications to support group working. Decisions have been made concerning the type of support that the framework should provide and a practical attempt has been made to tackle the tailorability issue.

A prototype application will be built for the spatial planning domain using the framework. It will be evaluated and the findings fed back into a subsequent design. Thus, the software practice of iterative development and formative evaluation will be followed.

In order to convey the concepts that have been incorporated into the framework, the activity is considered as requiring three types of interrelated support: communications support, task support and group support. These are discussed in Sections 2.4, 2.5 and 2.6, respectively.

2.4 Communications Support

McGrath (1984) indicates that for tasks involving conflict, rich interpersonal information is required in addition to information concerning the task. It is necessary to provide high bandwidth communication between the participants to enable interpersonal communication. Full multimedia conferencing facilities are provided to support this capability. These include face-to-face video and audio links between the participants. The communications support is provided by a low level infrastructure external to the framework.

There are still shortfalls in communication between the participants. It is not possible for participants to be as aware of others as they might be in a meeting environment. In addition, there are technological limitations which need to be overcome. Some of these shortfalls can be compensated for by mechanisms specified in Section 2.6.

2.5 Task Support

As suggested above, the negotiation process might require tools to assist the group in arriving at its decision. Tools can be defined by the particular decision support capability they provide. Traditionally, conventional tools, such as a site plan, might have been used. However, more sophisticated computer tools are now available, which help users to try out possible solutions. For example, a geographical information system is required by the particular activity outlined in Section 2.2.

The tools should be capable of supporting a task that the users and the group might wish to perform. Participants might employ a number of tools to perform a task, therefore the tools should be integrated. In addition, participants need to be equally adept at using the tools (Greenberg 1991), which requires that they are highly usable.

Many tools exist that provide the required functionality, but are not directly supportive of the task and are difficult to use. Edmonds and McDaid (1990), in work associated with the FOCUS ESPRIT project, have developed an architecture that incorporates existing systems and extends their usage by adding an intelligent front-end. The front-end consists of user support components that directly support the task, a user harness that greatly improves the usability of the tools, and a back-end manager that maps an application-independent specification into an executable specification, thus integrating the applications. The components are located within the architecture as shown in Fig. 2.2. They communicate via an abstract interaction language which enables the system to operate in a heterogeneous and distributed machine environment (Edmonds et al. 1992).

The user support agents negotiate with the user for information that the application requires to perform the necessary functionality. If the user does not provide the information, then, depending on its importance, the agents might inform the user of the implications, make possible recommendations and take subsequent actions.

The user harness is composed of several components that address the presentation of information to the user. It provides this capability for heterogeneous machines and for workstations with different multimedia capabilities. In addition, the harness assesses the cognitive load of information and decides whether further information should be displayed or

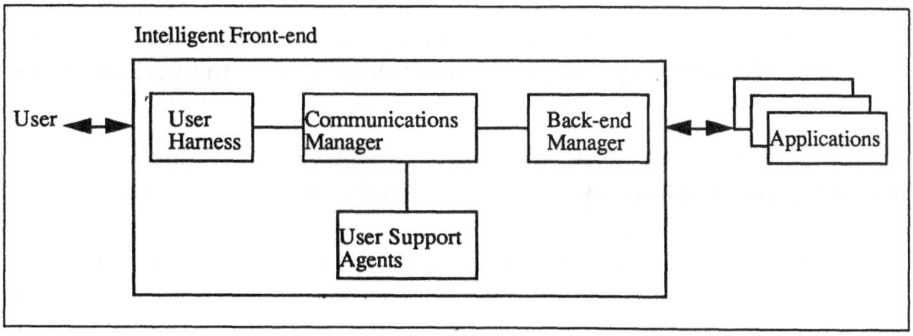

Fig. 2.2.

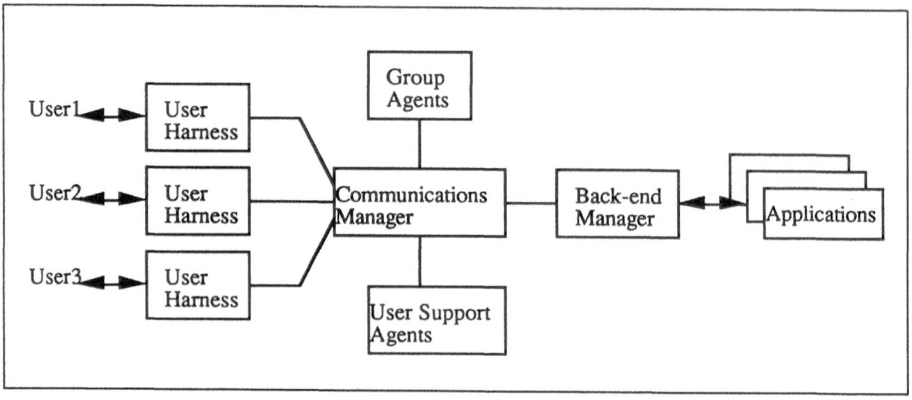

Fig. 2.3.

whether information that is on display should be removed. The user harness is an intelligent component.

The framework presented in this chapter extends the FOCUS system for group working. It incorporates existing systems, user support agents, a back-end manager and group agents (which are discussed in Section 2.6), and enables the addition of a user harness for each user, as shown in Fig. 2.3. In order that each user might interact with the applications, distribution facilities are provided by the communications manager. The distribution facilities enable the same information to be displayed to all participants and each user to utilize the functionality provided by the applications. The result is a system appropriate to and usable by a number of users.

The distribution facilities are limited, owing to the inherent design of the applications, which are built to support individuals rather than groups. Shortfalls in this area are compensated for by the group agents.

It could be argued that the group task is different to a single-user task and therefore imposes different requirements. Although, ultimately, developers will be able to write groupware by making calls to a library of function calls, experimentation is required to find out what this library should contain. In addition, front-ending existing applications has the advantage of decoupling the group functionality from the back-ends (for further discussion of architectures, see Chapters 4, 5, 6, 8 and 9).

2.6 Group Support

Group support addresses the support that the group requires to carry out its collective task and the benefits to be obtained by having an activity mediated by an intelligent system. In addition, group support compensates for the shortfalls that occur in communications support because of the restrictions placed on the interpersonal communication and the technical limitations. It also compensates for the shortfalls in distribution facilities because of the use of existing single-user systems.

The addition of group agents within the framework provides the group support requirements. The agents vary in their degree of autonomy: some group agents negotiate with users concerning group issues, others are completely autonomous, while some negotiate with agents in other parts of the system (for further discussion of autonomy, see Chapters 7 and 11).

An important consideration is to make the framework as usable and flexible as possible, though these can be opposing requirements. The framework is based on object-oriented principles (see Chapters 4 and 6), which enables developers to modify its components to suit the application. Group agents have been identified and are detailed in the following sections.

2.6.1 Conference Agent

The conference agent handles conference initialization and termination, and the joining and leaving of participants. The conference agent interacts with the conference initiator and with other users. It maintains a record of the participants in the group and informs participants of conference members.

Three types of conference are supported. Firstly, it is possible to initiate conferences for a predetermined group of users. The conference agent sets up the conference and invites the participants. Secondly, the conference initiator is presented with a selection of possible participants. Once the initiator has chosen the participants, the conference agent invites them to join. Thirdly, it is possible to have open conferences, where any user can join when they wish. Participants are also given the option to leave the conference when they wish. The conference agent coordinates with the facilitator agent when a member joins or leaves the conference (see Section 2.6.6).

Permitted users can terminate the conference. These might include: any participant, the conference initiator, the facilitator, the floor holder (see Section 2.6.2). The conference agent coordinates with the facilitator agent at the initiation and termination of the conference.

2.6.2 Floor Agent

The framework supports collaboration-transparent applications; that is, single-user applications that handle serial input and output. The framework enables developers to extend these applications to support group working and multiple users. In order to maintain the integrity of interaction with the application, serial input is obtained either by filtering the input to a single response or by permitting only one user to enter input at a time. If each user's input were delivered to the application, it is possible that two users could respond to the same application state, but the first response would alter the state so the second response would not have the expected effect. The choice of filtering input or restricting input depends on the type of floor policy selected.

Various types of floor policy are supported, including: pre-emptive, explicit request, first come, baton or ring-passing, round-robin and facilitated. The conference agent negotiates with users over the choice of floor policy. If the choice is not the pre-emptive policy, it becomes necessary to control the floor according to the policy. This entails setting up the floor permissions and enabling changes in the floor control.

Human actors that have been identified include: the floor holder, users who have requested the floor control, the conference initiator, any user and the facilitator (for further discussion relevant to floor control, see Chapters 5 and 11).

2.6.3 Representation Agent

Because participants have different interests in the task, it may be appropriate to have different representations of the same underlying data. Some applications provide this capability, such as geographical information systems. The representation agent extends this capability to the group by coordinating with the application, the user harnesses and the conference agent.

Individual users may have different preferences concerning, for example, the presentation of information at the workstation. The user harnesses already support this functionality (but see Section 2.6.5).

2.6.4 History Agent

The history agent cooperates with the user support agents to maintain a record of the actions that the group has performed. It might also negotiate with the group about the importance of recording particular actions.

2.6.5 Workstation Agent

The representation agent enables participants to have different representations, and the user harnesses support personalization of the workstation. However, it may be necessary at particular times to share the same representation between participants or to ensure that certain information is "visible" at participants' workstations. The workstation agent negotiates with users and with the user harnesses, and coordinates with the group agent.

2.6.6 Facilitator Agent

A facilitator is traditionally someone who understands group processes and assists a group to understand its problems and find solutions. Viller (1991) explains the role of the facilitator in greater depth.

The facilitator agent provides tools to enable the group to conduct the conference, such as creating and maintaining an agenda and time-keeping aids. It provides tools to the participant who takes on the role of a facilitator, such as a record of requests for floor control and the degree of participation in the meeting by each member of the group.

The facilitator agent might take a more proactive role. It might assist in setting the context of the meeting by using the results of the history agent from previous meetings to run through decisions that have already been taken. In addition, it might use the results of the history agent in this meeting as an aid in wrapping up the conference. When latecomers join the group, they can be brought up to date with decisions using the history agent. The facilitator agent performs these functions in negotiation with participants and with the history agent.

The facilitator agent might formally welcome a new member and inform the group when a new member has joined (a procedure in addition to updating the participant list). Similarly, it might formally inform the group when a member departs.

In addition, the facilitator agent might be more interventionist and recommend a particular floor policy, given a particular situation or at a particular time in the running of the conference. For example, at the beginning of the conference, it might be appropriate for a round-robin floor policy to be used to enable the participants to introduce themselves. The facilitator agent needs to coordinate with the floor agent. The facilitator agent might also prompt users who have not contributed to the discussion.

Other agents actually subsume part of the traditional duties of the facilitator, such as the history agent, the floor agent and the conference agent. Thus, the facilitator agent needs to coordinate with participants, the facilitator, the history agent, the conference agent and the floor agent.

2.6.7 Data Agent

Several issues arise concerning the ownership and security of data used in a conference. For example, if material is produced as a result of the conference, who becomes its owner, and if users bring material to the conference, does the material remain the original owner's property or does it become the property of the conference? Greif and Sarin (1988) cover these issues in greater depth. The framework recognizes the necessity of a data agent but does not currently support it.

2.7 Conclusion

The framework outlines the explicit provision of agents to support negotiation between the human actors, between the human actors and the software system and among the intelligent agents within the system. It tackles the important issue of tailorability that has been raised in the field of CSCW. Particular agents that are required to support negotiation are identified within the framework: user support agents, which help a user to perform a particular task; user harnesses, which present the information to users; a conference agent, which initiates and terminates a conference and enables users to join or leave; a floor agent, which handles the floor policy; a representation agent, which handles different presentations of the same underlying data; a history agent, which records actions taken during the meeting; a workstation agent, which handles the sharing of presented information; a facilitator agent, which supports some of the tasks performed by the traditional facilitator; and a data agent, which handles the sharing of data.

Acknowledgements The work reported is funded partly by SERC in the context of the MUMS project, IED4/1/1256, in collaboration with Queen Mary and Westfield College, London.

Chapter 3
Environments for Cooperating Agents: Designing the Interface as Medium

A. Dix, J. Finlay and J. Hassell

3.1 Introduction

Various interface styles suggest paradigms for understanding interaction. Direct manipulation (DM) suggests the interface as a passive entity, providing tools for the user to control. Intelligent interfaces suggest instead an active interface, a colleague which (or even who) cooperates with the user on the task in hand. Each of these paradigms seems useful in different contexts. Matters become more complex when we consider systems with multiple applications or multiple users. We can no longer see the interface as part of a two-participant dialogue, involving human and computer. Instead, we look towards an environment where several active participants – some human, some automatic – cooperate.

In this chapter we propose that viewing the interface as a *medium* allows us to make sense of the interplay between passive and active components of an interface, and, indeed, of that between human users. Within an interface we will distinguish the *objects*, the passive elements; the *agents*, the active; and, most importantly, the *medium*, the environment within which agents act upon the objects and communicate with one another. We consider how this model can support our understanding of the interaction, taking examples from intelligent interface design and Computer Supported Cooperative Work (CSCW). Consequently, we must design the interface as a medium of communication: an environment in which both human and artificial agents can cooperate effectively (for further discussion of cooperation, see Chapters 1, 2, 5, 6, 9, 10 and 11).

3.2 History

The analysis of an interface as composed of *Agents*, the *Medium* and *Objects* (AMO) was proposed by the authors some years ago as a way of understanding the interplay of passive and active elements within single-user interactive systems (Dix and Finlay 1989). Of particular importance is the medium, the environment within which the user interacts with the objects and other agents, human or automated, in the system. The application of AMO to single-user systems made use of images drawn from day-to-day interpersonal communication to understand the human–computer dialogue. We now bring the approach full circle by focusing again on multi-user and multi-agent interfaces. The chapter is based partly on older, but previously unpublished, material and partly on more recent implementation and analytic work. Several ideas which seemed "off the wall" when we originally discussed the AMO model are now only relatively simple extensions of current systems and metaphors. However, although concepts such as identifiable interface agents are now part of the normal vocabulary of Human–Computer Interaction (HCI), the medium itself is not. But it is through the medium that human users cooperate with artificial agents and with each other, and thus our emphasis must shift towards the positive and explicit design of the medium itself.

We begin in Section 3.3 by discussing the background of active and passive paradigms in single-user interaction. This is used as a springboard for the discussion of the AMO model in Section 3.4. The model is used to discuss design issues for adaptive interfaces (Section 3.5), concluding that the agent of adaptivity should be *embodied* in some form within the interface. In Section 3.6 we discuss an experimental system which exemplifies this principle of embodiment: an adaptive "buttons" orientated interface. We then shift our attention, in Section 3.7, from artificial agents to other people. We see how a medium-orientated perspective casts light on some design issues in electronic conferencing and communication. Finally, in Section 3.8 we give some suggested design heuristics for the medium, incorporating both other agents and other users. However, this discussion is not intended to be complete; the suggestions are, we hope, useful, but not crucial. The primary goal is to establish the central importance of the concept of, and design of, the interface as a medium.

3.3 Active and Passive Interfaces

Different interaction styles suggest different paradigms for understanding interaction. DM interfaces emphasize the passivity of the interface: the user is interacting with *things* in an artificial world (for example, on a desktop). This interface style is highly popular, partly because of the naturalness of the physical metaphors used, partly because of the immediacy of response (if you want something to be done you do it, rather then telling the system to do it). In addition, the very passivity of the system gives the user a sense of control; the initiative lies with the user. There is a danger that such user-controlled dialogues will be *under-determined* (Thimbleby 1990), but this is largely obviated by the graphical presentation of the objects of interest.

Successful as such interfaces are, the concept becomes dangerously stretched when extended beyond those applications which are most well suited, such as drawing and simple word processing. In an application such as statistical analysis you clearly want the machine to *do* something *for* you rather than you doing it for yourself. DM is an excellent paradigm for the production of tables of data, but when faced with analysis, especially non-standard analyses, the limitations become obvious. DM techniques can be used to draw a diagram describing the statistical processes required, and enabling intermediate results to be seen, so encompassing many of the positive points of DM. However, in the end, you want the machine to do the actual calculations: after all that's why you're using it.

Even the classic what-you-see-is-what-you-get (WYSIWYG) word processor starts to fail when more complex facilities are demanded of it: style sheets are added to paragraphs, and alternative views may even be given, containing, essentially, text formatting languages. Basically, when the issue is simple page layout or simulated typewriting then DM is sufficient. However, as soon as the focus changes to document processing then issues such as consistency of style make us demand that (again) the computer works for us.

Intelligent interfaces, on the other hand, emphasize the active nature of the interface. The interface sits between the user and the application, and uses its knowledge of system semantics and (possibly) of user understanding to present the application to the user in what it deems is an appropriate fashion. Adaptivity may identify the user's understanding of a topic in order to provide a restricted functionality (cf. Training Wheels, Carroll and Carrithers 1984) or alter the presentation of the system's functionality according to commonly used commands (Mason and Thomas 1984). Alternatively, an adaptive system may alter the view of the domain in order to reflect the user's actions (Greenberg and Witten 1985). Regardless of the aspect of the interaction which is adapted, there is a danger that the user will suffer due to loss of control over the interface and a sense of instability.

Traditional User Interface Management Systems (UIMS) fall between these two paradigms. They act as a bridge between the user and some set of underlying functionality (of which the statistical system would be a good example). Applications know little about the specific user interface and are addressed purely at the application domain. The job of the UIMS is then to produce a means of accessing the functionality, and presenting and manipulating the objects in the application domain. This philosophy of interface independent applications (and even sometimes application independent interfaces!), and the language models that underlie it, has been the subject of an extensive critique, which more modern UIMS are attempting to address. In particular, many try to be more "DM-ish", but of course they are addressing the application areas where DM has trouble.

One issue that has been a problem with older UIMS is that the UIMS's knowledge of the application was restricted to a type-syntactic description of function calls available. In order to produce sensible interfaces, deeper semantic knowledge is often needed. To address this, several recent UIMS proposals include knowledge bases and expert systems components which overlap to some extent with the intelligent and adaptive interfaces.

In both the traditional UIMS and the intelligent interface the user interface is seen as a *mediator* between the user and application. The user communicates intentions to the interface agent, which then processes these and passes them on to the application. In order to obtain reasonable performance, many UIMS allow direct semantic feedback – the user talks directly to the application – largely obviating the original intentions of separation. In each case we have a three-agent communication.

3.4 The Interface as Medium

In Section 3.3 we saw two very conflicting views of the interface. One, DM, emphasizes the system's passivity, but has difficulty coping with active applications. The other, represented by both the adaptive interface and the UIMS, has a far more active interface component, but lacks that feeling of directness and control that makes DM so popular, especially among the computer naive.

We take a third view of the interface, as a *medium*, which allows us to make sense of the interplay between the passive and active components of an interaction. The word "medium" here is taken to include the whole software/hardware amalgam, with both its functional and aesthetic attributes. In particular, it is not limited to the information theoretic concept of a channel or the physical characteristics of a device, although these will both be facets of the medium. In this paradigm, we decompose a system into *agents* (human or machine), the *medium* and *objects* (Dix and Finlay 1989).

Objects here are not those of an object-oriented system; only the agents are capable of autonomous action. The image is of a physical object: it doesn't *do* anything but it is manipulated by the various agents in the environment. The term "medium" is drawn wider than its use when we say that oils are an artistic medium. We would also call a style, such as Cubism, a medium encompassing a whole set of conventions and constraints. Similarly, television as a medium includes not only the technical limitations but also the cultural, legal and economic constraints.

The medium through which you communicate, and in which you operate, determines the way in which you frame your actions and interpret your perceptions. In our context the medium is the environment through which agents interact with one another and with objects. We are interested in both qualitative and quantitative attributes of this medium.

A motivating example for this approach is traditional mail and communication systems. Clearly when viewed as theoretical communication channels most such systems are similar: they differ more in the qualitative aspects of the interface. The important thing to note is that these non-functional differences, such as pace and ease of interaction, can make profound differences to the content of communication. This is typified by the differences between face-to-face, telephone and paper mail communication.

In the mail example, the total system consists of the medium and the people who are communicating. The medium is (relatively) passive and the people active. In general, systems have active members other than the humans and we refer to both types of active member as *agents*. The final classification, *objects*, refers to those components that are passive, but not merely artefacts of the interface, for instance data files. As with many such classifications it can be carried out at various levels in the system description. For example, at one level the postal system is a medium through which agents communicate, whereas, at another level, it involves the letters as objects being manipulated by the postman, an agent. Another example is a washing machine: this is an object when it is being lifted out of a van, but an agent when washing clothes.

When we first used the AMO model, the principal agents within a system were the applications and perhaps other users. The term was a way of identifying the active parts within systems, but was not normally used by the systems themselves. Now, of course, the idea of agents has become commonplace, but it is still important to look for interface elements that are not designated "agents" by the developer and yet exhibit autonomy – we will see examples of this later.

It is also important to note that agents within the system may have different levels of autonomy and intelligence. An automatic mail reply tool is an agent which acts autonomously, but without intelligence. An adaptive macro generator acts with some intelligence. Human agents obviously are fully autonomous and intelligent!

3.5 Adaptive Interfaces

The distinctions introduced can be used purely descriptively or normatively in judging existing or putative systems. An example of an interface issue that can be addressed is that of adaptive or intelligent interfaces (see also Chapter 10). These are sometimes justified by analogy with human dialogue (Kass and Finin 1988). When we enter a dialogue with other human agents we expect them to adapt the level and style of the dialogue to their perception of our abilities, knowledge and aims; the same type of adaptive dialogue, it is argued, should be possible with computers. On the other hand, such adaptive systems may be unpredictable to use, leaving the users feeling lacking in control, as the system continually tries to second guess them, and unsure of the response from (and even the method of achieving) system operations. Again, we see the conflict between a user-controlled passive (but stupid) interface and a more active, intelligent, and independent one. Can the AMO distinctions help us to resolve this conflict?

By analysing appropriate real-world situations in terms of agents and media, we can make recommendations as to which parts of a computer system should be subject to adaptivity. If we examine again the analogous human–human dialogue, it consists of two agents, the participants, and the medium through which they communicate. In the case of face-to-face conversation the medium would include the air through which the sound waves travel, the language used, the non-verbal visual cues, and, in a wider setting, the room in which the conversation is taking place. The important thing to note is that it is the other participant (the agent) who adapts and the medium which remains relatively stable. We would find it extremely disconcerting if the air around us began to vary its properties in sympathy with its model of us, perhaps reducing the speed of sound to a few centimetres per second in order to slow the rate of dialogue down, or adding echoes if it thought we were missing things. The closest effect one could imagine would be chatting next to a sound sensitive disco light controller!

Of course, changes of medium do occur. However, these tend to occur at a low rate and/or under the mutual agreement of the parties. For instance, if telephone conversations are interspersed with written letters, the change in pace and context of the medium is rather obvious. One can consider more dynamic situations, such as a technical "brainstorming", which swap between use of direct speech, whiteboard, and pencil and paper. However, in this case, the alternative media are supplementary rather than representing a total change in the medium of dialogue.

If we look again at adaptive interfaces, the situation is similar to human–human dialogue – we have two agents, the user and the application, and the interface, which is the medium between them. However, in this case, it is not the other agent (the application) which adapts but the medium itself. That is, the supporting analogy breaks down on who and what is adapting. It is not surprising, then, that the user may feel out of control, as the very means of communicating with the system is neither predictable nor stable. Users must possess such a *deterministic ground* in order to have a context from which to view and interact with the less predictable parts of a system (Dix 1990, 1991). A possible solution is to introduce an active agent into the system which will cooperate with the user on the task in hand. The adaptivity is thereby shifted from the medium (the interface) to another agent. The interface retains its consistency and the adaptivity is localized.

We can think of this approach as *embodied adaptivity*. There are two ways in which adaptivity can be embodied in the interface. The first is if the adaptive agent itself is given an embodiment. Hewlett-Packard's New Wave agents are an example of autonomous agents, embodied in an icon in the interface. One can imagine similar agents given an element of intelligence and thus being a focus for interface adaptivity. An example of an existing system where the adaptivity is given such an iconic embodiment is EAGER (Cypher 1991). This system looks for commonly occurring command sequences and when it thinks that it can predict your future commands, a smiling cat appears, highlighting its suggestion for your next command (menu selection etc.). This can either be ignored or the prediction confirmed.

The second way of embodying adaptivity is to embody the *results* of adaptivity. In the Xerox Buttons environment snippets of Lisp code, which act on the user's electronic environment, are attached to on-screen buttons (MacLean et al. 1990). When the buttons are clicked, the Lisp code is executed on the user's behalf, a form of sophisticated macro. Buttons can be copied and amended by the user, making them a focus for the user's own *adaptation* of the interface. However, although the buttons are autonomous, in that they perform tasks *for* the user, they are not intelligent, and are thus adaptable but not adaptive. Similar facilities are now becoming available on commercial word processors and spreadsheets, but with more limited macro languages, and tied to particular applications. As well as being more flexible, the buttons are *first class*, that is, they are manipulable items in the interface. In particular, they can be mailed (locally) from person to person. This happens frequently because the users who require adaptation may not always be sufficiently proficient Lisp programmers, so one user may produce a button and then give it to another user. Thus, the button has also become a focus of adaptivity within the social group. The agent of adaptivity is the colleague, a human agent. It is only a small step to consider using the non-intelligent button as the embodiment of the results of an adaptive interface. This is precisely the approach taken in the experimental system described in Section 3.6.

3.6 An Experiment in Embodied Adaptivity

Current work in user modelling for adaptivity has mostly been restricted to the application level, despite the fact that much of the information contained in the model has a wider applicability than the scope of the application domain in question. It seems a waste that this domain-independent information, which has been acquired at some considerable cost, is only allowed to affect the operation of the application in which its model resides.

The different levels of generality of the information stored in the model seem to indicate that the information should be stored in a hierarchical structure with the more application-independent information further up the hierarchy and the more application-specific information being stored closer to the leaves (which in this case could contain information relating to the current instance of the application usage, for example, information specific to the current document being worked upon).

This hierarchical structure provides an efficient way of storing user modelling characteristics and also allows for inheritance of general characteristics by any new tools introduced to the system. The reverse operation – of specific information propagating up the hierarchy as it is inferred to be more general than the level of the hierarchy at which it resides – also aids the process of task recognition in a global system-wide context.

The advantages of this structuring are obvious. With current advances in multi-window, multi-tasking operating systems, people are adopting a more concurrent tool-based approach to work. The boundaries between applications are no longer rigid, and interfaces are becoming more data-orientated rather than application-orientated. These new work styles require adaptation to break out of its application-specific role and to have effect on the system as a whole if it is to be useful in any real sense. The hierarchical structuring of the information parallels closely the way in which tasks are repeatedly broken down into subtasks, until the subtasks can be achieved by an application.

This approach to whole-system modelling allows any agent, whose job is to perform adaptation, to range over the entire user environment (the medium), thus giving it scope to provide a consistent adaptive interface to the system as a whole.

As an initial trial of the ideas presented here, an experimental system has been designed. The domain chosen for the prototype is that of document processing under LaTex on UNIX graphic workstations. There were a number of reasons for this choice: firstly, this is the environment that a good number of the researchers at York use for their document processing requirements; secondly, the production of documents using the system requires the use of many diverse tools, and the set of these and the environment in which they are used has been shown through questionnaires to be a matter of personal preference; and finally the complexity of mastering the tools, methodologies and command syntax is substantial.

The concept of the system is essentially simple – a button-dock is introduced to the machine's work surface with buttons that automate the user's habitual tasks (for example, there may be buttons for *print*, *spell-check* and *preview*). These buttons can be seen as intelligent agents working in the environment. Buttons are created or destroyed automatically by an adaptive filter working on a trace of the user's interaction with the command line and also with the buttons themselves (the collection of which is transparent to the user).

The filter builds up a hierarchical model of the user's interaction, starting at the lowest level of the tree – the specifics of the document in question. Commands that are used habitually are migrated to a button with a script specific to the current document. Over time, inferencing techniques within the agent recognize similarities between the scripts of buttons at the same level in the hierarchy and automatically form a more general script at a level one higher than the specific scripts. Any new document then inherits the general buttons of the levels above it to give a default button-dock for the new instance. As buttons are created automatically, so their traced use is also subject to adaptation, and buttons that are not used will gradually be destroyed and replaced by others.

To ensure stability of the interface, and to comply with the argument that the medium should not be subject to adaptation, the addition of the buttons to the interface does not in any way change the methods with which the user can get the job done. The buttons are a simple adaptive addition to the interface, the introduction of new agents, and can be completely ignored by the user if he or she so wishes.

The application of the AMO paradigm to this area provides important design heuristics to constrain the adaptivity in the system when the agents in question are autonomous adaptive agents. In Section 3.7 we change our focus to consider how the paradigm can be used to analyse human–human communication in computer supported conferencing systems.

3.7 Conferences and Cooperation

Imagine a physical conference room. What is it like? Typically, you would expect to see chairs and tables, an overhead projector, a whiteboard, a screen, and, if it is in use, people with many bits of paper. They do not constitute a conference in the same way that, say, a collection of pipes, boilers and turbines might constitute a power plant. Instead, the conference room is a medium in which the participants are able to make for themselves a conference. Often, the basic geometry of the room is varied from meeting to meeting, some groups opting for a linear "boardroom" effect, others placing chairs and tables in a circle, others stacking the tables and having ranks of chairs looking forward at the speaker. It is usually the case that such furniture shuffling takes place prior to the meeting proper. That is, the meeting has two phases: in the first the room is the medium and the chairs and tables are objects to be manipulated; in the second, the conference proper, the geometry becomes part of the medium itself.

In special-purpose rooms, such as lecture theatres or boardrooms, where the range of use is well understood, the geometry may be fixed. This usually renders such rooms virtually unusable for other purposes. This has been recognized in many areas, for example in church interiors, where the fixed, forward facing Victorian pew is now often replaced by movable chairs to allow different geometries for Sunday worship and for alternative weekday activities.

Occasionally technical constraints may force the room's designer to fix the geometry. This was the case with the design of Capture Lab (Mantei 1988), a computer assisted meeting room. Mantei describes how difficult this design process was, and the many different design options that were considered. However, the eventual design, the product of much careful thought, still conflicted with the participants' social expectations – the participants had to learn the new positions of power and cooperation that went with the new environment. To some extent this re-orientation was an inevitable consequence of new technology, but it underlines the complexities of designing a system for conferencing, even where the main elements are physical and well understood.

A medium-orientated approach to electronic conferencing would suggest that the emphasis should be on producing a medium for communication, which the participants should shape to their needs, like the conference room with chairs and tables; that is, a collection of shared items and tools that the participants can structure to their own needs. One would not dream of designing a physical conferencing room around a model of a typical meeting agenda. However, that is precisely the approach of structured communication systems such as Coordinator (Flores et al. 1988). More in line with the medium-orientated approach would be locally structured conferencing systems such as the Amsterdam Conversation Environment (Dykstra and Carasik 1991), where the system has minimal structure, allowing the participants to build the conversation or conference of their choice.

On the whole, conferencing and communications systems, even the most loosely structured, stand apart from normal single-user interaction. However, the participants in the physical room would bring in objects from other work contexts: briefcases, piles of papers, overhead acetates. Similarly, we should eventually look towards a communication medium which is seamless with the normal single-user medium, rather than a conferencing "application" separate from the rest of the interface. The closest extant system to this ideal is probably the Doors metaphor (Cook and Birch 1991), which is similar to Rooms (Henderson and Card 1986). As in the Rooms metaphor, the user can move between several virtual rooms, but, unlike the original metaphor, some of the rooms are private workspaces – normal electronic desktops – and some are shared. The user can carry objects back and forth between these private and shared rooms. A more mundane, but more prevalent, example is the growing sophistication of "enclosures" mechanisms in commercial LAN-based email systems.

3.8 Designing the Medium

We have seen how important it is to distinguish the adaptive agents from the medium within an interface, and discussed a medium-orientated approach to electronic communication. We now address the more general question of how to design the interface as a medium within which the user can cooperate with other users and with electronic agents in a unified manner. The medium should be invisible to the users themselves: it is the environment within which they work – natural and transparent. But to obtain that effect it must be highly visible to the designer. All interfaces constitute a medium – the issue for the designer is not whether to design a medium, but whether the design should be implicit, an accident, or whether to make the design of the medium explicit.

In many circumstances, the medium is largely "given", part of the operating system or window manager. Developers can build upon this given medium, as an artist adopts a particular style in the use of oils, but they operate under strong constraints – the effect on the medium of these pervasive, underlying systems is enormous. However, these pervasive media, designed for single-user/single-application interaction, will become increasingly strained as integration between users and between applications increases, and autonomous agents (surrogates, filters, helpers) become commonplace. To encompass these diverse developments we need a fresh look at the design of these underlying systems and the media they portray.

We do not attempt a complete answer to the difficult problem of designing the medium, but suggest a few useful heuristics and directions: active/passive separation, equal access, use of existing multi-user and of single-application media. However, the important issue is that the medium *needs* to be designed.

3.8.1 Separation

One issue that has already arisen is the separation of the active and passive parts of a system. It is easy to let active functionality "creep" into those parts that ought to form the user's deterministic ground. This is frequently a problem in modern hypertext systems. Early descriptions of hypertext gave the impression of a passive system, a sort of highly connected electronic book. This is still the impression given by, say, address book applications and is largely the model portrayed to the hypertext viewer. However, in many authoring systems the implementation is very different. Each button on a card triggers a piece of code, one possible action of which is to move to another card. This allows more complex systems than the simple book metaphor would suggest.

For an example of this problem consider a tourist information system. It has one card in which hotels are listed alphabetically, but the user can also look at an area map and then navigate to a list of all the hotels in that area. If you take a passive model of the hypertext, then you know that every time you return to the hotel listing the same information will be displayed, but you have no guarantee (except the accuracy of the data input) that the alphabetic and the area listings are consistent. An active view, where the lists are seen as computed, does guarantee consistency between views, but not necessarily through time – we all know systems where each time we ask the same thing we get a different answer. Which model should the user adopt? The clues as to which is the appropriate model are often absent and yet the models make very different predictions about the system. If the developer is careful, a hypertext need not suffer this problem, but it is an easy trap to fall into.

Designers, whether of hypertext or any other interface, should be clear in their own minds as to which elements of the interface are active and which passive. This should be communicated to the users, by documentation and by clues in the presentation as to the affordances of the objects.

3.8.2 Access

In real life, through social and physical constraints, we do not have equal access to all objects. However, when cooperating closely with others it is often the case that the principal objects and the medium of communication itself are equally available to all. This is close to Thimbleby's principle of *Equal Opportunity* which suggests (among other things) a blurring between the items in the interface used for input and output (Thimbleby 1986, 1990). If we design the interface as a medium, we expect it to behave in roughly similar ways when sending information to and from the user. However, the facilities normally available to the user and to the application are very different. Happily, there are some exceptions.

Took's Presenter system (Took 1990) treats the interface graphics as a data structure. Items may be moved, resized and edited, by the application and by the user. This is not an anarchic situation as the movability constraints and the groupings of items can be set so as to mimic standard interface widgets (and novel ones). However, the overall impression is that the surface interface is an area of negotiation between the user and application, a medium of communication.

Another example of good practice is the HyperCard *development* environment (Apple 1987). If the programmer wants a script to draw a filled circle, then the script selects the circle from the toolbox, clicks at one corner, clicks at the other (drawing the outline), then selects the paint can from the toolbox and clicks in the middle of the circle (filling it). The script performs exactly the same actions as the developer would to paint the circle by hand. The card surface is the common object upon which the programmer and the programmer's scripts are working, using the shared medium of the toolbox. This, of course, is the situation for the HyperCard *programmer*; the user may, depending on the skills of the programmer, suffer exactly the paradigm problems described earlier.

3.8.3 Using Models of Interpersonal Communication

One way to design the medium is to take an existing electronic human–human communication mechanism and use this for communication with other non-human agents. Email systems are an obvious candidate, and, indeed, it is possible to send email messages to special mailboxes which act as "servers", perhaps mailing back a document, or adding you to a distribution list. Structured mail messages, such as those in LENS (Malone et al. 1986), offer more opportunities for communication with other agents. Indeed, the Mailtrays system (Rodden and Sommerville 1991) is described in terms of "a federation of cooperating, distributed agents" which communicate using structured email – the medium. For example, to compile a program, one mails a "compile" form to a compiler agent, which returns a "report" form when the compilation is (successfully or otherwise) complete.

To return, yet again, to hypertext, this is used as the object of cooperation or the medium of communication in several conferencing and shared editing systems (e.g. ACE or Quilt). The hypertext in such systems is clearly passive – the agents of change are other participants. Social protocols, locking schemes or automatic change notifications are used to inform the participants of one another's actions. This suggests that hypertext may be used as a medium itself between user and intelligent agents. This gives a possible way forward for the separation problem in hypertext: the text itself is passive, but it is altered in specific places and times by a cooperating agent.

3.8.4 Using Models from Application Interfaces

One can also look at application interface paradigms and ask whether these can generalize to ways of communication with other users, or multiple agents. In the earliest interfaces, the interaction was restricted to a single application. This single focus has been developed in two quite different directions in more modern multi-window graphical interfaces.

One paradigm is seen in Macintosh and Next systems: the screen has windows representing objects from different applications, but only one application is active. There is an implicit address to the user's actions, the current application. One can view this in two ways, either as looking through the application to the desktop (as suggested by the Macintosh's menu border), or as looking at the windows, with the application by one's side. This "over the shoulder" view of the application would suggest multi-user interfaces of the "shared window" or "shared screen" type.

The other paradigm is exemplified by the many UNIX window systems. In these, the application is embodied within a window. There is still a single active application, but this is *within* the active window. The visual clues which emphasize this are the fact that menu bars and status information tend to be placed within the windows, as opposed to on the desktop. The interpersonal communication suggested by this paradigm would be where a user was embodied within a window, basically a "phone" type connection.

Both paradigms have the data objects within the applications. This is less clear in the Macintosh type interface, but true of both. Indeed, this is how applications are traditionally coded, the data is read (in a proprietary format) into the application, the application portrays the object to the user and updates the object for the user, and finally the object is saved. This paradigm does not easily admit cooperation either with other users or with autonomous agents.

The emergence of various forms of object linking, the embedding of objects produced by one application with those of another, may change these paradigms. However, this is changing the way one looks at documents; they no longer "belong" to a single application. At present, the outcome of editing an embedded object is, in effect, to flip to that application, focusing on the embedded object, but this accommodation of the new paradigm within the old is rather strained. A new paradigm is needed where the applications, together with the users, look at and act upon the document. Such a medium-orientated paradigm will make it easier to include other users and agents in this cooperation.

3.9 Conclusions

We have seen how the AMO model has allowed us to analyse several areas, often by structuring analogies with physical examples. In particular, it has suggested an approach to adaptive interface design, and gives us a basis for evaluation of conferencing systems. However, the general approach is wider in scope than these examples. As computer systems begin to incorporate various active agents, and as we expect to work closely with other people, the electronic environments in which we work must change.

Such environments must be places where cooperating agents can work together and yet must retain the advantages of the DM paradigm. To do this, we must design the interface as a medium.

Acknowledgements Alan Dix is funded by SERC Advanced Fellowship B/89/ITA/220, and Jonathan Hassell by a CASE studentship from SERC, supported by DEC.

Chapter 4

Domain Knowledge Agents for Information Retrieval

D.R. McGregor, C.R. Renfrew and I.A. MacLeod

4.1 Introduction

Civil and structural engineers require access to changing information from a wide variety of sources, such as standards, design guides and journals. Our approach is to propose an agent-based information retrieval architecture. Central to our architecture are active information agents, each of which is trained to be an expert in a particular topic on behalf of a user. This chapter describes the agent architecture and its implementation.

The architecture consists of three distinct types of agents: document agents that know about individual documents; knowledge agents that contain domain knowledge about a collection of documents; and query agents that match knowledge agents with a particular query. In the current implementation, one method of constructing the knowledge agent is by analysing document collections for word co-occurrence information in order to automatically extract quasi-synonyms. The user can then interactively refine an agent's internal representation until it is satisfactory. Such an agent can then be applied to other libraries or news streams. When a user presents a query, a query agent is invoked to find the best matching knowledge agent. The knowledge agent then finds the documents for the user. A major feature of this architecture is that it can provide a consistent interface across different information sources.

4.1.1 Scope of Chapter

Information retrieval is concerned with the problem of enabling users of computers to find documents from large on-line libraries. This chapter describes a prototype architecture (and its implementation) based on the *agent* metaphor (Nelson 1990). Agents are proactive autonomous software entities responsible for some function in the system. In their original conception, responsibility for actions is devolved from the user to the agent. As will be seen, the agent architecture also provides a natural mechanism for an automatic news or mail reader (for example, see Rodden 1990).

The work in this project was motivated by the discipline of civil engineering. The engineering process requires consultation of large amounts of information (for example, standards and product information) from diverse sources. Our central notion was the idea of a *knowledge agent* that would contain domain knowledge about particular topics. This knowledge agent would then know the appropriate documents on its own topic to retrieve. This chapter describes how the internal representation of such a knowledge agent is derived.

Overall, our experience suggests that the agents represent a powerful technique for searching and interacting with document libraries. Our knowledge agent provides a mechanism that allows domain knowledge to be accumulated and, importantly, shared among separate users. Finally, the agent metaphor maps particularly well onto an object-oriented implementation (see also Chapters 2 and 6) and so allows the software implementation to be efficiently achieved.

4.2 Agent Architecture

For the task of information retrieval we identify the three types of agents shown in Fig. 4.1. Each major component of an information retrieval system is represented as an agent in this architecture (for further discussion of architectures, see Chapters 2, 5, 6, 8 and 9).

4.2.1 Document Agents

The purpose of a document agent is to provide a simple consistent interface between the raw documents and all the other agents. Each document is assigned to its own agent, which knows its whereabouts and can answer simple questions about it, such as the presence or absence of a word. The abstraction provided by a document agent could, in principle, support access to documents across separate libraries. The document agents have auxiliary agents, described in Section 4.3, that act on the documents independently, but this extra complexity is hidden from other agents.

4.2.2 Knowledge Agents

The goal of a knowledge agent is to be a domain "expert", that is, it knows the keywords that index documents on a specialist subject such

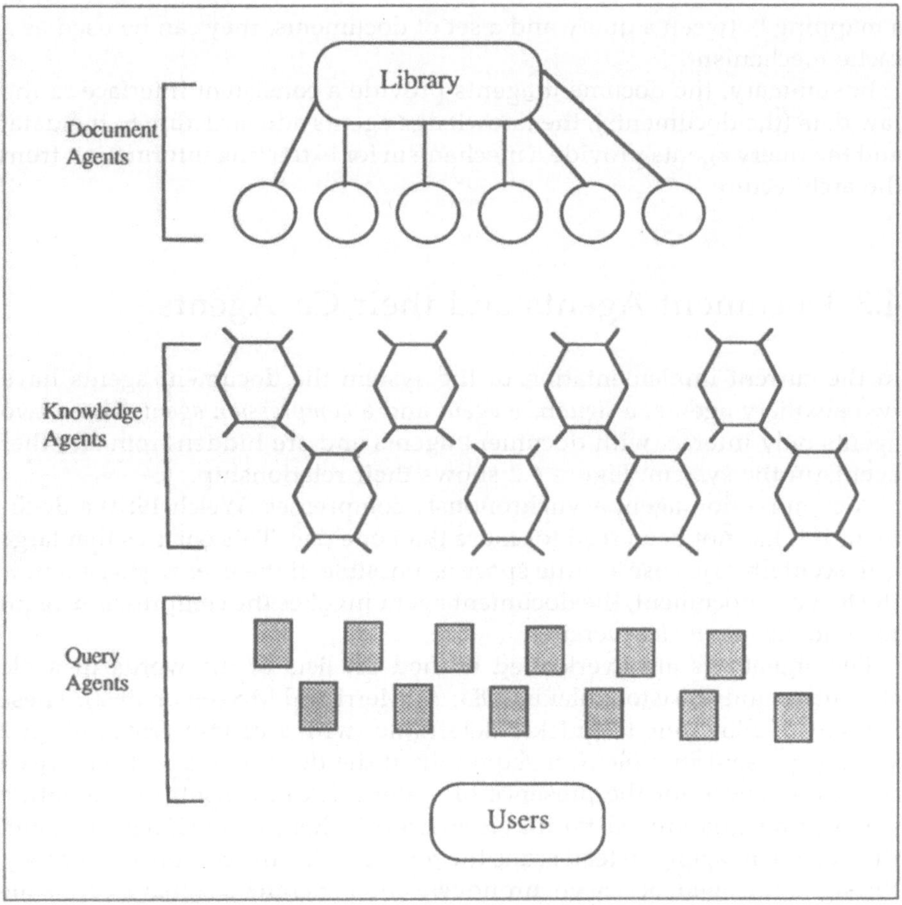

Fig. 4.1. Three types of agents for information retrieval. The document agents present the individual documents, knowledge agents hold domain-specific knowledge and query agents are used to find the appropriate knowledge agents.

as concrete or pitched roofs. Each knowledge agent interacts with the library solely through the document agents. Section 4.4 describes how knowledge agents can be constructed by hand, or automatically using machine learning techniques.

4.2.3 Query Agents

Query agents are responsible for mapping a user's query onto one or more knowledge agents and then returning the appropriate documents. The query agent is responsible for navigating among the knowledge agents to find one or more that satisfies the query. Since each query agent represents a mapping between a query and a set of documents, they can be used as a cache mechanism.

In summary, the document agents provide a consistent interface to the raw data (the documents), the knowledge agents add structure to the data, and the query agents provide a mechanism for extracting information from the architecture.

4.3 Document Agents and their Co-Agents

In the current implementation of the system the document agents have two auxiliary agents, a *signature agent* and a *compression agent*. These two agents only interact with document agents and are hidden from all other agents in the system. Figure 4.2 shows their relationship.

A compression agent asynchronously compresses (Welch 1984) a document if it has not been read for more than one day. This ensures that large quiescent libraries use as little space as possible. If the user wishes to view the text of a document, the document agent invokes the compression agent to generate an *en clair* version.

File signatures are overloaded hashed bit lists of the words in a file (Faloutsos and Christodoulakis 1984; Al-Merri and McGregor 1992). These signatures allow one to quickly determine (with a certain error rate) if a word is present in a file. Consequently, if the document agent receives a request to check for the presence of a word, it can consult the signature agent (if a signature exists) for an answer. If there is no signature agent, the document agent instead scans the text file. Like the compression agent, the signature agent acts asynchronously and generates a signature for a file

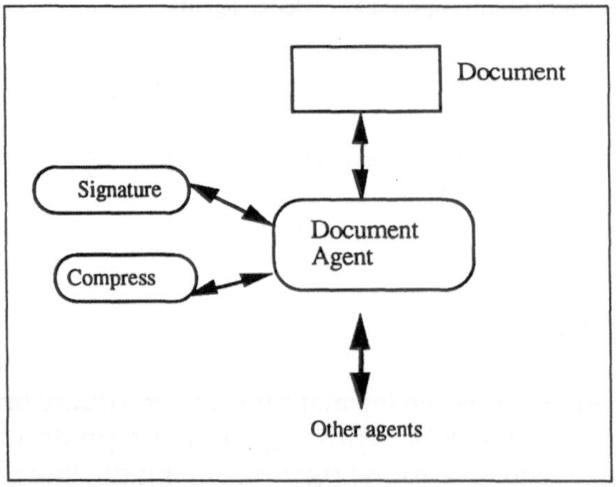

Fig. 4.2. The document agent and its two auxiliary agents.

if it does not have one or if the signature is out of date (the compression and signature agents are invoked at night by the UNIX *cron* daemon).

The presence of the signature agent and compression agent makes the task of the document agent more complicated because it must be explicitly aware of the effects that these autonomous co-agents might have on a document. However, the interaction between these agents is hidden from other agents.

4.4 Knowledge Agents

The knowledge agents carry the domain knowledge concerning topics of interest to the users. In this model there are three distinct types of knowledge agents that have different internal representations and different methods of generation. The first type of agent is constructed semi-automatically using the "AgentMaker". The second type of knowledge agent uses machine learning to derive a list of keywords. The third type is task-specific.

4.4.1 The "AgentMaker"

The domain of a knowledge agent is defined by an internal list of keywords. The keywords are used to match a knowledge agent document and this is achieved when a document contains all of the keywords. The user may also specify an optional threshold that allows approximate matching between knowledge agents and document agents. The keywords are stemmed automatically to ensure canonical comparison.

In this approach the internal representation is derived interactively using the AgentMaker. The user can manually specify the appropriate keywords for a subject. In order to help the process of choosing the most appropriate keywords for an agent, the AgentMaker also provides dynamic document analysis which generates words that frequently co-occur in documents indexed by the knowledge agent. This co-occurrence analysis (van Rijsbergen 1979; Rada and Martin 1987) finds quasi-synonyms that can be added to a knowledge agent's internal word list if required. Thus an iterative interactive process takes place where the user experiments with possible words and the synonym generator supplies other suggestions. Figure 4.3 shows the interface to the knowledge agents.

The matching mechanism used in knowledge agents (a list of keywords and a threshold) is not the most sophisticated (see van Rijsbergen 1979) because the main aim of this work is to experiment with the agent architecture and training techniques rather than with information retrieval engines.

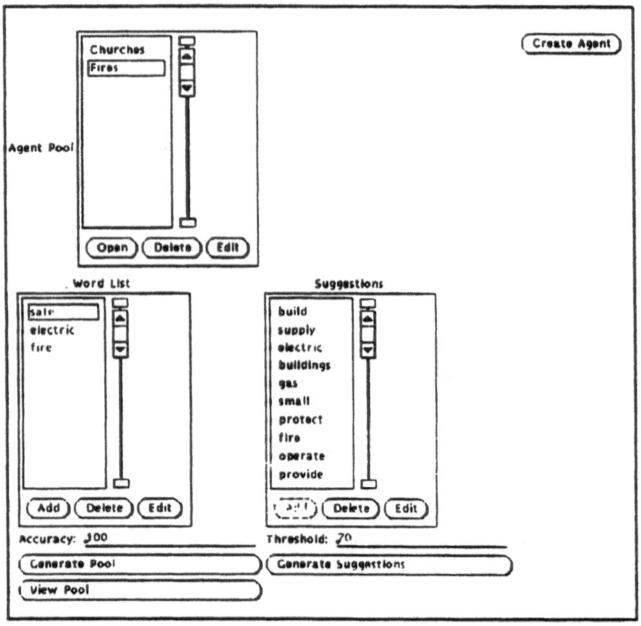

Fig. 4.3. The AgentMaker interface to the knowledge agents. The top panel shows the titles of the knowledge agents in the pool. The panel labelled "Word list" (bottom left) contains the list of words that define the topic of the knowledge agent. The "Suggestions" box contains the quasi-synonyms that are found from the document agents by co-occurrence analysis. The threshold determines the percentage of times a word co-occurs with the list of keywords within the knowledge agent. The example library consists of 750 documents on the care and preservation of historic buildings. The knowledge agent on display is about electrical fire safety and contains the keywords "fire", "safe" and "electric".

4.4.2 Automatically Generated Agents

The AgentMaker provides a mechanism for generating knowledge agents semi-automatically. However, it is also possible to apply machine learning techniques to search for potentially useful knowledge agents. The general idea is that it is possible for the knowledge agents to find for themselves clusters or concepts that can usefully be used in retrieval.

The approach taken here is to search for a set of characteristic words that span many documents. The measure of "goodness" of an agent tries to maximize the number of keywords and the number of documents indexed by these words. After removing common words we search for the set of words that maximizes:

$$M = \left(1 - \frac{1}{|W|}\right)\left(1 - \frac{1}{|D|}\right)$$

where W is the set of keywords in an agent and D is the set of documents indexed by those keywords.

This metric effectively forces the knowledge agents to search for words that are common (and hence characteristic) across many documents. In its nature it is similar to the kind of factoring found in lattice processing (Oosthuizen 1988; Oosthuizen and McGregor 1988).

Recent work (Peat and Willet 1991) indicates that the most discriminatory words have the lowest frequency. This type of learning will, it is hoped, build characteristic low frequency terms (and useful co-occurring terms) into the knowledge agent's representation.

4.4.3 Task-Specific Knowledge Agents

Sometimes it is useful to build specific domain knowledge into a search process. This "bottom up" approach takes the form of software that is written to recognize specific types of information. Examples of such agents could be for finding telephone numbers, addresses, or people's names. The telephone number agent might contain specific knowledge about area codes and international numbers.

It is important to note that the architecture being proposed here is extensible in that the knowledge agents could take different forms. For example, the manual agents could be set up using techniques other than word co-occurrence information, and different machine learning algorithms could be applied to the automatic agents.

4.5 Object-Oriented Implementation

All of the agents described have been implemented using the Objective C object-oriented programming language (Cox 1986). An advantage of the agent approach is that it maps naturally onto objects. Figure 4.4 shows the currently implemented objects. Notice that the agents described are implemented as individual objects (e.g. *KnowAgent*) and collections of agents are implemented as pools (e.g. *KnowAgent Pool*).

4.6 Conclusion

This chapter has described a new agent-based information retrieval architecture. Our experience indicates that the agent metaphor confers several advantages. Firstly, the function of each type of agent is easily understood by users. Secondly, the agents can be easily rendered using object-oriented software. Thirdly, the knowledge agent provides a natural vehicle for a "nugget" of domain-specific knowledge. In principle, these domain knowledge agents can also be shared among many users. A fourth advantage of the agent architecture is that our experience suggests that it is

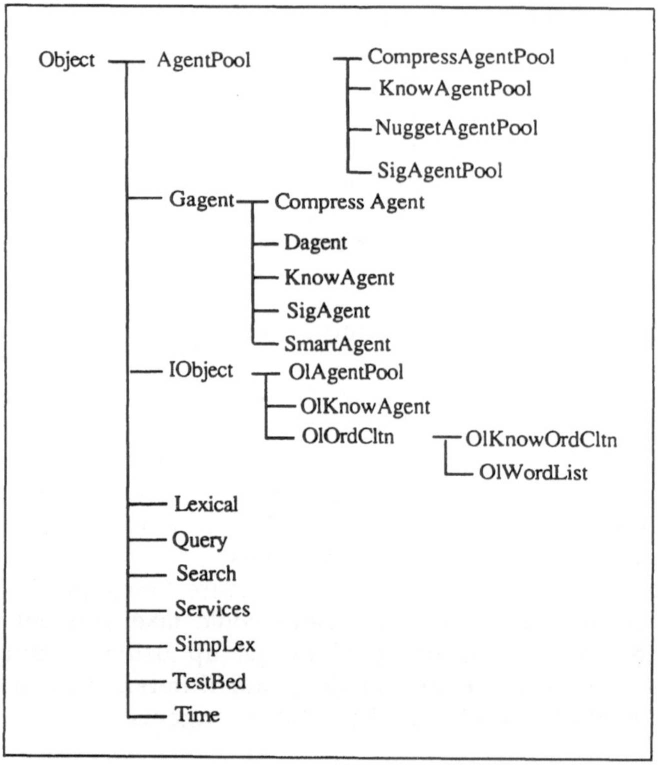

Fig. 4.4. The object hierarchy of the implemented architecture.

robust and extensible. For example, the compression and signature agents were added after the overall architecture of Fig. 4.1 had been designed.

This work has raised a number of issues that have yet to be resolved. A population of agents demands some control mechanism to ensure that redundant agents are removed. The architecture also poses the problem of mapping query agents onto (potentially different) knowledge agents.

Acknowledgements We gratefully acknowledge SERC, for support of this work (grant number GR/F/90813). We should also like to thank John Bankier, who implemented the user interface, Gordon McIntyre, William Wallace, Steven McInnes and our industrial collaborators, Hutton and Rostron.

Chapter 5

Autonomous Agents in the Support of Cooperative Authorship

G. Staniford and P.E.S. Dunne

5.1 Introduction

An architectural specification of independent communicating agents intended to form part of a system designed to support the cooperative writing of complex documents is described. The specification extends architectures designed to cope with non-communicating intelligent agents in a natural way, so that the complexities due to concurrency may be attended to.

The environment in which the agents exist is most suitably represented as a graph or network, and examples of such an environment are given based on document graph paradigms, using the formalization of these paradigms expounded in recent work. The formalism extends the document graph concept, which has been considered previously by several other authors, and can also model dynamic changes to document structure.

Such an approach has a number of advantages compared to less detailed techniques: it provides a general representation paradigm that can be used as a basis by document management systems, and it is easily customized to model different document graph structures, e.g. trees, directed acyclic graphs (DAGs), hypertext, etc. A direct consequence of this explicit formal structure is the ability to model, modify and study the behaviour of independent agents in a suitable "non-toy" environment. A model of cooperative authorship is presented and the ongoing work in building agents is discussed in relation to the model. Future approaches to the study of communication using dialogue analysis along the lines currently being followed at the University of Liverpool – for example, the Rapporteur Dialogue Model – and the inclusion of models of cooperation extending ideas such as "tit for tat" are indicated.

5.1.1 Scope of Chapter

Conventions have developed over time for the structural classification of meaningful documents. The understanding of and adherence to such conventions is a fruitful framework for the process of communication between author(s) and reader(s). Latterly, with the inception and development of powerful networked computing facilities, it has become possible to explore paradigms for computer supported writing systems. Such systems may provide an enabling technology for increasing authoring efficiency in the production of large, cooperatively written documents.

Many classes of document – from scientific papers to multi-volume technical publications, from joint reports to complex company plans – are written by groups of authors working in cooperation with one another on the creation of the final work. During the planning and creation phases of such documents, authors need support facilities to record and report on joint decisions and inter-author communication. The process of collaboration through structured dialogue is a common and valuable method of reaching an agreed position. One problem with this approach, however, is that the conclusions reached by a dialogue and the arguments by which they are arrived at may have to be consolidated into a single document reporting on the discussion. If this task is undertaken by one of the participants it is possible that the final report may fail to reflect truly the collaborative process. Ideally an external, independent observer – or *rapporteur* – should be employed to carry out this activity.

In this chapter we develop an architectural specification of independent communicating agents that provides the basis of a *cooperative authorship support system* (CASS) based around the concept of a *general document management system* (GDMS), which may be used by authors in the parallel production of structured documents. The system of autonomous agents is designed around the concept of a four-layer model of agent communication and cooperation. It is intended to enable the creation of documents represented in machine form using any form of graph-theoretic paradigm, and it employs knowledge engineering techniques to reason about its internal domain and to control the asynchronous interaction of multiple authors. We describe a model of cooperative writing together with a graph grammar representation of documents, and show how these elements may be combined with an agent to produce documents that summarize the content of a dialectical discussion. A simple model of dialogue structure and content, which captures certain elements of general discussion, is employed for this purpose. The system is based on the concept of formal dialogue games and employs graph modification systems as a mechanism for transforming the dialogue form into a document. It is based upon the Rapporteur System introduced by Bench-Capon in conjunction with the present authors (Bench-Capon et al. 1991), and follows the graph modification system introduced in that work very closely, but implements the concepts using agents designed in accordance with the architectural scheme outlined here.

In designing these architectures and systems the authors intend to provide a platform for the study of cooperation between autonomous communicating agents; this approach is discussed and future directions are outlined in Section 5.6. (For further discussion of architectures, see Chapters 2, 4, 6, 8 and 9.)

5.2 A Model of Cooperative Authorship

A cognitive model of communication which explains writing as the process of organizing a loosely structured network of internal ideas and external sources into a suitable hierarchy – section, subsection, paragraph, sentence, etc. – followed by mapping the hierarchy into a suitable linear form, is used by Smith et al. (1986). In this model the author is viewed as an independent process, creating text or complete documents without cooperation and communication between authors. Barlow and Dunne (1991) model authors as cooperating processes, jointly working with other authors on the same document. The author processes communicate at the level of parallel processes within a single unified system.

In our model we extend the ideas contained within the cognitive writing model to include and support the notion of communication between the authors at the conceptual level, so that they may cooperate on a jointly written document. This extended notion, coupled with the agent model, allows a description of writing that is flexible at the conceptual level and highly structured at the document level. The extended model includes the concepts of *exosystem communication* and *endosystem communication* to model the idea of authors as independent, communicating information processes (see Fig. 5.1). By exosystem communication we mean any channel, oral or written, by which authors communicate with each other. These communications may be exchanges of ideas, critiques of existing sections of the document, administrative matters, etc. To facilitate communication between members of a writing team, the model supports endosystem communications in textual electronic form. These internal communications may be channelled between authors without the intervention of any management system. However, when authors wish to record these messages they may treat them in a similar way to imported textual matter and store them as documents via the document management system. The features of this model have been encapsulated in the architectural design of a CASS (Dunne and Staniford 1992).

Quite clearly the author processes described can be viewed as human agents cooperating together in the document production process; in this chapter we are primarily concerned with the design of the autonomous

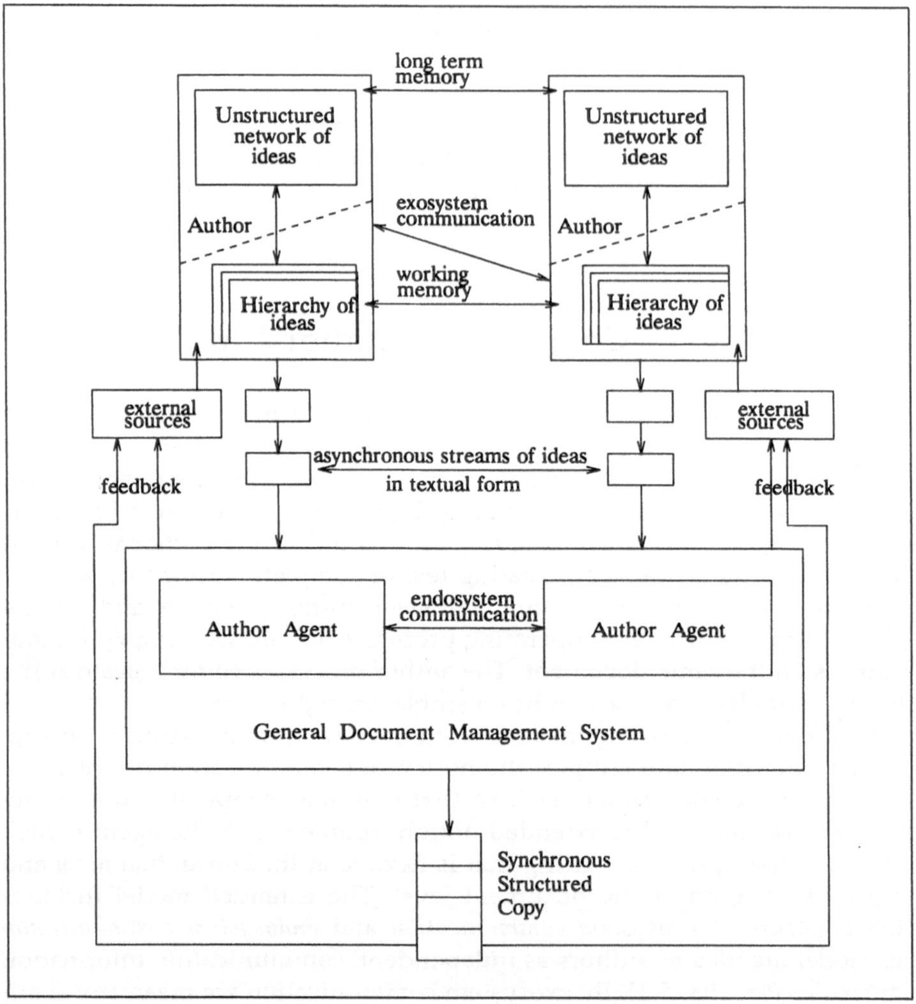

Fig. 5.1. Cooperative authorship model.

and semi-autonomous software agents that will be used to implement the many types of agents within the authorship support system.

5.3 The Definition of Loquacious-Agents and their Document Environment

Genesereth and Nilsson (1987) define four types of agent: *tropistic, hysteretic, knowledge level* and *stepped knowledge level,* in order of increasing sophistication and complexity. They then introduce the notion of a *deliberate* agent, which is a stepped knowledge level agent with certain restrictions on its set of actions. These agents are designed to exist in an environment in which they have the sole occupancy. There is no need for them to be aware of or to communicate with others of their kind. In this chapter we extend the architecture to enable agents to coexist, communicate and cooperate with other agents. For the sake of brevity we cannot summarize the work of Genesereth and Nilsson; the interested reader is referred to chapter 13 of their book for a full account. Note that for the sake of clarity all definitions in this chapter are presented in a simplified form, abstracted away from implementation level detail.

A *tropism* is the tendency of biological life forms to react in response to an external stimulus, and our simplest agent – the tropistic agent – is modelled with this metaphor in mind. Two functions are required to enable an agent to receive external stimuli:

$$\textit{see}: R \rightarrow S$$

and

$$\textit{hear}: T \rightarrow Q$$

where R is the set of states that characterizes the agent's world, and, in order to characterize the agent's sensory capabilities, we partition the set R of external states into a set S of disjoint subsets such that the agent is able to distinguish states in different partitions but is unable to distinguish states in the same partition. T is a set of words that characterize communications that the agent may receive from other agents, and, again, in order to further characterize the agent's sensory capabilities, we partition the set T of words into a set Q of disjoint subsets such that the agent is able to distinguish words in different partitions but is unable to distinguish words in the same partition.

These are sensory functions and are used to characterize the way in which an agent perceives stimuli external to itself. We use *see* to enable an agent to determine the local state of its environment, and *hear* to enable the agent to receive communications from other agents. It will often be necessary to define agents that carry out an action purely as a result of the influence of one or other of the external stimuli, and consequently it seems reasonable to keep the two functions separate.

Milner (1991) argues that a valuable simplification in modelling communicating agents with respect to the act of communication is to consider a communication channel to be a one-way system that provides a medium for acts of communication to take place. An act of communication is considered to be an indivisible event, taking place instantaneously between two or more agents. We adopt this simplification for our models and consider that if a message has been "sent" (see below) by an agent then it has been received by the agent or agents to whom it was sent. Similarly, we consider that any local attributes of a state in an environment that an agent can *see* will have been perceived by that agent as soon as they become available as a result of some state change within the environment.

Next, we need to turn our attention to the manner in which the state of an environment is changed. We assume that agents make local changes to an environment and consider that a state S_n changes to $S_{(n+1)}$ the instant that an agent makes a local change. Agents do not have the power to make global changes in an environment. In order that an agent may make changes we define two more functions:

action: $S \times Q \rightarrow A$

is a discriminatory function which maps each disjoint subset of states and inputs onto a particular action to provide an agent with the ability to choose which action to perform according to its perceived stimuli.

do: $A \times R \times T \rightarrow R \times W$

is an executory function which maps an action, state and input onto the new state and an output, providing the agent with the ability to change the local state of its environment and to communicate a message to another agent. W is a set of words that characterize the communications that an agent may send to another agent. We assume that the agent can distinguish all of its responses, so there is no need to partition W.

Unlike *see* and *hear*, we encapsulate acting and communicating in one function because although there will be occasions when we wish to communicate without changing a state, the converse is not the case. We do not allow an act that changes the state of the environment to take place without there also being a corresponding act of communication; hence the use of the word "loquacious" in our name for these agents. We wish to indicate that these two operations are closely bound together in order that we may simplify the coordination of the knowledge – between autonomous agents – that environmental state changes have taken place. The ability to communicate without state changes is in fact crucial to the notions of cooperation that we will develop later. Although we do not explicitly map W into a set of disjoint subsets, implicitly outputs fall into one of three categories: successful completion of a state change, failure to complete a state change and communications regarding cooperation. To avoid ambiguity we require that these categories do form disjoint subsets within W and, in fact, that there is an implicit bijection between the success and failure messages.

For our purposes, then, acts of observation – both visual and oral – must take place in the internal state of an agent, between changes in state of the external environment. In general, there is no simple linear correlation between the internal state changes within an agent and the external state changes of the environment. This presents problems for analysis and design, but we contend that these problems are more amenable to solution with the use of communicating agents than with simple non-communicating agents.

5.3.1 Definition 1

A *loquacious tropistic agent* in an environment is a 10-tuple of the form:

<*R, S, T, Q, W, A. see, do, hear, action*>

where R is the set of states that characterizes the agent's world. We partition the set R of external states into a set S of disjoint subsets. The function *see* maps each state in R into the partition to which it belongs. T is a set of words that characterize communications that the agent may receive from other agents, and we partition the set T of words into a set Q of disjoint subsets. The function *hear* is a sensory function which maps each word in T into the partition in which it belongs. W is a set of words that characterize the communications that an agent may send to another agent. A is a set of actions, all of which can be performed by the agent, and the function *do*: $A \times R \times T \rightarrow R \times W$ is an effectory function that characterizes the effects of the agent's actions by mapping each action, state and input into the state that results from the execution of the given action in the given state together with the resulting output. Finally, in order to characterize the activity of an agent, the discriminatory function *action*: $S \times Q \rightarrow A$ maps each state and input partition into the action that the agent is to perform whenever it finds itself in a state in that partition with an input in a particular partition.

5.3.2 Definition 2

A *loquacious hysteretic agent* in an environment is a 12-tuple of the form:

<*I, R, S, T, Q, W, A. see, do, hear, internal, action*>

where I is an arbitrary set of internal states. We assume that the agent can distinguish between all its internal states so there is no need to partition I. R is the set of states that characterizes the agent's world. We partition the set R of external states into a set S of disjoint subsets. The function *see* maps each state in R into the partition to which it belongs. T is a set of words that characterize communications that the agent may receive from other agents, and we partition the set T of words into a set Q of disjoint subsets. The function *hear* is a sensory function which maps each word in T into the partition in which it belongs. W is a set of words that characterize the communications that an agent may send to another agent. The set A is a set of actions, all of which can be performed by the agent, and the function *do*: $A \times R \times T \rightarrow R \times W$ is an effectory function that characterizes the effects of the agent's actions by mapping each action, state and input into the state that results from the execution of the given action in the given state together with the resulting output. The function *internal*: $I \times S \times Q \rightarrow I$ maps an internal state and both types of observation into the next internal state. Finally, the function *action*: $I \times S \times Q \rightarrow A$ maps each internal state, external state partition and input partition into the action that the agent is to perform whenever it finds itself in a particular combination of internal states, inputs and external states.

5.3.3 Definition 3

A *loquacious knowledge level agent* in an environment is a 12-tuple of the form:

$\langle D, S, T, A, R, Q, W, \mathit{see}, \mathit{do}, \mathit{hear}, \mathit{database}, \mathit{action}\rangle$

where D is an arbitrary set of predicate calculus databases, S is a set of external states, T is a set of partitions of S, A is a set of actions, R is a set of input words, Q is a set of partitions of R and W is a set of output words. The function *see*: $S \rightarrow T$ maps each state in S into the partition to which it belongs. The function *hear*: $R \rightarrow Q$ maps each word in R into the partition in which it belongs. The function *do*: $A \times S \times R \rightarrow S \times W$ maps each action, state and input into the state that results from the execution of the given action in the given state together with the resulting output. The function *database*: $D \times T \times Q \rightarrow D$ maps a database and both types of observation into the new internal database. Finally, the function *action*: $D \times T \times Q \rightarrow A$ maps each internal database, external state partition and input partition into the action that the agent is to perform whenever it finds itself with a particular combination of internal databases, inputs and external states.

5.3.4 Definition 4

A *loquacious stepped knowledge level agent* in an environment is a 12-tuple of the form:

$\langle D, S, T, A, R, Q, W, \mathit{see}, \mathit{do}, \mathit{hear}, \mathit{database}, \mathit{action}\rangle$

where the sets D, S, T, A, R, Q, W and the functions *see*, *hear* and *do* are defined identically to the corresponding sets and functions in Definition 3. The function *database*: $D \times N \times T \times Q \rightarrow D$ maps a database, cycle number and both types of observation into the new internal database. Finally, the function *action*: $D \times N \times T \times Q \rightarrow A$ maps each internal database, cycle number, external state partition and input partition into the action that the agent is to perform whenever it finds itself with a particular combination of internal databases, inputs and external states.

5.3.5 Definition 5

A *loquacious deliberate stepped knowledge level agent* in an environment is a 12-tuple of the form:

<*D, S, T, A, R, Q, W, see, do, hear, database, action*>

where the sets and functions are defined identically to those in Definition 4. The difference in defining agents in this class arises from the use of an automated inference method like *resolution* when defining the operation of the action function – the authors are currently actively investigating the use of Toulmin's Argument Schemas (Toulmin 1958) in deriving a sentence that indicates the required action on each cycle.

The names of the agents defined above, while giving a good descriptive feel, are too long to be used comfortably in practice. We will refer to the class of all such agents as *L-Agents* and will abbreviate each individual agent class from the set {*Lt-Agent, Lh-Agent, Lk-Agent, Ls-Agent, Ld-Agent*}.

Two important definitions of properties that *L-Agents* share with other autonomous agents, *weak* or *observational equivalence* and *strong equivalence,* are complex and protracted (see Milner 1980, 1991). For reasons of space we content ourselves with a simple explanation tailored to *L-Agents.* Two *L-Agents* are observationally equivalent if a third external agent cannot distinguish between them. This means that for every possible set of inputs the two agents produce the same set of actions/outputs. There is no requirement that the two agents should pass through the same internal states. Strong equivalence, on the other hand, requires that the inputs, internal states and outputs/actions are indistinguishable.

From an architectural viewpoint we see that *L-Agents* are intended to provide communicating software agents with different levels of reasoning and memory capabilities for the purpose of providing suitable units for design and implementation in a "top down" approach to applied Artificial Intelligence (AI) problem solving. *Lt-Agents* form the lowest level and would typically be used for simple operations on unstructured atomic elements of the environment. The next level in complexity, *Lh-Agents,* while still only working on unstructured atomic environmental elements, have a memory capacity and can be used in the solution of problems that require consideration of a previous external state. *Lk-Agents* with an internal database can be used to consider complex relations and will typically be used to operate upon structured complex areas of the environment. The difference between *Ls-Agents* and *Lk-Agents* is the dependence (in the case of *Ls-Agents*) of the database and action functions on the agent's cycle number. This means that *Ls-Agents* may be used in areas that require temporal reasoning. *Ld-Agents* represent a restriction upon *Ls-Agents* and are deliberate in the sense that they deliberate on each cycle about which external action to perform and which message to communicate.

Deliberation has considerable importance when considering consistency and fidelity, but these issues will be the subject of future publications and are not pursued in this chapter.

We leave further discussion of some of the practical properties of *L-Agents* until after we have defined and described the environment in which they are to operate. This does not imply that agents of this architectural design are only suitable for this type of environment; we believe that they have considerably more generality than that. However, it is much easier to set up examples of actual agents for discussion of their properties when a uniformly specified environment is available.

The environment in which the agents that we will discuss have their existence is the mathematical space of *document graphs*. In order to set the notion of a document graph in context we first consider ideas of document structure.

Furuta (1989) defines a taxonomy of document structures, which we describe briefly here. A document description can be divided into two major parts: the definition of the document's content and the definition of its structure. The document's content is formed from atomic objects such as words, figures, tables etc., combined together in such a way as to communicate the author's meaning to the reader. The document's structure specifies the form of the document, describing how the atomic objects are composed into higher level structures.

There are two quite different types of relationship defined in the content of a document: *composition*, which specifies the ordering of atomic objects and how these atomic objects are combined into higher level objects; and the specification *interrelationships*, which establish a connection from one part of the document to another.

We separate the structures that describe these relationships into *constituent structures*, and define them separately. Each constituent structure is defined over some partitioning of the document's content into atomic objects, but we note that the granularity of partitioning of one constituent structure may not be at an appropriate level for use in another constituent structure.

It follows, then, that we are, when describing the structure of an atomic object, specifying the *minimum addressable unit* of the constituent structure and therefore such descriptions are an essential component of a structure specification.

We divide constituent structures into three main types: *primary*, *secondary* and *auxiliary*. Primary structures are the structures that define the composition of atomic components into higher level components; secondary structures describe interrelationships among document objects, and auxiliary structures describe relationships between document objects and objects that are outside the document.

Directed graphs have been widely used to link the conceptual and abstract representations in an electronic document model. We use the term "document graph" to refer to a graph-theoretic representation of a document. There is a hierarchy formed by the three main types of directed graph in current use: *tree, DAG* and *general*. The acyclic graph has considerable advantages, being more flexible than a tree structure and less problematical to maintain than the general variety. Koo (1989) introduced the concept of *graph modification rules,* which formally are a set of production rules in a graph grammar. Nagl (1978) provides a good introductory account for general graphs. The rules are employed to control modification of a document graph in order to reflect changes in either structure or interpretation. The nodes of the graph represent objects within the document (see Furuta (1989) for a full analysis of this concept) and the edges represent the logical connections between different objects within the document.

Bench-Capon and Dunne (1989) give a comprehensive description of the advantages of using DAGs, and the interested reader is referred to their paper. We content ourselves with noting that an important feature of such graphs is that there is only a fixed number of finite paths permitted by the graph structure from source nodes to terminal points, and that we make the assumption that the sensible paths through any document are acyclic, stressing that this pertains to the high-level structural organization of a document and not to how it might be read when produced as hard copy.

To analyse common properties of graph-theoretic document representations, Dunne and Staniford (1991) introduced the concept of a *general document representation.*

5.3.6 Definition 6

A *document graph* is a DAG, $G(V, E)$, with a vertex labelling relation λ_V and an edge labelling relation λ_E. The vertices in V denote objects in the document and the edges in E depict logical connections between objects. Each object has an associated object type. This consists of two parts: a *data type,* which specifies the domain of possible data values for the object, and an *attribute type,* which indicates the domain of possible properties that the object may possess. The labelled directed graph structure $<G(V, E); \lambda_V; \lambda_E>$ is called the document graph of D.

5.3.7 Definition 7

A *document specification* consists of a pair $DS = (C, Init)$. Here, C is a finite set of constraints, $\{C = \{C_1, C_2, \ldots, C_k\}$, where each C_i is a (computable) predicate on document graphs. *Init* is a set of initial document graphs. Given a document specification DS and a document graph G, G is said to meet the specification DS if and only if $G \in Init$ or $C_{\{i\}}(G)$ is true for each constraint C_i.

5.3.8 Definition 8

A *general document representation, D,* is a sextuple:

$$D = <\Sigma; V; E; \lambda_V; \lambda_E; \psi>$$

where Σ is a finite alphabet of symbols, V a finite set of vertices, E $V \times V$ is a set of directed edges; λ_V is a vertex labelling relation; λ_E an edge labelling relation; and ψ is a vertex content relation.

In terms of the computer representation of documents a general document representation, D, may be viewed as follows: Σ corresponds to the set of character symbols used to describe the document: thus text and annotations on the text present in the representing structure. Note that this supports representation at a number of levels: the low-level physical storage, with $\Sigma = \{0, 1\}$ and a higher level "readable" form with, for example, Σ being the ASCII character set. A document is regarded as a labelled directed graph structure. The vertices of the graph correspond to different textual blocks in the document (and thus the relation ψ associates each block with particular textual content(s) – words from Σ^*). The edges group together text blocks (vertices) that are "logically" related, e.g. the paragraphs comprising the introduction or the definitions, lemmata and proofs relating to the development of a single theorem in a mathematical paper. In a number of document representation systems it is possible to associate parameters in addition to textual content with vertices. Thus, the relation λ_V specifies the labelling of vertices with other attributes (e.g. font size, section header, etc.); similarly the relation λ_E allows names to be associated with edges to describe the nature of the relationship in which vertices are grouped. It may be noted that no constraints are placed on λ_V, λ_E and ψ: specifically they are not required – in the general framework – to be mappings. Thus, a concept of history can be captured: ψ may associate a (possibly infinite) number of different textual contents with each vertex and these might represent the progressive changes made to a section before it is completed. Similarly, the attributes of a vertex given by λ_V may change, and the view of edge relations. For examples of specific representation classes and an extension of this discussion, see Dunne and Staniford (1991).

5.4 The Four-Layer Model of Agent Communication

Throughout the literature on the structure of social units there are many models. Three very pervasive models are *hierarchical, network* and *market* (see Thompson et al. 1991), and workers in the field of distributed autonomous agents are actively engaged in investigating the application and suitability of such models in various projects. For a survey, the reader may like to consult Bond and Gasser (1988). In the four-layer model of agent communication we make use of a combination of hierarchy and network to form an *authority structure* (Durfee et al. 1987).

There are two primary mechanisms that may be used to structure autonomous agents: the vocabulary of the agent may be used to prescribe which other agents are allowed to communicate meaningfully with it, and we can use the computational ability of an agent to implement cooperation strategies that enforce a hierarchy of control. We partition *L-Agents* into the four levels according to their inherent abilities (see Fig. 5.2). We have included both *Ls-Agents* and *Ld-Agents* in level zero, bearing in mind that *Ld-Agents* are a subset of *Ls-Agents* that are designed with particular internal functional methods in mind. *Atomic* agents are, informally, agents of any type that can not be subdivided into simpler agents. *Complex* agents, on the other hand, are agents that are composed

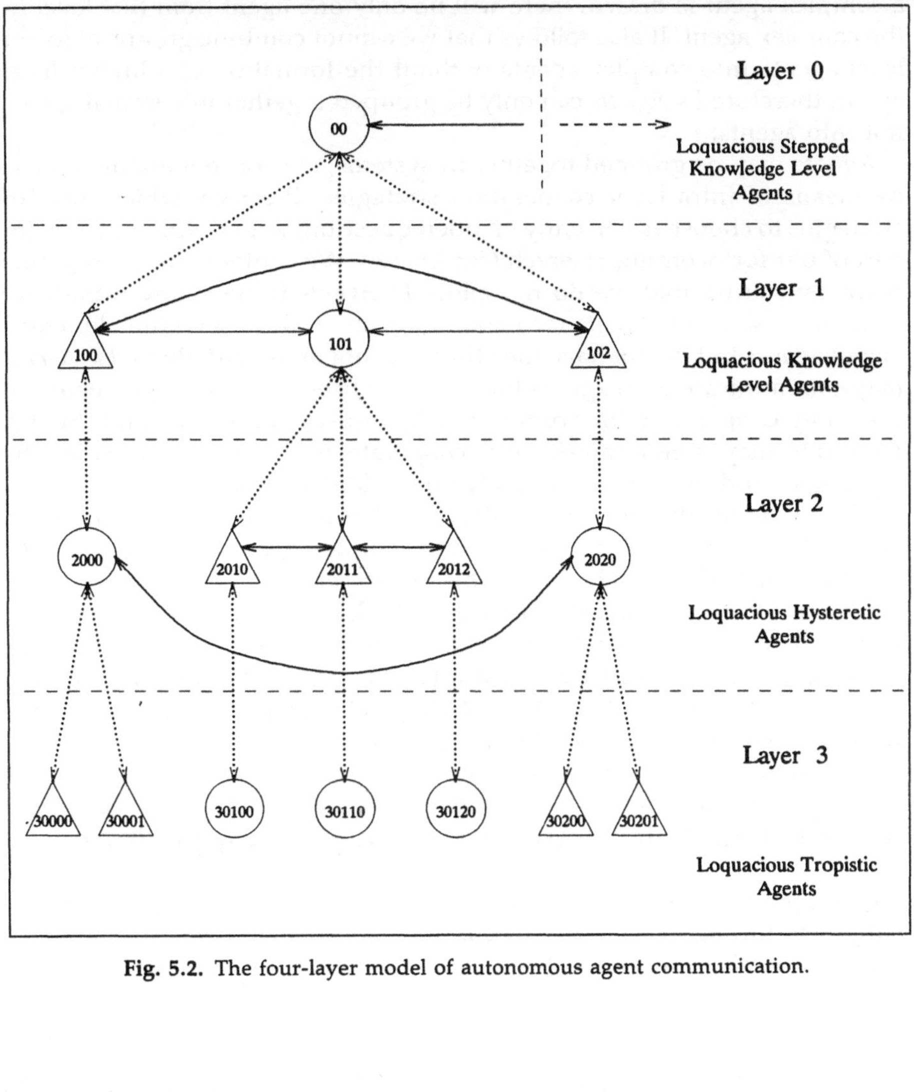

Fig. 5.2. The four-layer model of autonomous agent communication.

using at least two atomic agents from more than one level in the four-layer model. In a complex agent atomic agents will use *preemptive* cooperation in a downward direction, which leads to the principle that a complex agent embodies within it the notion of a hierarchical control structure. We use the term "preemptive cooperation" to allow for the situation in which lower level agents may refuse to accept a commission if they are already engaged upon an action commanded by some other higher level agent. This approach is necessary so that high level agents may share resources.

We do not view a number of agents on the same level cooperating upon a common task as a complex agent. Such a grouping is a set of autonomous communicating agents, which we might describe with collective nouns such as team, system, subsystem, society, etc. From the foregoing, it follows that, regardless of the level from which the highest level agent in a complex agent is drawn, there will be only one agent from that level in the complex agent. It also follows that we cannot combine groups of lower level agents into complex agents without the formation of a higher level agent; therefore *Ls-Agents* can only be grouped together into systems, etc., not into agents.

Agents may be grouped together in systems, etc., of cooperating equals by means of intra-layer cooperation strategies. Precisely which form of strategies to choose is currently an open question, which will form a major part of our forthcoming research (see below). We content ourselves at this point by stating that we do not allow *Lt-Agents* to have any intra-layer communication. *Lh-Agents* may communicate with observationally equivalent agents but do not have the ability to cooperate with them. *Lk-Agents* may communicate with agents that are not observationally equivalent but may only cooperate with observationally equivalent agents, and, finally, *Ls-Agents* may communicate and cooperate with both observationally equivalent and non-observationally equivalent agents.

We see, then, that we have networks of communicating agents being grouped into hierarchies to form more complex agents in a manner that is both rich and precisely specifiable. These notions, we contend, when taken with the agent architectures described, allow the design of systems that fit in very well with the ideas contained in the "top down" design philosophy first mooted by Dijkstra (1968), but enable the extension of those ideas to include the notion of cooperating equals in a system. (For further discussion of cooperation, see Chapters 1, 2, 3, 6, 9, 10 and 11.)

5.5 An Example Using an *Ls-Agent*: Rapporteur

One highly fruitful way in which people collaborate when working on a subject is through dialectical discussion: one person tries to establish a point while his colleague, either because of genuine scepticism or because he is playing devil's advocate for the purposes of the discussion, attempts to rebut the point. Such a discussion will help to structure the argument, clarify the position, and anticipate objections that require either additional exposition or refutation, or else that require the original position to be modified or withdrawn. When the aim is to produce a document, the discussion must be followed by a writing process, in which the resulting developed argument is committed to an electronic version of the document. In our system when such dialectical discussion occurs it is recorded by an autonomous *Ls-Agent* acting as a *rapporteur*, whose responsibility is to synthesize what may be a rambling discussion into a coherent document setting out the thrust of the debate. Our rapporteur agent is designed to support two or more authors collaborating through dialectic and to produce a report of their discussion. The report is linked as an auxiliary structure to the main document, where it provides the background supporting evidence for the conclusion of the argument, which itself makes up the textual content of one of the nodes in the main document graph. Of course, if it should be desired by the authors, the dialogue report can be included as textual content in the main document.

Rapporteur agents are designed to allow collaborative participation in a constructive dialogue game according to well-defined principles given below. One set of participants must adopt the role of proposer, making an initial assertion and then taking turns to provide arguments in support of that assertion. The other participant(s) adopt an opposition role in which challenges and objections to the proposer's assertion and supporting premises are put forward. The rapporteur agent allows counter objections and makes provision for both sides to modify earlier arguments. Either side can win the argument; in the case of the opposition being successful, the original assertion must either be negated or withdrawn.

Both sides take turn and turn about in presenting their respective cases, although one member of a side may take several consecutive turns for that side in order to present a particular line of thought. Game play takes place in a structured way which reflects the different roles that the two sides bring to the dialogue. The proposers are required to present an assertion, and are allowed to modify that assertion, provide supporting premises and modify those premises, refute objections from the opposition and require the opposition to continue objections and challenges. In their turn the opposition are allowed to challenge the assertion or premises, object to premises and modify those objections and require the proposers to continue the assertion, premises and refutations. Either side may accept defeat, the opposition by accepting it has no valid challenge or objection, the proposers by accepting they have no valid refutation. The rapporteur agent oversees the game and will only allow legal moves to be made. The general dialogue graph model that is realized by rapporteur agents cannot be included here because of space limitations. Interested readers are referred to Bench-Capon et al. (1991); sequences of legal moves can be worked out readily from this graph. (For further discussion relevant to the subject of floor control, see Chapters 2 and 11.)

A rapporteur agent has no notion of the semantics of any argument; it provides a way of enforcing a general syntactic structure to a dialogue represented by a graph. This structure is sufficiently flexible to allow the participants to conduct their dialogue using deduction, induction or indeed abduction as the mode of reasoning in their arguments (see Fig. 5.3).

A discussion report is a simple example of the more general document models described earlier. A report graph, $G_r(V_r, E_r)$, is a DAG. The vertices in V_r denote objects in the report and the edges in E_r depict logical connections between the objects. Each object has an associated object type which consists of two parts: a data type which specifies the domain of possible data values for the object (e.g. word, phrase, sentence, etc.), and an attribute type which indicates the domain of possible properties that the object may possess (e.g. font, size, etc.). Objects may also be labelled. A report specification consists of a pair $RS = (C, Init)$, where C is a finite set of constraints, $C = \{C_1, C_2, \ldots, C_k\}$ where each C_i is a computable predicate on report graphs. *Init* is a set of initial report graphs. Given a report specification RS and a report graph G_r, G_r is said to

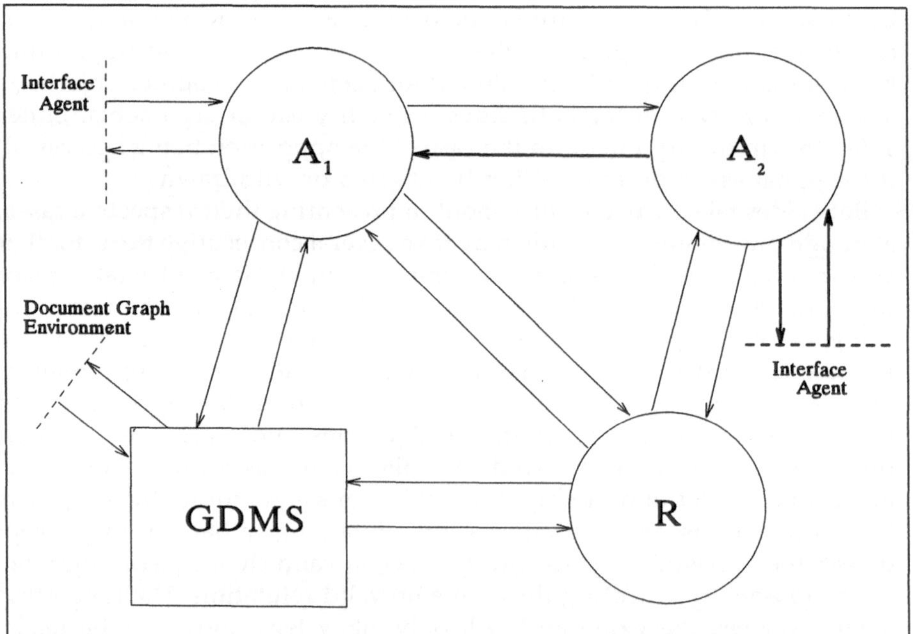

Fig. 5.3. A communicating sub-system of *Ls-Agents* with rapporteur providing support for two authors.

meet the specification *RS* if and only if $G_r \in Init$ or $C_i(G_r)$ is true for each constraint C_i.

Report graphs are abstract representations of report structure: the form that is manipulated during the generation of the report from the raw dialogue graph. Our objective is to have this abstract representation closely matching the dialogue participants' conceptual representation of an accurately summed up logical discussion.

We thus have two graphs, one – a directed cyclic graph – representing the realized dialogue space, and one – a directed acyclic graph – the model of a report of a dialectic discussion, both graphs containing single sources and sinks. The main task facing the rapporteur agent is to transform the former into the latter. This will, for example, include moves to enable the digressions common in dialectic, such as when a person puts forward a definition which is found by a challenge to be inadequate, and which is consequently modified, to be elided so that the report will show only the final form of the definition, and the debate which led to the modification will be included in the justification of that definition.

To this end, during the course of a dialogue, the rapporteur agent explicitly builds a set of nodes V_d, while implicitly following a set of edges E_d of the dialogue graph G_d (V_d, E_d). To achieve a mapping in between the two graphs the agent adopts the strategy of partitioning V_d such that a set of candidate nodes, SP_d say, includes all nodes in V_d that lie on the shortest path through E_d, and then discards nodes that lie in $V_d - SP_d$. Depending on which side won the game, the agent partitions SP_d to produce V_r as follows:

1. Proposer wins: then V_r includes all nodes in SP_d that are premises and in addition the assertion node. $SP_d - V_r$ is discarded.
2. Opposition wins: then V_r includes all nodes in SP_d that are accepted premises, all nodes in SP_d that are successful objections and in addition a node containing the negation of the assertion node. $SP_d - V_r$ is discarded.

To complete the report graph G_r (V_r, E_r) the agent produces E_r in accordance with the constraints present in the report specification. Upon termination of the dialogue, the author agent A_1 indicates to the GDMS agents whether the full report or just the conclusion of the argument is required as the textual content of the document node. In parallel the rapporteur agent communicates the report to the GDMS agents. In the case that just the conclusion is required the GDMS agents store the conclusion of the argument as the textual content of the document node and the full dialogue report as an auxiliary structure. We present a highly simplified example in which two authors are critiquing the work of a third:

A_1: Jones clearly intends that this place is a place where careless people have picnicked.

A_2: How do you arrive at that conclusion?

A_1: It is clear that all places where soiled paper plates and cups are scattered are either places where careless people have picnicked or places where rubbish has been accidentally spilled from bins.

A_2: Yes, but you still have not made the case. How do we know that rubbish has not been spilled from a bin?

A_1: In an earlier passage it was stated that "this spot was untouched by the hand of man" so we can assume that no person has installed bins there and it was stated at the beginning of this passage that "the place was littered with paper cups and plates".

A_2: OK! I am convinced.

This dialogue would generate the following text content of a node in the critique document:

> Jones clearly intends that this place is a place where careless people have picnicked.

and a report as an auxiliary structure to the critique as:

> It is clear that all places where soiled paper plates and cups are scattered are either places where careless people have picnicked or places where rubbish has been accidentally spilled from bins. In an earlier passage it was stated that "this spot was untouched by the hand of man" so we can assume that no person has installed bins there and it was stated at the beginning of this passage that "the place was littered with paper cups and plates".

therefore:

> Jones clearly intends that this place is a place where careless people have picnicked.

This example is necessarily contrived but we have tried to maintain a sufficient level of self-evident analogy between the argument we present and practical scenarios to provide sufficient realism for readers to envisage how rapporteur agents operate.

5.6 Discussion and Conclusion

We have presented an architectural model for autonomous communicating agents designed with a combination of hierarchical and network features. The environment upon which the agents act was specified as a DAG, which we view as being in a dynamic state by the use of graph grammars. The hierarchical element in the architectural model is produced by taking account of four levels of agent ability in conjunction with a very prescribed form of cooperation; the orthogonal network element is obtained using intra-layer communication to form networks of cooperating agents, the networks again being partitioned on the basis of agent ability.

We contend that this architecture provides a rich, specifiable model on which to build, predict and study the behaviour of autonomous communicating agents. The study of cooperation between such agents is an open question that we intend to address in our work in the immediate future. Much of the previous work that has been done (Axelrod 1984; Bond and Gasser 1988) has been concerned with much simpler architectures than the one presented in this chapter and we believe that we will need to carry out a considerable amount of empirical work in order to determine the best way or ways of building from that work as a base. To this end, we are currently experimenting with rapporteur agents as in our presented example, with a system of agents providing simple text processing, and in addition we intend to develop a set of agents to form a concordance/cross-referencer tool. We see these three approaches as providing a good experimental testbed for studying parallelism and cooperation between agents.

It is our belief that the practical consequences that will arise from our work will be an enhanced ability to design and build systems of authorship support tools that will reduce the cognitive burden on authors when they use a computer system to aid them in collaborative working.

Acknowledgement Geof Staniford is supported by an SERC research grant.

Chapter 6

Agency within CSCW: Towards the Development of Active Cooperative Working Environments

G.M.P. O'Hare, P. Dongha, L.A. Macaulay and S. Viller

6.1 Introduction

This chapter describes attempts currently being made within the Cooperative Requirements Capture (CRC) project to harness some of the work on "Agency". The CRC project is concerned with the development of a system that provides effective computer support for the CRC process. This process involves a multidisciplinary team, who actively collaborate in the capture of system requirements, specifically, in the context of this project, computer systems. This team, after an initial formulative meeting, return to their respective corporate positions and are, therefore, distributed both geographically and temporally. This contrasts with the traditional scenario in which design teams meet together frequently and discuss system requirements in a face-to-face setting, and identify requirements through the use of a particular methodology.

Each team member, or "stakeholder", has a particular portfolio of skills and experiences that are of relevance to the system under design. Consequently, each stakeholder has a particular objective, or set of objectives, that they are trying to preserve with a view to ensuring their adequate representation in the final agreed design. (See Chapters 2 and 7 for further discussion.) Like those of all other organizations, the social dynamics of the design team are highly complex and very important. Stakeholders often disagree: their objectives, of course, often conflict; individuals attempt, and sometimes succeed, to gain dominance; others feel alienated, resulting in a lack of participation; mutually beneficial allegiances are formed, and so forth. The "attitudes" of team members evolve and are revised as a result of the social interactions.

This social process must be managed effectively. In the traditional medium in which this activity takes place this is achieved by a facilitator. While a facilitator will still oversee the activities of the design team within the CRC project, they will, however, be performing their tasks in a computer mediated environment. This medium is less "rich" and as such considerable computer support is necessitated.

Within the CRC project a software environment – the "Cooperative Working Platform" – is under development which assists in the management of both the social process and the task. A particular component of an object-oriented methodology is supported and it is within this that the team members express their contributions.

The design of this platform has been greatly influenced by work within Distributed Artificial Intelligence (DAI). (See also Chapters 8, 9, 10 and 11.) The concept of "Agency" has been used to view the interactions of the stakeholders and their negotiations, and, furthermore, has been used as a metaphor for the design of the underlying software platform itself. Component tools within the platform have certain skills and deductive capabilities, and interact with each other in given circumstances. Consequently, they are perceived as agents and collectively constitute an "Active Environment".

This chapter describes our efforts toward the development of an "Active Cooperative Working Environment". Section 6.2 presents the research landscape within which this work was conducted, while Section 6.3 details the objectives, design and implementation details of the Cooperative Working Platform. Section 6.4 presents our conclusions.

6.2 Related Research

The work described here is, we believe, representative of the convergence of several research areas previously regarded as distinct. This work seeks to harness results from the areas of Group Decision Support Systems (GDSS), DAI, Computer Supported Cooperative Work (CSCW) and Software Engineering (SE).

Currently, work within the GDSS arena is reaching such a degree of maturity that influential systems have been developed and tested in the field. Examples include PLEXYS (Nunamaker et al. 1988) and COLAB (Stefik et al. 1987). However, more pioneering work is seeking to harness some of the capabilities of Artificial Intelligence (AI) to produce Decision Support Systems (DSSs) with a greater deductive capability and a greater degree of autonomy.

Several classes of system have emerged of late. Active DSSs represent those systems which, although capable of reactive support of the user's needs, can also provide proactive support. Such systems do not always operate under the explicit directives of the user, and, on occasion, can be seen to use their own "initiative". Manheim et al. (1991) define active DSSs as "decision support systems in which the computer works independently of explicit user direction to assist the user in working on the problem".

Symbiotic systems, on the other hand (Manheim 1989), represent a particular class of active DSS. Symbiotic DSSs (S/DSS) utilize a user model as the basis upon which to make logical deductions which determine the proactive computational processes performed by the system. It is, however, the intention that such computer support should be regarded as being adjunct rather than replacement in nature.

Work within DAI has addressed the problem of constructing intelligent systems but based upon a multi-agent metaphor where several computational cognitive entities coexist within the same environment. These "agents" are each equipped with a set of "skills" which they may or may not offer to their colleagues. This approach has, to date, largely been used as a conduit for the development, maintenance and evolution of intelligent systems. All too often, varying social metaphors have been imported into DAI and used as a prescriptive model upon which to base the social dynamics of the agent community. Rarely, however, have the experiences of interacting computational agents been exported to comparable social situations in collaborative working. Recent research has addressed the convergence between DAI and GDSS (Shaw et al. 1991), and work on participant systems seems to hold considerable potential.

SE has always advocated modular decomposition as a mechanism for facilitating the development, maintenance and evolution of large, complex software systems. DAI embraces this principle, and more recently synergy between the two research areas has resulted in the adoption of a new programming metaphor, that of Agent-Orientated Programming (AOP) (Shoham 1990). This can be viewed as a specialization of object-oriented programming. An agent can be considered as an object with a particular structure imposed upon it which characterizes its "mental state". This includes components such as beliefs, capabilities, commitments, choices and so forth. The mental state is thus captured in the normal way by the introduction of standard epistemic logic whose belief and knowledge operators are equipped with some awareness of time. Explicit operators are introduced to represent commitment, capability and choice. In addition inter-agent communication is considerably more stylized than in the object-oriented case. Agents are each empowered with communication operators which are strongly typed and are based upon speech act theory, including verbs like inform, offer, request, decline, promise and so forth. The methods associated with the agents will be dependent upon the epistemic state of the agent and other society requirements like honesty or consistency.

The work described in this chapter seeks to integrate these research threads. The Cooperative Working Platform picks up on the work on active DSSs and seeks to develop this. The platform we are developing seeks to include both reactive and proactive capabilities, with the latter being based on not merely a user model, but rather an analysis of the social dynamics of the cooperative capture team. In addition, it endeavours to accommodate work on intentionality in general in the provision of support for the social process. For example, conflict resolution strategies commissioned within DAI are being incorporated into the Cooperative Working Platform. The models formalized to represent agent intentions and those of its community may also be applicable for stakeholder models. These models are of use when reasoning about the behaviour of stakeholder(s) and providing advice to the facilitator.

6.3 The Cooperative Working Platform

6.3.1 Objectives

The primary objective of the Cooperative Working Platform is to develop a software environment that can actively support a multidisciplinary team engaged in the requirements capture and analysis process. We recognize within this work that effective computer support for collaborative work in its most general sense would necessitate a rich portfolio of tools. This set of tools would, among others, include tools with a capability to:

- Assist in analysis and strategic decision making.
- Support visualization and scenario building.
- Support the construction and maintenance of multimedia documents.
- Enable effective communication.
- Assist in the management of the social process.
- Assist in the management of the particular task undertaken.

This work seeks to focus on the last three of these areas. Within the Cooperative Working Platform we are attempting to provide support for a requirements capture team whose members are distributed both geographical and temporally. The stakeholders within this team will, typically, engage in numerous distinct activities concurrently. The anticipated communication mode is therefore asynchronous in nature. The Cooperative Working Platform will need to be one application of many that can be supported by stakeholder workstations.

Specifically, the Cooperative Working Platform seeks to:

- Support effective textual communication between stakeholders.

- Provide support for the social process, and particularly for the facilitator who oversees this process. This support could be system initiated or facilitator initiated via, for example, Social Meters (graphical icons that represent group dynamics), the capacity to recognize various social syndromes, or Avoid, Recognize, Resolve Conflict.
- Provide support for the particular task of requirements capture, using a particular fragment of an object-oriented methodology. It seeks, however, not to preclude the importing of other methods.
- In part, help with the preparation of a requirements capture document.

For further discussion of cooperation, see Chapters 1, 2, 3, 5, 9 and 10.

6.3.2 Design of the Cooperative Working Platform

The architecture of the Cooperative Working Platform is comprised of the following computational agents:

- Communication Agent
- Listener Agent
- Interface Agent
- Method Control Agent
- Facilitator Support Agent

A computational agent has a particular set of capabilities and an ability to communicate with other software agents with whom it is acquainted. Figure 6.1 presents a top-level description of the Cooperative Working Platform. Stakeholders communicate with each other via their workstations over a local area network. Each stakeholder can communicate with those stakeholders with which it is acquainted by sending "messages". Each stakeholder has locally an Interface Agent which is responsible for enabling them to visualize the underlying software system and enabling their effective interaction. Messages are packaged so as to conform to a particular communication protocol prior to communication via the network. The associated encoding and decoding of messages transmitted along the network is the responsibility of a Communication (Comms) Agent. Upon decoding or encoding a message, the Communication Agent forwards it to the appropriate agent. An agent in this sense can be either the Listener Agent, Conversation Analysis Agent, Method Control Agent or any of the Interface Agents associated with an individual stakeholder.

While the messages are decoded by the Communication Agent, the actions taken as a consequence of their receipt are performed by the agent

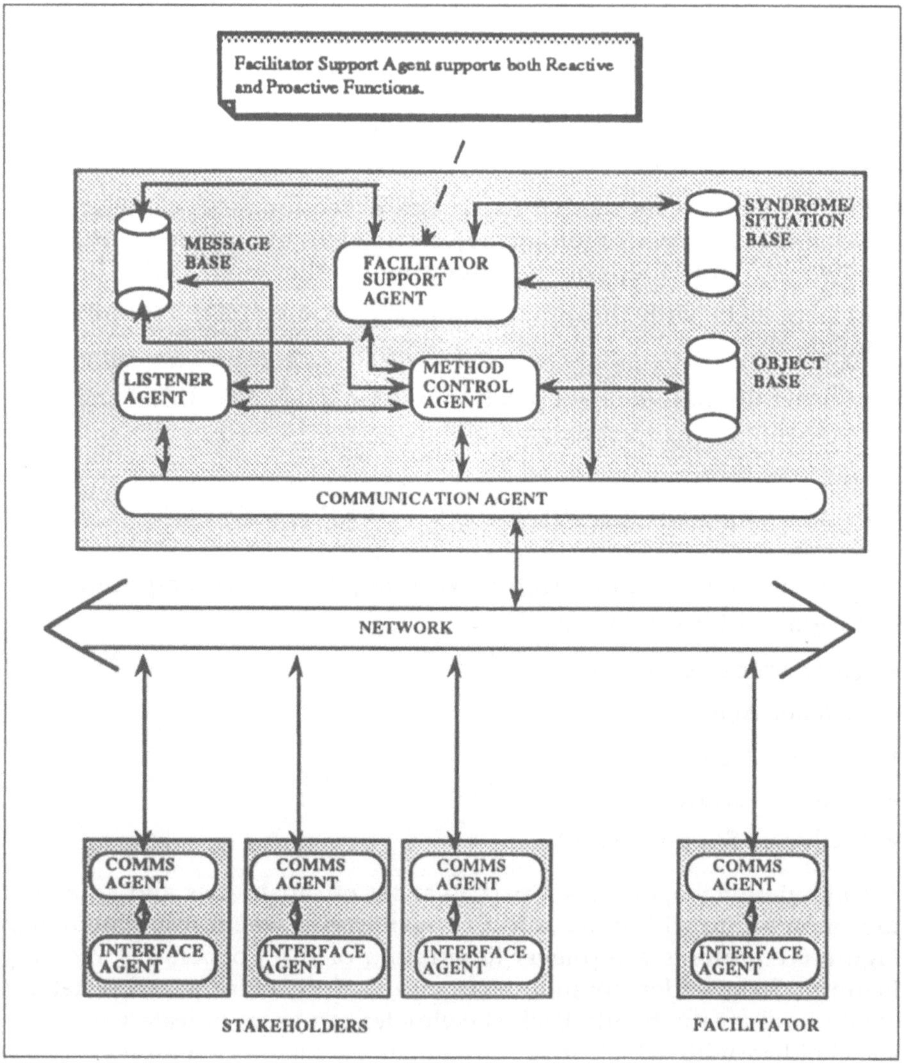

Fig. 6.1. The structure of the Cooperative Working Platform.

to whom the message is forwarded. The Listener Agent is responsible for recording all messages and generally archiving network traffic in the Message Base. The Facilitator Support Agent, on the other hand, performs various analyses on the Message Base in an attempt either to diagnose a particular situation or to predict the likely occurrence of such a condition.

Finally, the Method Control Agent has direct responsibility for overseeing the particular requirements capture method being employed. It will maintain the evolution of the Object Base as the various discrete stages of the method are undergone. In order to regulate the progression of the method, the Method Control Agent will necessarily have to communicate with the Facilitator Support Agent and the Listener Agent, together with interrogating the Object and Message Bases.

Section 6.3.3 will consider each of these agents in turn, providing a greater insight into the implementation of the platform.

6.3.3 Implementation Details

While this research adopts an underlying multi-agent model, it was felt that the current state of AOP languages represented an inappropriate base upon which to build; Agent0 (Shoham 1990) and Elephant2000 (McCarthy 1990), for example, are largely in the development stages.

There have, however, been moves to integrate the object-oriented paradigm with other programming paradigms. Successful marriages with the functional model have been achieved in the form of two early Lisp-based object-oriented systems, namely Flavors, developed at MIT, and Loops, developed at Xerox PARC. More recently, and perhaps to be the most influential, is the Common Lisp Object System (CLOS) (Gabriel et al. 1991).

The Cooperative Working Platform was developed using CLOS and resides on Sun workstations connected via an Ethernet. The Cooperative Working Platform currently encompasses five agents; the Communication, Listener, Interface, Method Control and Facilitator Support Agents. These are considered in turn in Sections 6.3.3.1 to 6.3.3.5.

6.3.3.1 The Communication Agent

As stated earlier, the Communication Agent is responsible for controlling access to the network. Messages need to be preprocessed to ensure that they adhere to a particular communications protocol; detailed consideration of this is beyond the scope of this chapter. As can be seen, additional information must be augmented to the actual message itself in order to ensure that the message arrives at its intended destination. Such transmitted messages are referred to as "message packets" or simply "packets". Figure 6.2 shows the structure of the Communication Agent, which comprises two subsystems, the message handling subsystem and the registration handling subsystem.

The message packet structure is comprised of two layers of protocol. The first is referred to as the *Network Protocol* (NP) layer and the second as the *Application Protocol* (AP) layer. The use of these two layers is best demonstrated with an example: user Linda (the group facilitator) wishes to dispatch a message to all those on the cooperative requirements capture team. The following steps are executed in constructing, delivering and interpreting a packet which contains this message:

1. User Linda selects her preferred editor, types the body of the message (simple text) into a text editor, and indicates that the message is for a particular group whose alias has already been created. She does this by selecting the appropriate menu option, namely "group", and then selecting the "send" operation from a menu on her user interface (see Fig. 6.9).
2. The communication agent at Linda's workstation encodes the following packet:

   Group . User-message . <message>

   The NP layer contains the token "Group" and the AP layer contains the token "User-message". This packet is sent in the first instance to the Listener Agent (all messages originating from a user are sent first of all to the Listener Agent before being forwarded to the intended recipient(s)).
3. The Listener Agent picks up the packet and proceeds to decode the

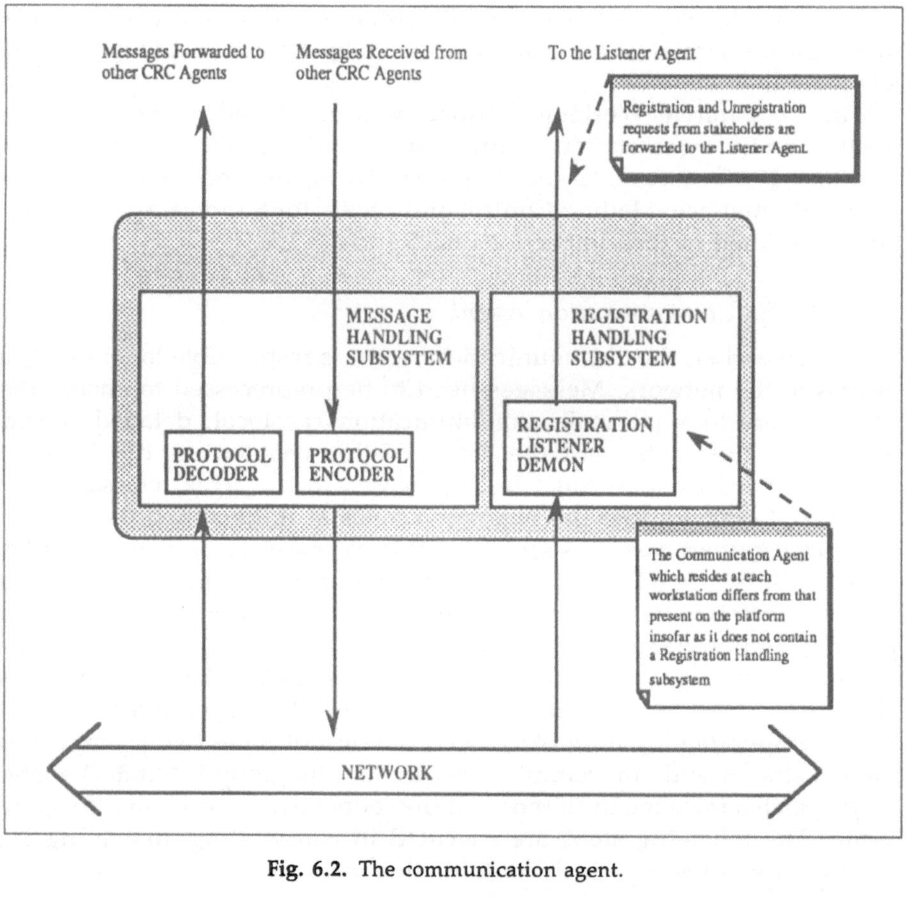

Fig. 6.2. The communication agent.

network protocol. The network protocol indicates that this message is to be forwarded to the CRC team. The network protocol is removed from the packet and the remainder of the packet is left unchanged. The new packet is:

User-message . <message>

This packet is then sent on the network to each member of the group.

4. The participant's Communication Agent picks up this packet at some time in the future and decodes the AP. Notice that the NP is not required because the message is now effectively in the possession of the recipient(s), who will only be interested in the AP. The AP "User-message" indicates that the message originates from Linda and is a text message. This information and the <message> part are passed on to the Interface Agent on each recipient's workstation.
5. The Interface Agent then interrogates the body of <message> in order to discover the sender and the text of the message. The user interface is affected by the Interface Agent to indicate that a new message has arrived (see Fig. 6.10).

Note that a packet that is to be sent from a user to another user needs to have a NP since it will be processed by the listener before it is passed on to the intended recipient(s). However, a packet that is sent from a system agent to a user need only have an AP since user Interface Agents do not need to decode NPs. The message handling subsystem of Fig. 6.2 consists of two processes: one which encodes messages into the appropriate protocol (Protocol Encoder) and another which decodes messages, thus extracting only the message information (Protocol Decoder). The former receives messages from CRC agents and adds or removes any protocols before forwarding or transmitting them, while the latter receives messages from the local area network, disassembles the packet received, and thus enables the message to be extracted, decoded and subsequently forwarded to the appropriate agent.

The second of the two subsystems, the registration handling system, is concerned with stakeholder requests for registration on the system. The Communication Agent initially invokes a registration listener daemon. This daemon resides on the monitor and is continually waiting for participants to start a CRC session. The wish to initiate such a session is indicated by the participant typing "crc" at their workstation. As a result, a registration request packet is transmitted via the Interface Agent to the monitor. Upon recognition and decoding of such a packet the registration listener daemon thereafter creates a connection with the originating participant, effectively registering them with the monitor. The registration listener daemon consists essentially of:

PROCESS Registration Listener Daemon;
BEGIN

```
WHILE the monitor is active DO
BEGIN
  IF a participant attempts a connection THEN
  BEGIN
    get participant's username;
    check valid username
  END
  IF valid username THEN
    Send "Register New User Request" to Listener Agent
  ELSE refuse the connection
 END
END;
```

6.3.3.2 The Listener Agent

The function of the Listener Agent is essentially one of receiving messages from the Communication Agent, storing them in the Message Base, taking a copy of each message and forwarding the copy to the intended recipient(s). Not all messages will be stored in the Message Base. For example, a "Die" message, indicating a participant's wish to terminate a session, will not be stored.

The Listener Agent can be thought of as actively waiting to invoke numerous processes. For each participant registered with the system, four processes exist which are placed on wait queues awaiting the occurrence of different events. Two further processes exist, one of which deals with the registration of participants. The Reader, Inspect and Decode, and Writer Processes collectively place messages in the Message Base and subsequently forward copies of these to the in-trays of those for whom the message is intended and in turn to the recipient(s) themselves. Each of these processes has an associated "guard" (as in the Dijkstra sense), and once any of the guards is satisfied its associated process then becomes a candidate process which can be activated. As can be seen from the pseudo-code below, the guard associated with Writer(N) process is that the in-tray(N) is not empty. If several candidate processes exist, then one is chosen randomly by the scheduler and becomes active for an allotted time-slice, or until it becomes suspended on a wait queue. The general structure of the Listener Agent is depicted in Fig. 6.3.

```
AGENT Listener;
BEGIN
  REPEAT
    IF Register User Request(N)    →Register(N);
    IF NOT (out-tray(N) empty)    →Inspect & Decode out-tray(N);
    IF User N Registered          →Reader(N);
    IF NOT (in-tray(N) empty)     →Writer(N);
  FOREVER
```

```
END;

PROCESS Register(N);

   PROCEDURE Create Participant Processes(N);
   BEGIN
      create Out-tray(N);
      create In-tray(N);
      create Reader(N);
      create Writer(N);
      create Inspect & Decode Out-tray(N);
   END;
```

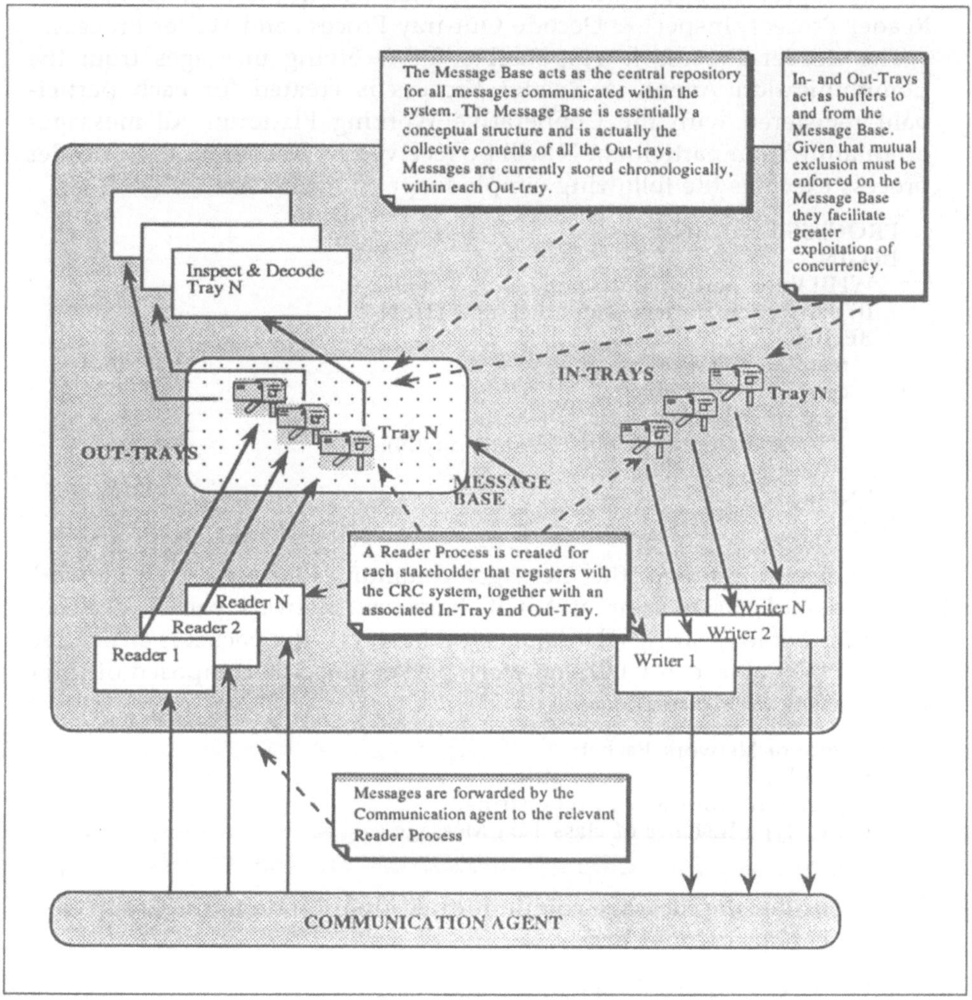

Fig. 6.3. The listener agent.

```
PROCEDURE Establish Connections(N);
BEGIN
  FOR participant(N) DO
  BEGIN
    connect Reader Process(N) to Out-tray(N);
    connect between the In-tray(N) and a Writer Process(N).
  END
END;

BEGIN
  Create Participant Processes(N);
  Establish Connections(N)
END; (* Register *)
```

Three subprocesses for each user are created within the Register Process: Reader Process, Inspect & Decode Out-tray Process and Writer Process.

The Reader Process is responsible for receiving messages from the Communication Agent. A Reader Process is created for each participant registered with the Cooperative Working Platform. All messages originating from participant N will be received by Reader N. Each Reader process executes the following simple loop:

```
PROCESS Reader(N);
BEGIN
  WHILE the participant is still connected DO
  IF the participant has sent a message THEN
  BEGIN
    read the message;
    create message object;
    lock out-tray(N)
      write the message object to out-tray(N)
    unlock out-tray(N)
  END
END;
```

As has been described, the messages communicated across the network are necessarily in the form of ASCII characters. Network packets are thus comprised of long strings. Upon receipt, however, the packet is structured into a CLOS object. A CLOS network packet object is composed of three components (attributes):

```
(Instance of Network-Packet:
  network-protocol      : type string
  application-protocol      : type string
  body : type Instance of class Text Message
)
```

If we consider the message communicated from Linda to the group then the CLOS object would be:

```
(Instance of Network-Packet:
  network-protocol "Group"
  application-protocol "text-message"
```

```
    body (Instance of Text Message
      Id  mg-id-number (generated by listener agent)
      From "Facilitator"
      To  "Group"
      Date "17th June 1992 14:34:01"
      Subject  "Stop Brainstorming"
      Keywords " "
      Body "OK Folks, I think that is enough for us to be going on with now.
      How about starting on evaluating what we've got? We can always add
      more as they arise while doing this."
      In Reply To NIL
      Status "unread"
  )
  )
```

Coercion needs to take place in order to convert a message from one representational form into another. Two functions exist: those of structuring and unstructuring. The former accepts a message in the form of a large string and converts it into an appropriate CLOS object. Unstructuring (the inverse operation) converts a CLOS object into a large string containing all the attributes of the CLOS object. Structuring and unstructuring are totally transparent to the listener and to the interface. The structuring and unstructuring operations are implemented as methods that are specialized dependent upon the type of CLOS objects that are passed as parameters.

At present the messages are stored persistently in the form of CLOS objects, thus enabling all manipulations of messages within the system (except of course network transmission) to be expressed in terms of methods associated with the network packet class.

The Inspect & Decode Out-tray subprocess manages the interaction between the participant's out-tray and the appropriate in-trays. A separate process (for each participant N currently registered) poles the out-tray for user N. Upon identification of at least one message within that tray, a copy of the message is retrieved, unstructured and decoded. Decoding involves inspection of the network protocol. If the message is a "Die" message then an Unregister process will dispose of the processes associated with the participant who sent that packet. If, however, the message protocol is either "Broadcast" or "Addressee" then the message will need to be forwarded and consequently passed to the in-tray(s) of the intended recipient(s). Because the in-trays constitute a resource shared among all the Inspect & Decode Out-tray processes currently in existence, and the Writer process associated with each stakeholder, mutual exclusion must be enforced. This is achieved by the simple locking and unlocking of the Message Base. In a similar fashion access to each out-tray(N) must be controlled as these are shared by both the Reader(N) and the Inspect & Decode Out-tray(N) processes. The Inspect Out-tray process is described in the following section of pseudo-code:

```
PROCESS Inspect & Decode Out-tray(N);
BEGIN
  WHILE participant(N) is connected to the monitor DO
    IF NOT (out-tray(N) empty) THEN
    BEGIN
      lock out-tray(N);
        read and copy message object from the out-tray(N);
      unlock the out-tray(N);
      destructure the message;
      CASE message OF
        "Die"   : Unregister(N);
        "Broadcast" OR "addressee"  :
      BEGIN
          FOR each recipient(N) DO
            lock the in-tray(N);
              write copy of message
            unlock the message base;
          END
      END
    END
END;
```

The final process, the Writer process, manages the dispatching of messages to users logged onto the Cooperative Working Platform. Each Writer(N) continually polls its respective in-tray and upon identification of a message it is removed from the in-tray and dispatched to the Communication Agent to be sent via the network to the recipient:

```
PROCESS Writer(N);
BEGIN
  WHILE participant(N) is connected to the monitor DO
    IF NOT (in-tray(N) empty) THEN
    BEGIN
      lock in-tray(N);
        remove a message from the in-tray;
      unlock in-tray(N);
      pass the message to Participant(N);
    END
END;
```

6.3.3.3 *The Interface Agent*

The basic cycle of steps for handling the interface (Fig. 6.4) is encapsulated within three modules: screen event monitor, screen event decoder and screen handler, which form part of the Interface Agent.

The screen event monitor continually awaits any actions taken by the user that are intended to effect changes to the user interface. These actions are typically referred to as events. For example, the screen event monitor notices events such as mouse movements, mouse clicks and key strokes. However, no distinction is made between events at this stage; the presence of an event is simply noticed:

```
PROCESS Screen Event Monitor;
BEGIN
  WHILE (user is logged into the CRC system) DO
  IF (event queue not empty) THEN
  BEGIN
    pop next event from event queue;
    invoke the screen event decoder with current event
  END
END;
```

The screen event decoder is then responsible for interpreting events noticed by the screen event monitor. For example, a mouse click event will be interpreted by the screen event decoder, which then decides what action needs to be taken as a result of a mouse click within a particular situation – for example, pop up a menu if the mouse button was depressed over the frame of a window or expose the window under the mouse if the mouse button was depressed inside the window:

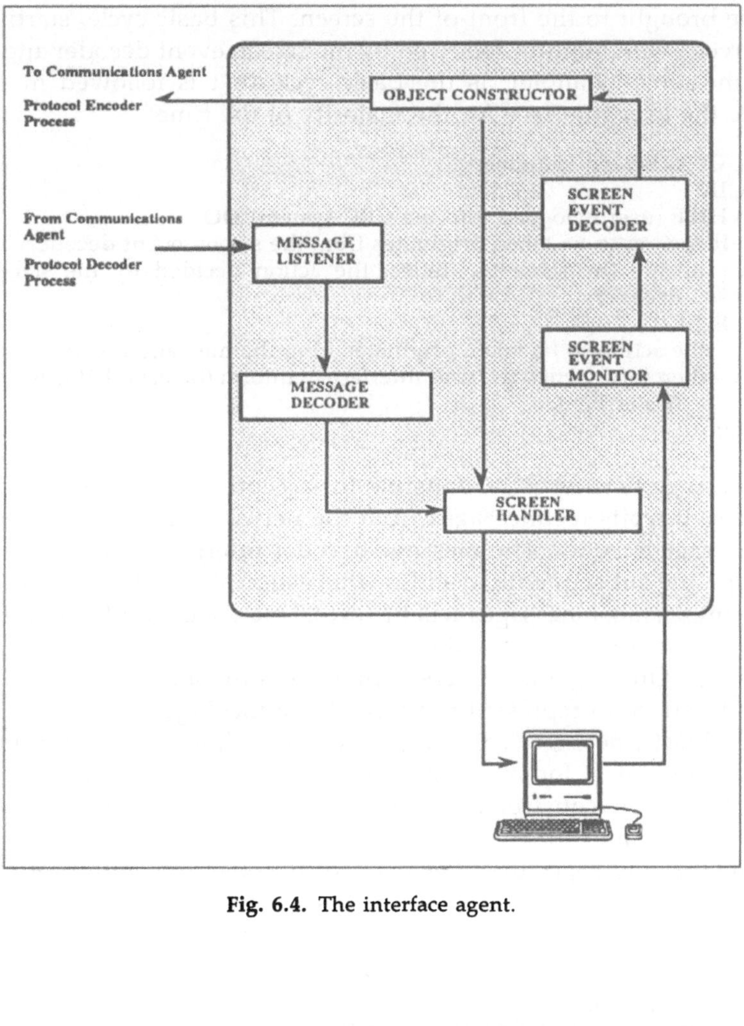

Fig. 6.4. The interface agent.

```
PROCESS Screen Event Decoder;
BEGIN
  WHILE (user is logged into the CRC system) DO
  BEGIN
    decode the event;
    decide what action needs to be invoked;
    IF (action is one of sending a message) THEN
    BEGIN
      invoke the object (message) constructor passing to it the message
        to be sent;
      pass the message to the Communication Agent
    END
    ELSE pass the action onto the Screen Handler
  END
END;
```

The screen handler is then invoked. It is responsible for executing the actions decided by the screen event decoder. For example, a menu will be displayed on the user interface as a result of a mouse click or a window will be brought to the front of the screen. This basic cycle, starting from the screen event monitor followed by the screen event decoder and ending with the screen handler, is the basic cycle that is followed in order to handle the user interface for the majority of the time:

```
PROCESS Screen Handler;
BEGIN
  WHILE (user is logged into the CRC system) DO
    IF (action to be taken originates from the screen event decoder) THEN
      update the screen to reflect the action decided by the screen event
        decoder
    ELSE
      the action to be taken originates from the message decoder
      therefore change the user interface to inform the user that a new message
        has arrived;
END;
```

The message listener is responsible for accepting messages intended for the user. It waits for messages from the network and passes them on to the message decoder. The message decoder interprets the protocol of the message and subsequently decides what action should be taken as a result. For example, most messages will be textual messages similar to those on an email system, in which case the user needs to be informed of the arrival of a message. Once again, the screen handler is invoked, which updates the user's interface to represent the arrival of a message.

The object (message) constructor is responsible for creating messages that are intended for recipients other that the user. For example, the user may have constructed a message and may wish to send it to other participants in the group. The user will make a menu selection to send the message, the screen event decoder will interpret the send request and invoke the object (message) constructor accordingly. This module constructs an object (in the object-oriented programming sense) and then passes it to the protocol encoder process (which packages the message, including in it the appropriate protocols, and eventually passes the message on to the monitor). At the same instance the screen event handler is invoked to effect a change on the user interface which should inform the user that a message has indeed been sent:

```
PROCESS Message Listener;
BEGIN
   WHILE (user is logged into the CRC system) DO
   IF (incoming message queue not empty) THEN
   BEGIN
      remove the first message from the message queue;
      pass the message onto the message decoder
   END
END;

PROCESS Message Decoder;
BEGIN
   WHILE (user is logged into the CRC system) DO
   BEGIN
      interpret the protocol of the message;
      decide on action based on the protocol of the message;
      pass the action to be taken to the screen handler
   END
END;
```

6.3.3.4 *The Method Control Agent*

The Method Control Agent is responsible for monitoring the progress of the team of stakeholders with respect to the particular method under commission. Within the CRC project we are not concerned with methodological issues *per se,* but rather, given a particular requirements capture method, how we can utilize this within a computer mediated environment, and, particularly, what computer support can realistically be provided in the pursuit of CRC. As a frame of reference for this project we are concerning ourselves merely with a very small component of the overall requirements capture process. The project has adopted an object-oriented approach (see also Chapters 2 and 4), and such an approach underpins the medium within which we elicit our requirements. We are focusing on the early stages of requirements capture, which comprise the identification, agreement, prioritization structuring and description of objects within the particular problem domain. Figure 6.5 describes the portion of some generic method that we are addressing.

At present computer support exists only for the identification, prioritization and description of a list of objects and the constructing, sending and viewing of textual messages from one participant to another. The animation of this process can be seen in part in Figs 6.6–6.10. Figures 6.6 and 6.7 depict the screens of two stakeholders engaged in brainstorming.

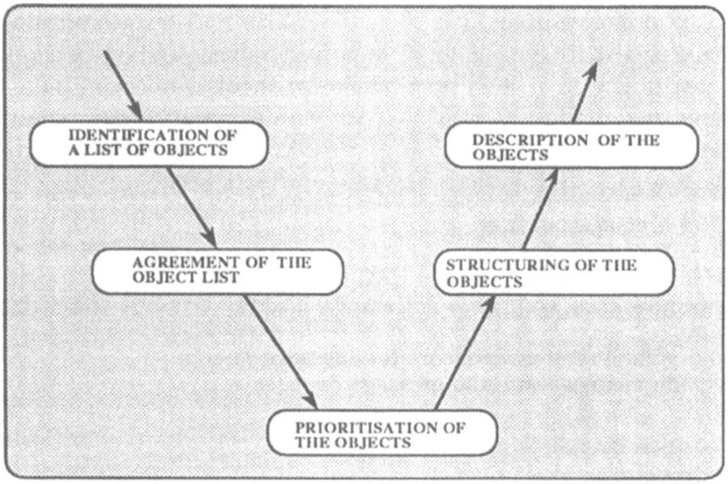

Fig. 6.5. Discrete stages in the "method" under consideration.

The public window can be seen to represent an aggregation of the individual brainstorming windows. Figure 6.8 illustrates how descriptions are attached to the active object regions on the public window. Figure 6.9 captures the process of the facilitator constructing and dispatching a message, while Fig. 6.10 shows the receipt and subsequent inspection of this message by a stakeholder. At present the Facilitator Support Agent can recognize the "situation" whereby this task is complete. Clearly, this merely involves invoking a reactive function which seeks to identify when the list of objects has reached an equilibrium state. Similar social situations can be recognized, such as a team member being alienated or the team developing into a two-headed beast.

The design of mechanisms to support the second stage of the method, that of agreement, is under way. The overall design of the Method Control Agent is complete. Figure 6.11 describes the structure of the Agent. It comprises three processes: the Method Selector, the Agenda Executor and the Agenda Manager.

The Method Selector, upon direction from the facilitator, selects the appropriate method from a Method Base. This agent is generic in that it is designed so that it can oversee numerous requirements capture methods. While this has been a design consideration, we will not concern ourselves with providing, or indeed importing, a collection of methods. The Agenda Executor is the process responsible for the execution of each of the tasks which collectively represent the method. This task level description of the method is installed on the Agenda. This is subsequently interrogated by the Agenda Executor, and the Agenda Manager completes the cycle by updating the agenda when the task has been completed. Completion can sometimes be difficult to detect, and assistance may need to be sought from the Conversation Analysis Agent. We hope that by invoking

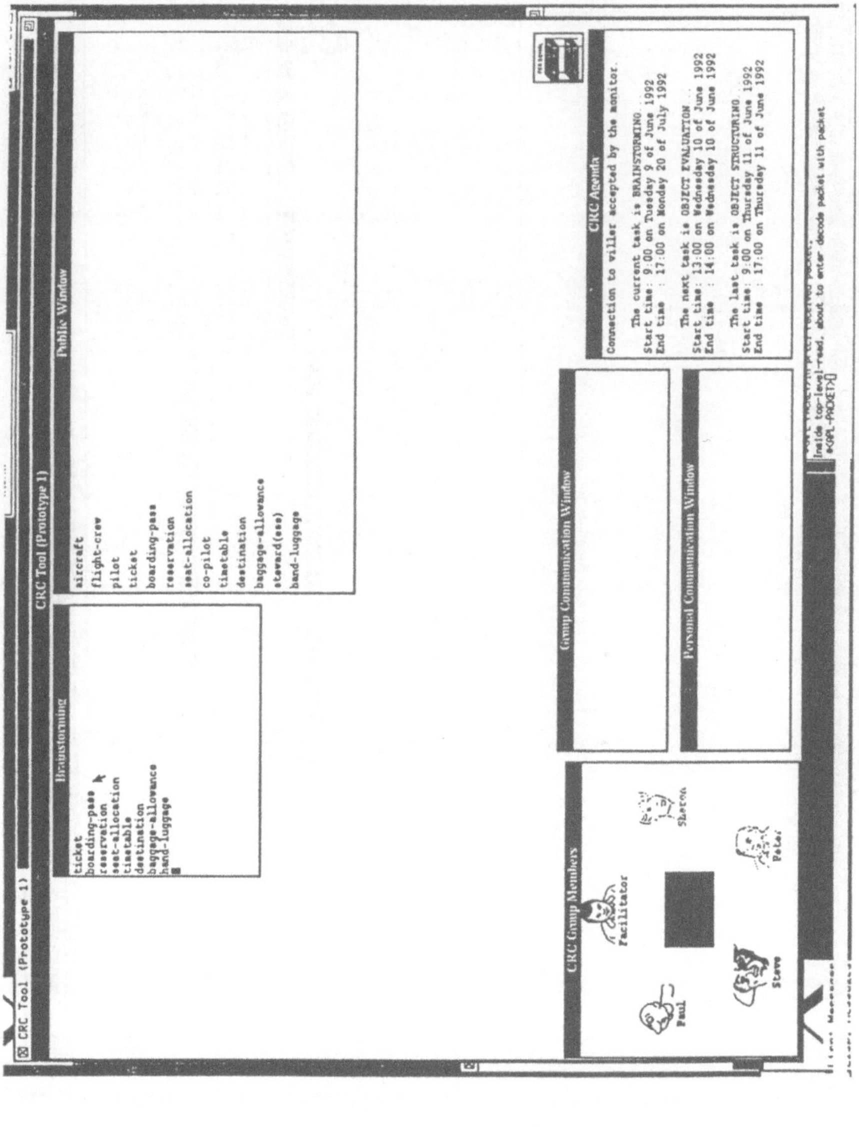

Fig. 6.6. Brainstorming in progress, stakeholder 1.

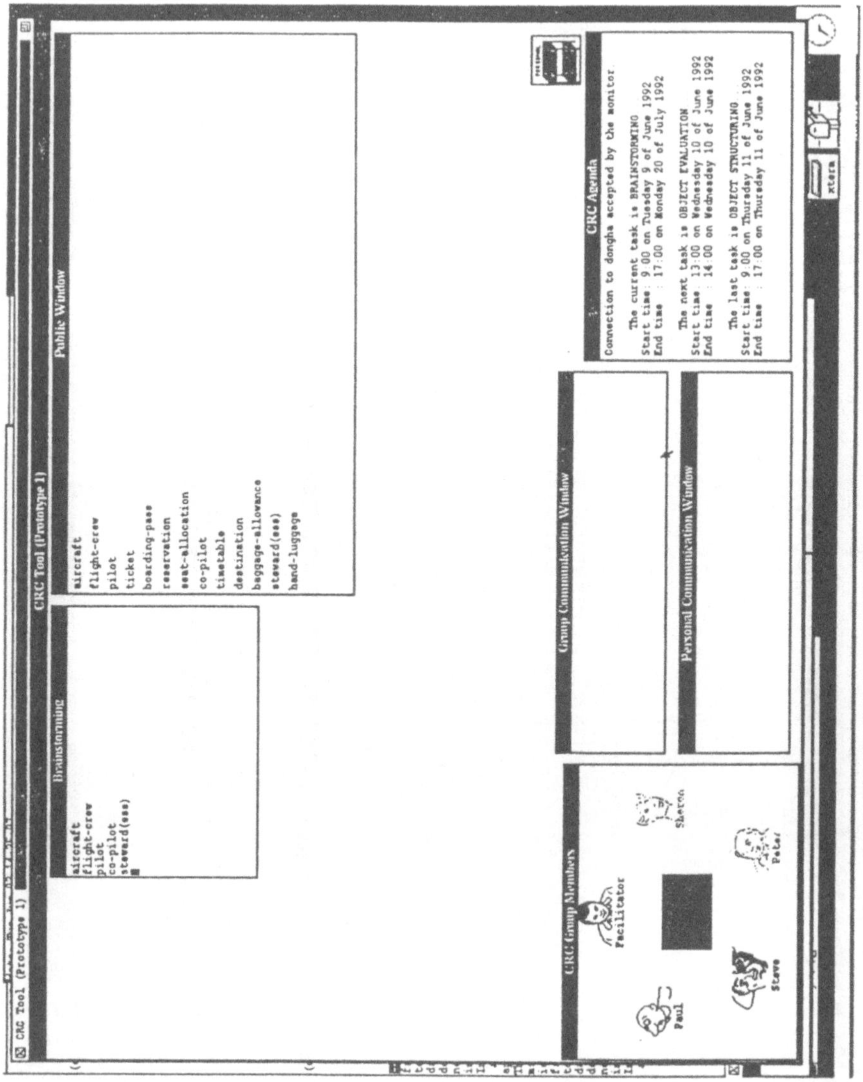

Fig. 6.7. Brainstorming in progress, stakeholder 2.

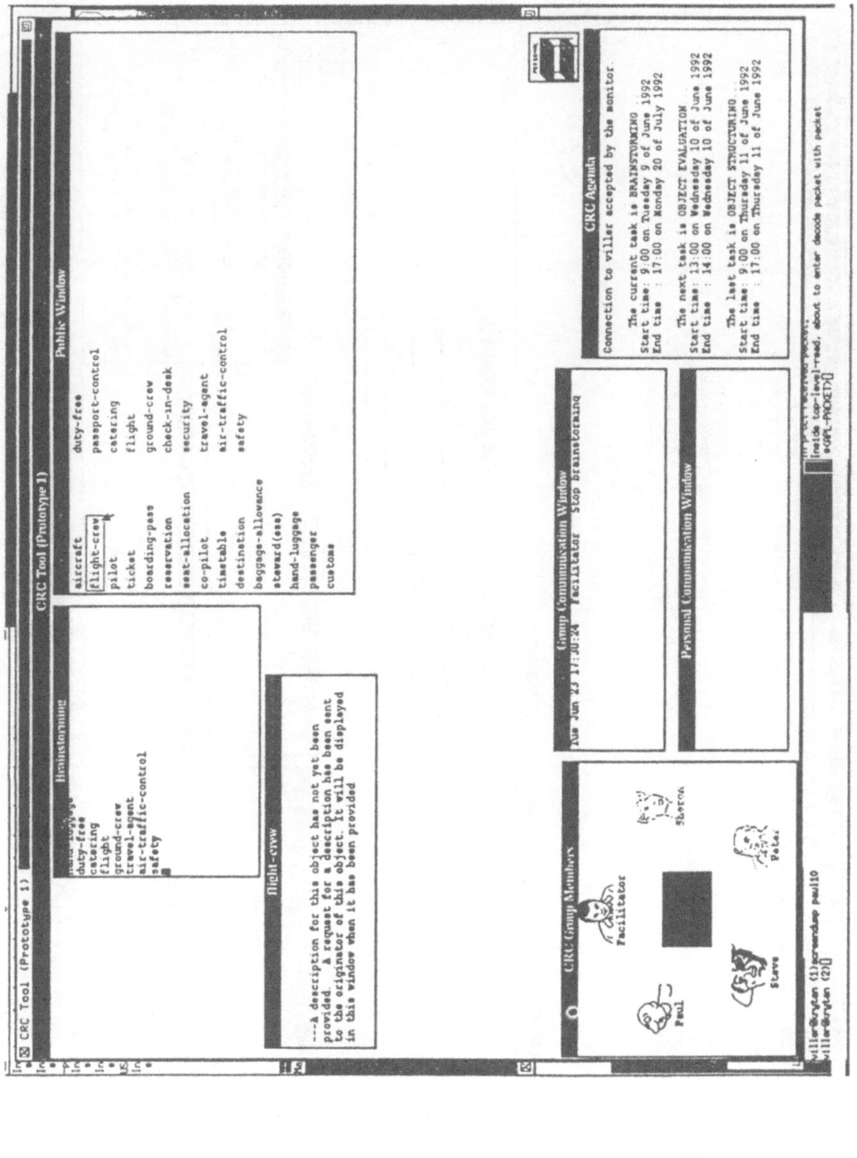

Fig. 6.8. Object descriptions.

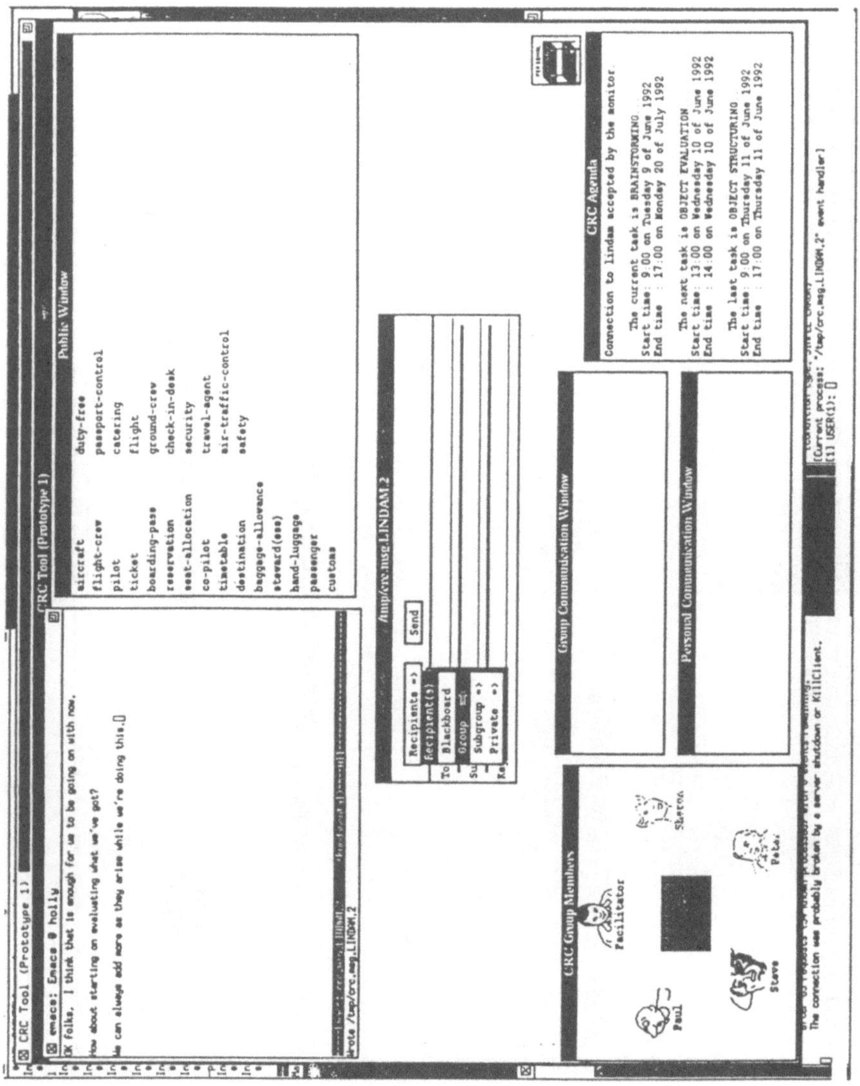

Fig. 6.9. Message construction and dispatch.

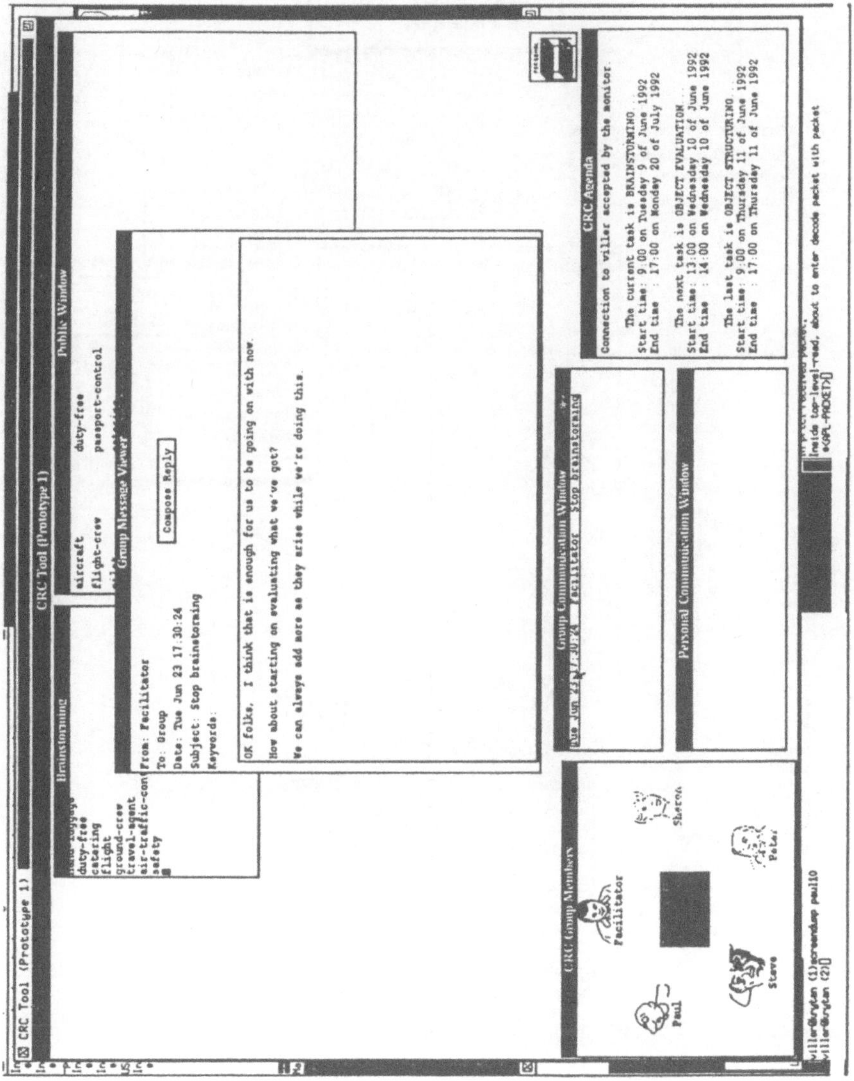

Fig. 6.10. Message receipt and interrogation.

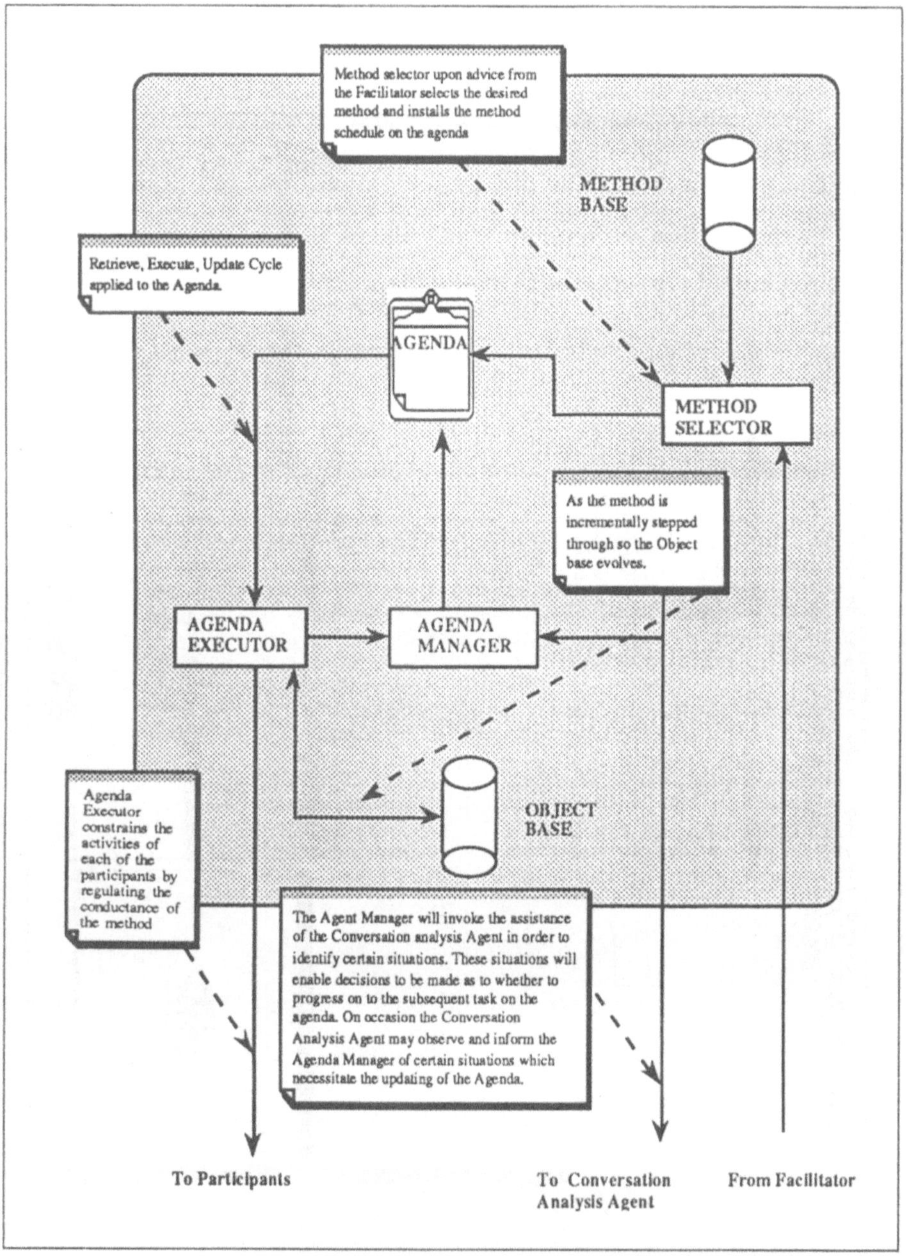

Fig. 6.11. The method control agent.

reactive functions the state of the team activity can be ascertained and the method regulated accordingly. In a similar manner the Facilitator Support Agent may as a result of the invocation of proactive functions inform the Agenda Manager of "social conditions" affecting the team's productivity. For example, a conflict may develop between two participants, and this may necessitate the installation of several tasks on the agenda which, when executed, should result in resolution of the dispute.

6.3.3.5 *The Facilitator Support Agent*

The Facilitator Support Agent is shown in Fig. 6.12. It supports two classes of function: those of a reactive nature and those of a proactive nature. The former are queries tendered by either CRC agents or participants. Upon receipt, such a request is first decoded by the reactive function decoder. Thereafter, the associated function is retrieved from the reactive function base and subsequently executed, returning the result of this computation. Examples of such functions are similar to database queries, for example: Who has actively participated between time period t_1 and t_2? When was the last time participant P_1 contributed?

The second class of functions are those of a proactive nature. They demand a conversation monitor continually analysing the team's discourse and recognizing certain situations and syndromes by comparing them to "situation patterns" that have been captured in the situation/syndrome base. At present this agent is still at a relatively rudimentary stage. Nevertheless, several simple reactive and proactive functions, similar to those mentioned above, are supported, which currently assist the facilitator. Figures 6.13 and 6.14 illustrate two such functions and the social meters provided for the facilitator.

6.4 Conclusions

Within this chapter we have sought to describe our work toward the development of an Active Cooperative Working Platform. It is "active" in the sense that it takes cognizance of the social dynamics of the cooperative requirements capture team and provides support for the facilitator and the individual team members on this basis. This work has incorporated DAI principles at two levels. Firstly the design of the platform is based on a multi-agent paradigm, with various interactions and collaborations taking place within the software agents. These software agents are collectively working toward supporting the participants in the cooperative requirements process. Secondly, at the team level various techniques utilized in achieving agent coherence and resolving agent conflict are being applied to the design team.

In terms of its objectives, the Cooperative Working Platform does

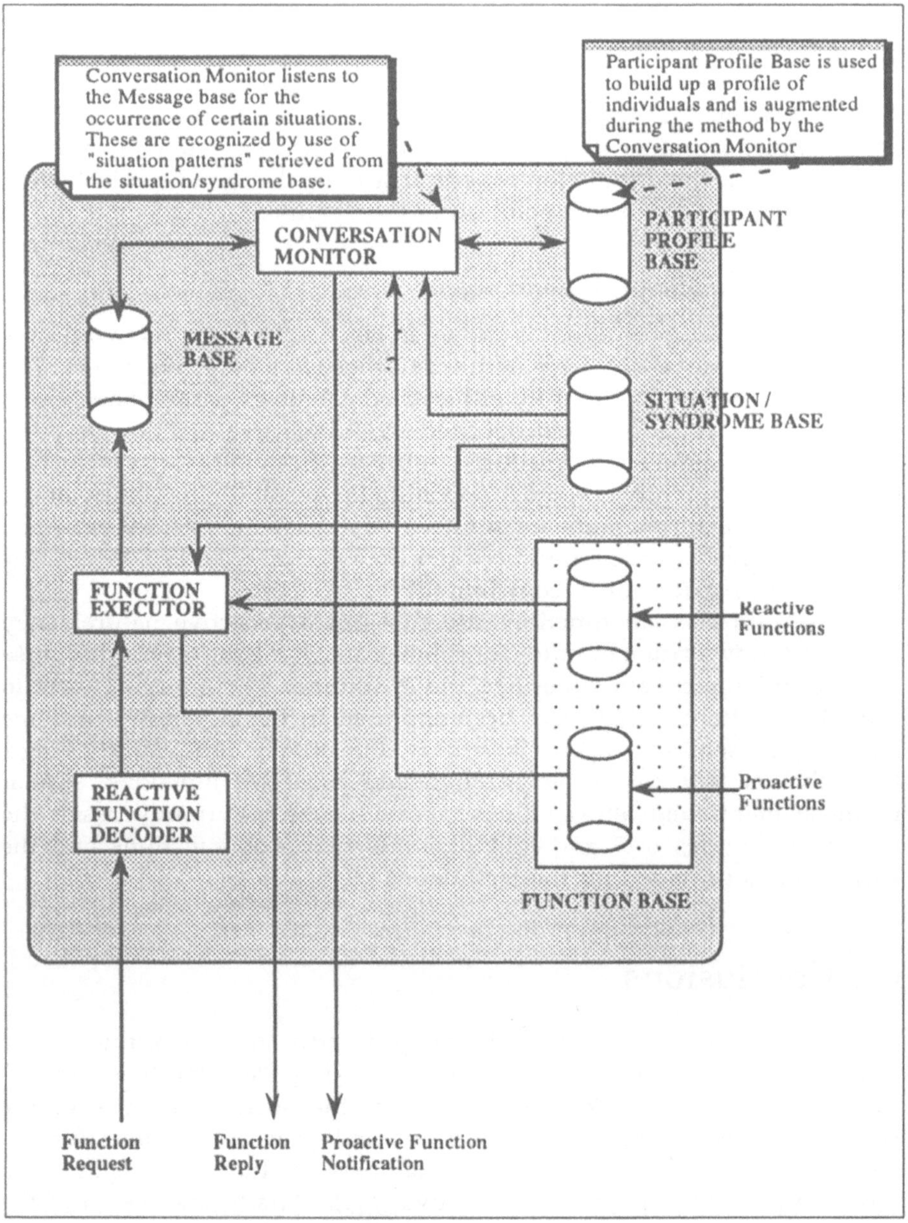

Fig. 6.12. The facilitator support agent.

support effective textual communication. Support for the social process is provided, though the recognition of the more complex social syndromes and the assistance of stakeholder conflict are some way off. The support of the requirements capture method is currently being extended so that the structuring and agreement phases will be fully supported.

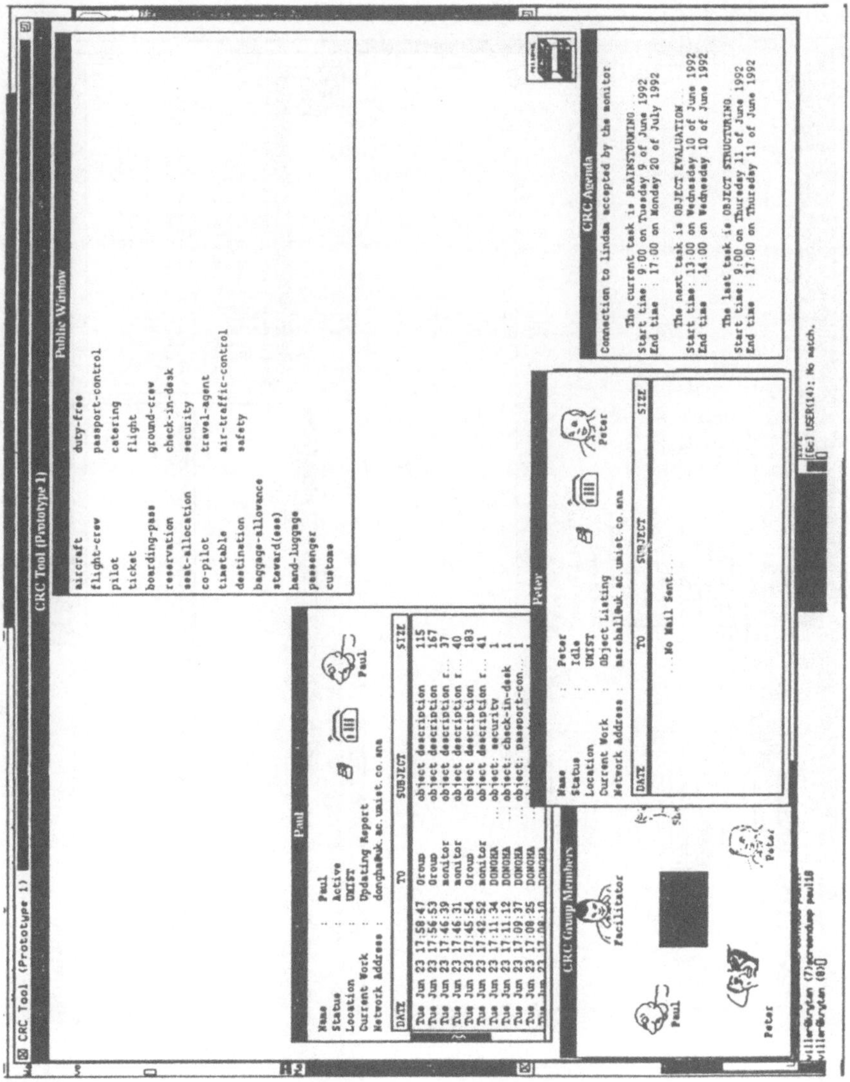

Fig. 6.13. Facilitator support 1.

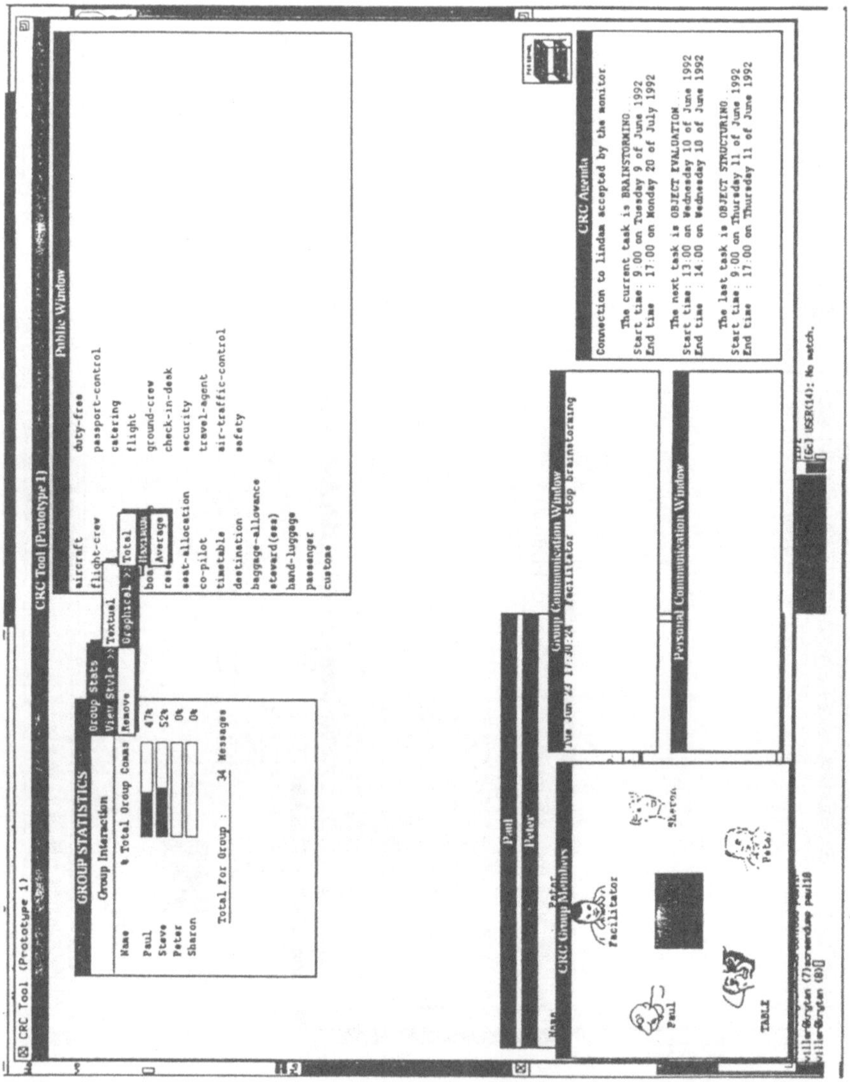

Fig. 6.14. Facilitator support 2.

At present the platform is still very much evolving. However we hope that, from this brief description, the reader acquires a feel of the spirit of the work that has been and remains to be undertaken.

Acknowledgements We would like to acknowledge useful discussions held with Dr A. Hutt of ICL, E. Trodd of Brameur, and M. Edwards and Professor E. Edwards of Human Technology Ltd. The Cooperative Requirements Capture (CRC) project is funded under the IED/DTI Advanced Technology Programme (project number 1130) and is a collaborative project involving the participation of the Department of Computation UMIST, ICL, Brameur and Human Technology Ltd.

Chapter 7

A Model for Supporting Interacting Knowledge Sources

J.G. Gammack and R.A. Stephens

7.1 Introduction

In this chapter we use a Distributed Artificial Intelligence (DAI) perspective to describe a formal model for representing and reconciling disparate viewpoints in knowledge-based problem solving for Computer Supported Cooperative Work (CSCW) and team decision making. We view the role of Artificial Intelligence (AI) within CSCW as one of providing knowledge representation formalisms and inference techniques to mediate information between socially distributed agents.

In many organizational and industrial domains knowledge and decision making is distributed across a number of experts, and these have typically proved resistant to Intelligent Knowledge-Based System (IKBS) modelling. Traditional IKBS formalisms which focus on modelling a single expert's knowledge do not adequately support domains with such a decentralized nature, and there arises a need in knowledge engineering for models that support inter-expert communication or multi-expert problem solving. Such models must not only accommodate the local knowledge of different experts, but also make provision for their intercommunication and knowledge sharing in a unified system. As recognized in the work on multi-agent planning, knowledge supplied by one knowledge source will modulate or constrain the recommendations made by another. In highly connected systems, involving intricate information exchange, the powerful computational techniques of constraint satisfaction and parallelism apply. We describe one model which uses a constraint-propagation algorithm on a distributed matrix-based knowledge representation to resolve problems with decentralized contributions. By representing a problem as a set of constraints, or relations among relevant components, provision is made for contributions from any number of experts, and their interaction can be effectively modelled. This model is suited to multiprocessor implementations, and effectively represents the knowledge of functionally and/or geographically distributed specialists and supports their communication. Using real-world examples from a manufacturing domain, we illustrate how the model can be used to support knowledge-based cooperative problem solving.

7.2 The Scope for AI in CSCW

AI has tended to follow the physical symbol system hypothesis, whereby symbolic tokens act as the building blocks of meaning, guaranteed by correspondence with objects and features in the real world. The limitations of representational hypotheses have been increasingly recognized in recent years (e.g. Winograd and Flores 1987; Brooks 1991b) as it has become realized that symbols can act only as *vehicles* for meaning, conveyed between (human) intelligences who interpret and impute meaning in specific contexts. The indeterminancy of meaning in symbols is an inevitable problem for AI and implies a different approach based on this recognition. This is particularly true when the system is explicitly concerned with the transfer of communicative intents via computer-based media, such as in computer supported group decision making applications. Symbols encode regularities in the use of language that make information processing meaningful. But, as Winograd and Flores (1987, p. 64) say, these regularities "grow out of mutual coupling among language users . . . but this does not mean that formal accounts are useless . . . computers can play a major role as devices for facilitating human communication in language".

AI offers a set of formal structures that are well understood, often mathematically founded, internally consistent and relatively unambiguous, which allow a sophisticated manipulation of symbols and processing of information to be effectively conducted via computers. The type error has, it seems, been made that the symbols equate with the meaning, and thus symbol systems contain knowledge, when in fact the location of the knowledge, intelligence, interpretive ability and meaning is in the minds of the human agents using those symbols in specific ways. If an agent is one who acts or intervenes in the world, clearly both humans and machines can have this capability. Only humans, however, are capable of referencing their activities to contexts meaningful beyond that assumed by the original design. Although agents can be human, artificial or both, autonomous artificial agents are likely to be successful only when dealing with fairly static, Platonic domains, such as arithmetic and numerical calculation, or in a few linguistically tokened domains with trivial semantic content. For changing environments, more ambitious designs are required, but rather than burdening the representation inappropriately, we must ensure that the ultimate responsibility for meaning rests with the human who interprets for some purpose.

Nonetheless, the full power of knowledge representation technologies and other AI techniques can be exploited within the context of a different philosophy of design. One essential difference in design philosophy pertinent to CSCW is the locus of agency, and the scope for autonomy (see also Chapters 1, 2 and 11). Whereas AI has tried to locate agency within automata, user autonomy is a fundamental principle within CSCW. Philosophically, intentional agency is uniquely a human property, and designers must recognize that the responsibility for action rests in the social domain. Given the inevitable tension between the computer requirement for formalism and the necessity of interpretive freedom even in bureaucratic practices (Taylor et al. 1988), there is a requirement for design paradigms to have a greater sensitivity to the interaction between work and technology. Giddens' structuration theory has been advanced as a foundational paradigm for CSCW by Lyytinen and Ngwenyama (1994), who define computer support for cooperative work as "the integration of computer mediation into cooperative practices in a way which supports the emergent character of the agency/structure duality". We view the role of AI within CSCW as one of providing knowledge representation formalisms and inference techniques to mediate information between socially distributed agents. Accordingly, the formal level provides a common reference point, which can be considered as regular and predictable by participants (Robinson 1991).

7.3 Organizational Decision Making and Interacting Knowledge Sources

The nature of decision making in organizations is often at odds with the conventional models provided by expert systems researchers and cognitive scientists. AI approaches emphasize the content of decision sequences with little regard to the process of decision making. Expert systems tend to be task-specific, prescribing from a predetermined and closed set of choices to a single user. While such formal models can solve routine problems, problem solving in organizations often involves novel situations, adaptation and feedback, both from peers with their own interests and requirements, and more widely from non-local stakeholders. Because human experience and action takes place in specific contexts and is radically affected by them, it is not possible to formulate laws for each of an indefinite number of contexts, or general laws indifferent to context that are powerful enough to be of some use (Vickers 1981). In a dynamic environment it is more important for successful organizations to be open to change than to reiterate obsolescing classifications. Decisions leading to innovative practice *emerge* from the interaction of creative people, each bringing specialized knowledge and distinctive ideas. For effective decision support, it is important to provide communicative mechanisms to facilitate this collaboration and ensure coordination without imposing regulation.

Within organizations important problems tend to be unfamiliar and are largely defined in terms of their anticipated consequences (Preston 1991). Frequently, the magnitude of such problems cannot be grasped by any one individual, but require several people to resolve conflicts of perception and value. Very often these can only be articulated in the process of solving a problem. As recognized in the work on multi-agent planning (Georgeff 1987), knowledge supplied by one expert will modulate or constrain the recommendations made by another. This extra information provides the constraining and enabling conditions for a set of decision options, articulating both opportunity and restriction.

When a number of workers collaborate, the inputs from these different knowledge sources form a web of constraint which shapes the problem representation in its operational context. In highly connected systems, such as a complex organization, where intricate information exchange is involved, the powerful computational techniques of constraint satisfaction and concurrency apply. By representing a problem as a set of constraints, or relations among relevant components, provision is made for contributions from any number of specialists, and their interaction can be modelled effectively. We now go on to detail a computational model for communicating the specialized knowledge of agents in a distributed decision making context.

7.4 A Model for Supporting Interacting Knowledge Sources

The specialized information of a human or artificial knowledge source may be recorded in a tabular formalism representing relations between category values (Gammack et al. 1989). Such representations may be expressed computationally as a constraint graph, in which each category is shown as a node and arcs between pairs of nodes indicate the existence of inter-category relationships or influences. In the simple case the specific constraints between category values are given in a binary matrix associated with an arc where 1 and 0 mean an admissible and an inadmissible relation, respectively. It is also possible to represent and manipulate continuous values when these are known (Gammack et al. 1991).

An arc is directed such that each column corresponds to a value for the head of the arc and each row to a value for the tail node, as shown in Fig. 7.1. Using an example from quality control in the steel industry, the two labelled nodes show the relation between steel quality and car manufacture. Low quality finished steel is admissible for the frame but not for the body or component.

In problem solving, as specific information becomes known, values are assigned to particular categories and the implications are propagated through the graph according to the given admissibility matrices. As well as propagating known values, what is implicitly known of the possibility of every value should also be propagated. The representation most suited to this task is a vector containing one element for each value in the category, assigned the value 1 if it is a possible state or 0 if it is impossible.

The matrices operate on this vector representation by the operation of vector–matrix conjunction. This is similar to matrix multiplication, but using AND and OR instead of multiplication and addition. An update procedure determines if and how a variable should change when the result of the conjunction is combined with the previous state. Constraints between two variables can be identified by simply taking their vector intersection. Partial orders over representational states are a good way to describe this kind of operation in constraint systems, where one state is

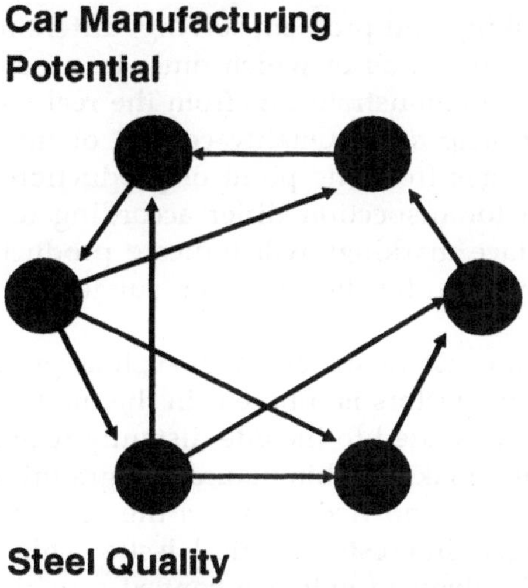

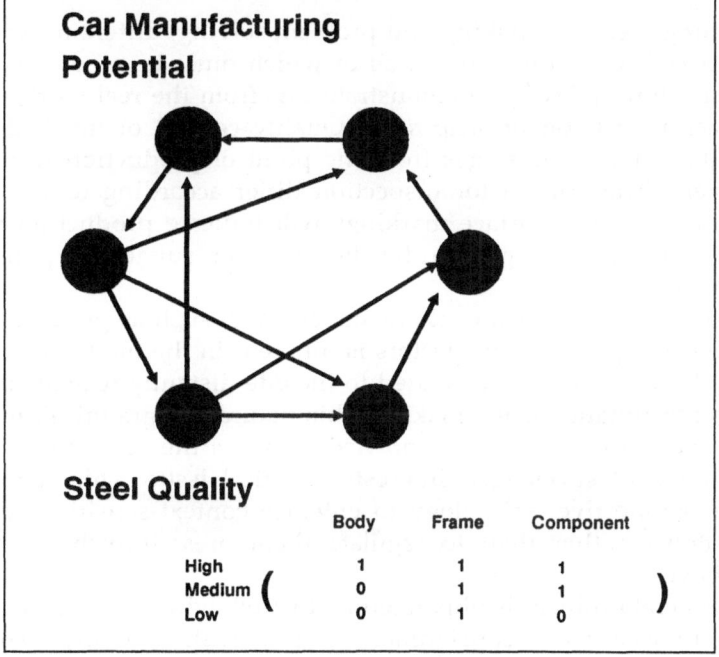

	Body	Frame	Component
High	1	1	1
Medium	0	1	1
Low	0	1	0

Fig. 7.1. Constraint graph for quality control in the steel industry, showing a typical admissibility matrix for one arc.

above another if the former logically contains the latter. Partial solutions get tighter as constraints are added: the update procedure can then be understood as finding the least upper bound of two states (Battle 1990).

Every variable has an initial state of a vector of 1s, where every value in its category is a possibility. By direct entry or inference, certain values may be found to be impossible, making the solution progressively tighter. The effects are carried over into the next cycle so the final solution reflects the conjunction of all the inputs made in a single session.

Each node in the constraint graph is a separate unit, activated only by data reaching it along its own arcs. This corresponds to the process model of computation described by CSP (Hoare 1985), and has been implemented as a concurrent system written in OCCAM running on the transputer.

Having suggested that knowledge representations are best evaluated in terms of their communicative power, and having described one model that addresses the issue of mutual influence, we now consider whether this formalism can be used to provide support in a collaborative decision making context.

7.5 Modelling Communication in Multiparticipant Settings

In planning, decision making and problem solving, different experts will make specialized contributions, all of which must be accommodated in the final solution. We can demonstrate this from the real-world example of surface inspection of strip steel. Quality control of finished steel is undertaken at various stages from the point of production to the point of delivery. The criteria for inspection differ according to the issue at hand; in particular, surface markings will indicate production faults to an engineer or metallurgist, or, for the customer, suggest its potential for manufacturing.

The complementary expertise of stakeholders such as production engineers, metallurgists and inspectors is inherent in the quality control process, and the list may be extended to include distantly related specialists such as accountants or toolmakers. This natural geographical, functional and temporal distribution of knowledge makes the communication and coordination of specialized interests a critical issue. This coordination requires supportive technology to enhance context-sensitive communication flows, rather than to regulate them prescriptively, as it were, from above.

The general problem is illustrated by the following example, in which a customer rejects a steel consignment as "not finished quality". This information is then propagated to the inspection and production engineers, who use this category to diagnose whether this is due to inadequate vision inspection or to a production fault. Arcs between the nodes representing these stakeholders provide the relevant communication channels in the model. Total quality management requires producers to be sensitive to market fluctuations, so the definition of full finish quality reflects particular consumer demands and is not simply determined at the point of production. There is a systemic relationship between production capability and customer requirement, which must be negotiated in the context of the market. A defect, therefore, is defined not by objective physical properties, but by a consensus of the interested parties. Multiple viewpoints are naturally accommodated in the model, and consensus is represented by shared terms, labelling the matrices between nodes.

Different pairs of nodes may share category schemes at different levels of precision: to give a simplified example, the vision inspector and metallurgist identify 15 different grades of steel, but a customer may only distinguish three. The best of the vision inspector's 15 categories may be identified as "unblemished", and the customer's categories may be "finished quality" (high), "industrial quality" (medium) and "serviceable" (low). If the entry in the cell representing the intersection of "unblemished" and "finished quality" is 0, implying that the customer's categorization of the quality of the steel is incompatible with the manufacturer's, then a solution is not immediately possible because the critical category is overconstrained. As we have noted, however, the solution to a problem is not simply defined by any one agent, so having detected a possible incompatibility of definition, negotiation can now come into play. For example, the customer may (i) accept the product as industrial quality (perhaps at a lower cost), or (ii) re-evaluate their standard for finished quality (relax that constraint). Alternatively, the producer, if possible, may undertake to improve the process before delivering the order as originally specified.

So far the model has highlighted potential conflict between stakeholders, but our second example shows a more complex interaction, in which the model conveys useful information between distributed specialists to promote more effective local decision making.

The vision inspector realizes that the steel being produced has a "defect", and reports it to the process controller, who needs to decide, and quickly, whether or not to stop the process. To decide effectively, information is needed.

One option is to stop the process, diagnose and correct the fault, which, especially in a continuous production system, may incur substantial cost. Alternatively, if production is continued, can an outlet be found for this steel even if it violates the schedule profile? This decision requires consideration of a number of new influences: the economics of storage, knowledge of possible markets, production practicalities, etc. – all specialized areas of expertise, contributing to a collaborative decision. These specialists are unlikely to be at the point of decision but we suggest, through appropriate technology, the relevant expertise can be located and accessed to produce a more informed decision. Consider the influence of specialized knowledge about outlets. If there is no immediate customer, continuing the process will necessitate storing the steel. If the market is saturated, however, this may not be viable. A third specialist can advise on the availability and cost of storage, if required. This specialist, however, may not be a human, but an autonomous agent with access to a database with the relevant facts and figures. A daemon-like agent can receive and rapidly process a request, informing other involved agents as necessary, through constraint propagation.

The collaborative decision to stop the process or to continue it is thus made by propagating the relevant information among the specialists involved. The systems analysis aspect of the problem is to identify the relevant information flows. The model can represent this information as constraints, and update the specialist on each node with the local decisions that are being made.

7.6 Conclusion

AI has provided powerful formal representations and technologies for building models but has limited value as such for CSCW. In attempting to model prescribed goals, decisions and choices, AI necessarily compromises human agency by reducing interpretation, contextual ambiguity and uncertainty through the application of precise logics and additional knowledge representations. The CSCW foundational tenet of user autonomy cannot be subordinated to this project; rather, the formalisms provided by AI can mediate collaborative work in an open context.

A model has been presented which propagates information among distributed specialists, and we have described its extension to multi-participant decision making with reference to organizational settings. The requisite semantic coordination between specialists is naturally accommodated by locating the responsibility with the user agents rather than with the knowledge representation.

Chapter 8

A Functional Model of Interacting Systems: A Semiotic Approach

D. Benyon

8.1 Introduction

Recent developments in Human–Computer Interaction (HCI), Computer Supported Cooperative Work (CSCW) and Distributed Artificial Intelligence (DAI) share a common problem: communication. We are moving towards a situation of multiple interacting systems. Some of these systems will be humans, others will be "intelligent" agents and still others will be "dumb" devices. Agents may be human or software systems. Unless we are clear as to the capabilities of these systems, serious misunderstandings and impoverished HCI will result. This chapter seeks to provide the basis of a theory of interaction within which communication can be understood and the capabilities of systems to communicate are brought to the foreground.

For example, Hans-Werner Hein has suggested that in the not-too-distant future we can expect to see robots cleaning the floors of railway stations and other public buildings. We must demand high quality human–robot interaction. We do not want robots sweeping up people or children's toys. We should expect robots to adapt to circumstances both individually and collectively – if we have persuaded one robot not to clean a particular piece of floor, we do not want another robot to move in. Robots are autonomous agents, intelligent to some degree, and must communicate with humans and with other robots. What must the architecture of such machines be?

If multi-agent systems are to arrange our meetings for us (Kearney et al. 1991) – finding suitable times and places and acting as secretaries – what knowledge and capabilities can we expect such systems to have? How will we know what such systems understand? What constraints pertain to a particular agent? Which activities lie within its scope and which do not?

The answer to these questions lies in making explicit the abilities of agents to communicate and reason. To do this we need an architecture which reveals the significant components of the agent with respect to its abilities to interact. (For further discussion of architectures, see Chapters 2, 4, 5, 6 and 9.)

8.2 An Overview of Interaction

Interaction between any two systems involves the physical exchange of signals. It would be reasonable to argue that the picture hanging on my wall is interacting with the wall (through an exchange of energy), but it would be stretching things too far to suggest that it is interacting with a book on the book shelf. I may perceive a relationship between the picture and the book, but then it is I who am interacting with the book–picture system (through an exchange of photons). Signals are the "elementary particles", the basic units of interaction. These may be auditory signals, radio signals, atomic or chemical signals and so on. Without the exchange of signals, interaction cannot occur. Signals are units of transmission (at some level of abstraction) which travel through a communication channel (e.g. the auditory channel) (see Chapter 10). In order to send signals a system requires a transmitter function, and in order to receive signals it requires a receptor function. This model of interaction (Fig. 8.1) is

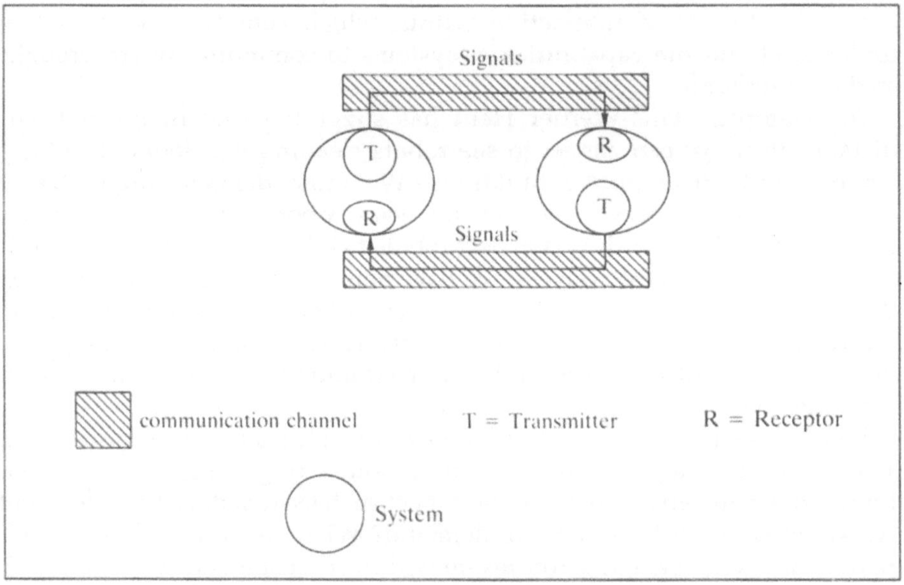

Fig. 8.1. General model of system–system interaction.

generally accepted within systems theory (e.g. Laszlo 1969), information theory (Shannon and Weaver 1949), communication theory (Cherry 1966) and linguistics (Lyons 1977). Providing a semiotic perspective, Eco (1976) defines a communicative process as "the passage of a signal, from a source, through a transmitter, along a channel to a destination" (p. 8).

The sort of interaction that is the concern of CSCW, HCI and DAI involves not just the exchange of signals, but the exchange of signals that *mean* something. Meaning may be defined as the relationships that exist between some signals and existing knowledge. If those relationships are not present, meaning will be absent. MacKay (1969) defines the meaning of some signals for a recipient system as the "selective function" which those signals have on the system's knowledge. For example, if I perceive someone waving two flags in a particular manner, I might realize that he or she is using semaphore. However, since I do not understand the signals, I cannot obtain any meaning from them.

Two other definitions are relevant. *Information* is the value added, or "surprise value", arising from the receipt of some signals. Information is to do with things that were unknown, or that could not be known, before the information was derived. In our case, we are not concerned with syntactic information, which is the subject of information theory (Shannon and Weaver 1949); we are concerned with semantic information. *Knowledge* is a representation (MacKay 1969) which we may view as a network of beliefs and propositions possessed by a system. *Semantic information*, then, is defined as "an increment of knowledge' (Tsrichritzis and Lochovsky 1982) – an enhancement of the network of beliefs and propositions. (Note that enhancement does not imply that the network is always increased: semantic information may cause propositions to be retracted.) Information about X is obtained by a system if the receipt of signals enriches the system's representation of X.

If systems only interact by exchanging signals, then how does a system derive any information or meaning from this exchange? To answer this, we must look inside a system that has received some signals. As shown in Fig. 8.2, we can then identify three major processes that are necessary if information is to be obtained from those signals.

The receptor process (process 1 in Fig. 8.2) receives the signals and transforms the raw signals into a structured set of signals called a *message*. To do this, the process employs algorithms, rules, heuristics and other operators embedded in it along with existing, stored representations (knowledge), in addition to the contents of signals.

Process 2 in Fig. 8.2 (derive semantic contents) transforms the message (again making use of existing knowledge) into a representation of the *semantic contents* of the message. It may be necessary for the message to be re-formed and the signals can be passed back to process 1 for this to occur.

Process 3 in Fig. 8.2 derives *information* from the semantic contents of

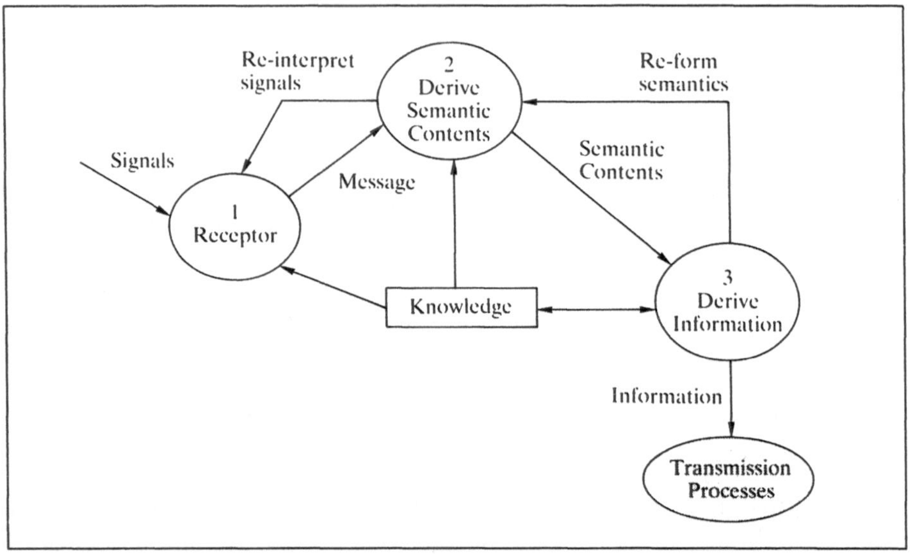

Fig. 8.2. Main processes involved in receiving and interpreting signals.

the message and updates the store of knowledge (i.e. changes the state of the system's representation). If information cannot be derived from the semantics of the message, process 3 may pass the message back to process 2 where the semantics can be re-formulated.

In the following sections, each of these parts of the functional architecture is examined in more detail. Of course, not all systems possess all these functions. By examining the functions at a finer level of detail, we can see the role of each part of the architecture and hence identify the abilities of different systems.

8.3 A Detailed View of Interaction

Semiotics is the study of signs and has been exploited in many areas of human endeavour, such as linguistics, anthropology, psychoanalytic psychology and literary theory (see, for example, Sturrock 1986). This wide range of applications has resulted in a number of different views on the role and structure of semiotics. In computer science semiotics has – surprisingly – been left relatively untouched.

Signals are units of transmission. They travel along a channel between the source and the destination system. Individually, signals do not mean anything; they do not signify. Signals exist in time and space and have characteristics associated with these dimensions (Cherry 1966), such as the duration of a sound or the location of a mark on a page in relation to other marks. Signals may be considered to be binary, in that they either exist or do not exist.

For example, the letter S is to be transmitted through the auditory channel as three tonal blips, thus: blip, blip, blip. A comma indicates a short period of silence – the absence of a "blip". It should be clear that:

blip, blip, blip

is different from:

blip,blip,,,,,,,,,,,blip,,,,

and it is likely that any system will interpret the first in a different way from the second. The transmission of signals therefore requires some structure to be observed, and if this structure is not as anticipated, the signals may be taken to signify something other than what was intended. This problem is nicely illustrated by a child's handwriting, in which the gaps between the letters are often larger than the gaps between words. Interpreting the signals is extremely difficult because the usual convention for parsing the signals has been lost.

When signals are received and interpreted they may become signs, i.e. they may signify something else. In order to signify something, a signal must be placed into a context of a system of signification which links the purely syntactic expression of the signal(s) to a semantic system. Meaning may be derived from this relationship. It is this relationship – between the signal(s) and the things signified – that is a sign. Eco (1976, 1984) emphasizes that it is the relationship that is the sign, by saying that a sign is always a sign-function. Also following Eco, we may use the terms *sign-vehicle* for the syntactic part of the sign (i.e. for the signals once they are associated with a semantic system) and *sign content* for the semantic part of the sign. "Symbol" is used by a number of authors (e.g. Rasmussen 1986) to indicate the thing that the receiving system "understands' – i.e. the sign contents. A symbol is the conceptual side of a sign. Pierce uses the term "interpretant" for this (Eco 1976; Cherry 1966).

Following and interpreting Eco (1976), who bases his model on Hjelmslev (1961), we may define:

- The signifier (or sign-vehicle), which is the signals when placed in a relationship with a system of signification.
- The signified (or sign content), which is the (conceptual) entity associated with a signifier when put in relationship with a system of signification.
- The sign (or sign-function), which is the relationship between the signifier and the signified.

Both the sign-vehicle and the sign content have a substance representing what each is and various different forms, or representations. A signal (e.g. a "blip") is the substance of the sign's expression. The term "symbol" is reserved for the substance of the sign content.

8.3.1 The Receptor

The receptor is the mechanism that receives the signals and produces a coherent structured set of signals (a message). Hence it is most important that the receptor is tuned to the form of the sign's expression (i.e. that it can receive the signals). The sensitivity of the system to the signals is a feature of the receptor. Also, the receptor has to actively process and organize the signals it receives.

In Morse code, for example, the letter S is to be transmitted as three tonal blips. The receptor of any system that is to receive these signals has to be able to:

1. "Recognize" a blip.
2. Recognize what is not a blip.
3. Remember that there have been some previous blips.

The receptor also has to be sensitive enough, yet robust enough, to deal with difficulties and noise.

In terms of the model presented here, the receptor is passive with respect to the signals it can receive. Issues concerned with how a system focuses attention, or with the active seeking of signals in the world, may be attributed to some higher level function of the system which organizes and directs the receptors available, perhaps tuning them or making them more or less sensitive.

Figure 8.3 illustrates, conceptually, the operation of the receptor function. This type of diagram has already been used in this chapter (Fig. 8.2). We may call such diagrams "sign-flow diagrams" following the notion of dataflow diagrams (DeMarco 1979; Gane and Sarson 1979). Sign-flow diagrams describe the type of signs that are communicated between the functions (or systems) illustrated by the circles. Boxes show the knowledge stores that are logically necessary for the function to do its work. The labels used on sign-flow diagrams are themselves sign-vehicles. They need to be linked to some system of signification if readers are to derive meaning from them. A description of the labels is a necessary part of the diagrams. A particularly useful feature of sign-flow (or dataflow) diagrams is that of hierarchy. The processes numbered 1.1, 1.2, etc. are a true, finer grained description of process 1 in Fig. 8.2, and all sign-vehicles shown flowing into or out of a process are shown at each appropriate level.

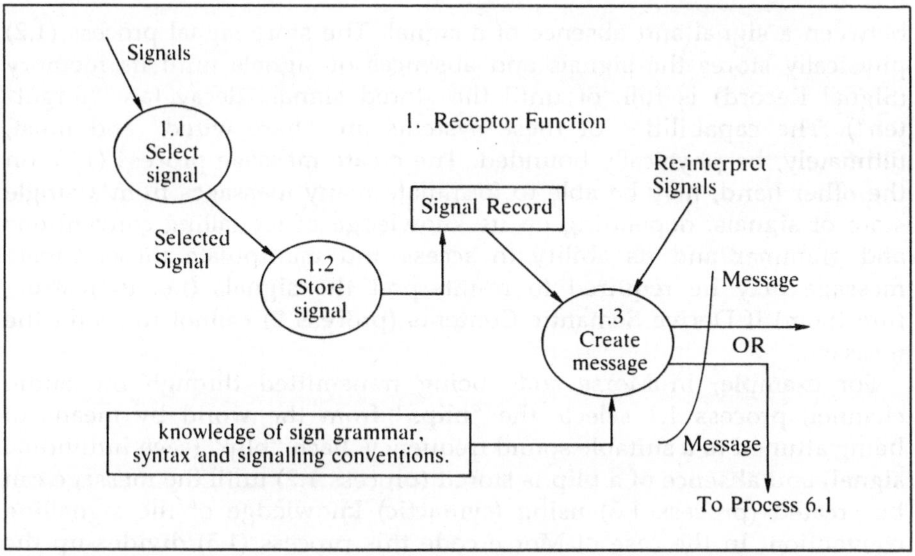

Fig. 8.3. The functioning of a receptor. Signals, the elementary units of communication; selected signal, the signals that the system is capable of receiving; message, a structured set of signals; re-interpret signals, the message returned along with contents indicating why it could not be interpreted.

Figure 8.3 may be interpreted as follows:

1.1. Through this process, the receptor has to sense the signals. It will be tuned to the type and intensity of the signal and its position in time and space. It has to separate the signals from the noisy world.

1.2. Selected signals are then stored in some (short-term) memory or buffer, called the Signal Record. This memory must be short-term because its purpose is simply to enable the message to be created. The capacity of a system's Signal Record (both in terms of the number of signals it can hold and the length of time before the representation decays) is an important determinant of the ability of the system to create messages from signals.

1.3. The create message process forms the signals into a message, which is a coherent, structured set of signals. This process provides enough structure for the next stage of the interaction (see Fig. 8.4). Some systems ("dumb", syntactic systems) that are incapable of communication send the message directly to the transmission process (see below, Fig. 8.7). In order to structure the signals, the create message process needs access to a syntactic system (the grammar of the signalling system).

Notice that the select (1.1) and store (1.2) processes do *not* need access to the grammar of the signalling system. The select process (1.1) is physically tuned to receive a certain type of signal and to distinguish between a signal and absence of a signal. The store signal process (1.2) physically stores the signals and absences of signals until its memory (Signal Record) is full, or until the stored signals decay (are "forgotten"). The capabilities of these systems are "hard-wired" and must, ultimately, be physically bounded. The create message process (1.3), on the other hand, may be able to formulate many messages from a single store of signals, depending on its knowledge of signalling conventions and grammar and its ability to access and manipulate these. Create message may be required to re-interpret the signals (i.e. to restructure them) if Derive Semantic Contents (process 2) cannot interpret the message.

For example, in Morse code being transmitted through the audio channel, process 1.1 selects the "blips" from the world by means of being attuned to a suitable sound frequency. Each "blip" (each individual signal) and absence of a blip is stored (process 1.2) until the message can be created (process 1.3) using (syntactic) knowledge of the signalling convention. In the case of Morse code this process (1.3) divides up the individual "blips" according to the length of the gaps between them. Once three blips have been arranged into a message, the message is sent to process 2 of Fig. 8.2 so that the semantic contents can be derived.

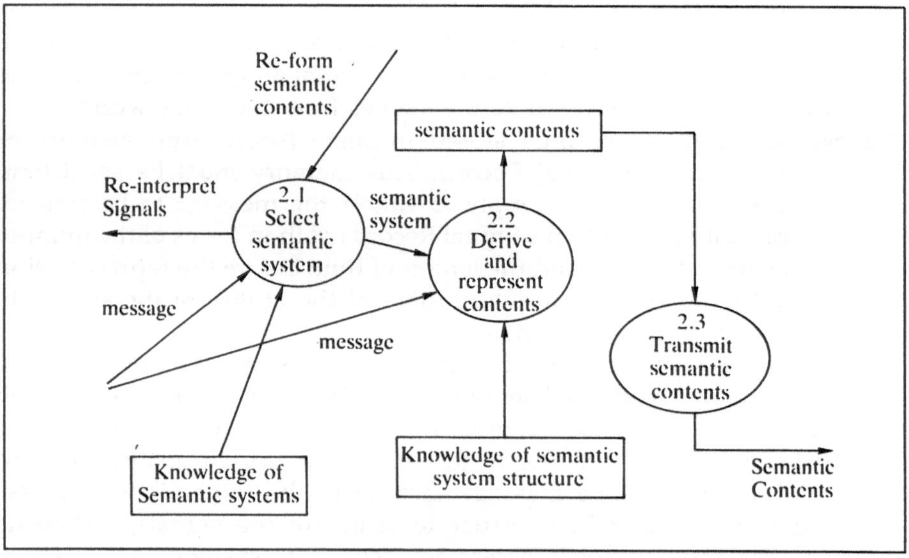

Fig. 8.4. Deriving the semantic contents. Message, a structured set of signals; re-interpret signals, the message returned along with contents indicating why it could not be interpreted; semantic system, description of the semantic system selected; semantic contents, the content of the sign (the result of applying the semantic system structure to the message); re-form semantic contents, semantic contents along with contents indicating why it could not be interpreted (see Section 8.3.5).

8.3.2 Deriving Semantics

Meaning does not simply reside in the message. It has to be derived in relation to previous knowledge. Once the system knows what is being referred to (signified) it has obtained the semantic contents of the message.

The processes involved in this are illustrated in Fig. 8.4. The message is received by process 2.1, which is responsible for selecting a suitable semantic system (the system of signification). This structure is passed to process 2.2 along with the message so that the semantic contents can be derived. If the semantic contents subsequently have to be re-formed and are passed back by process 3 (see Fig. 8.2), a new semantic system may be required. The message is then "decoded" (process 2.2) by referring the message to the semantic system in order to determine the semantic contents. These are represented in some form in the system and stored in a memory called "semantic contents". Process 2.3 subsequently transmits a suitable contents to the derive information process.

For example, process 2.1 receives the message "blip, blip, blip". The semantic system of Morse code is selected and hence the message can be connected to the concept of a letter S (process 2.2). This is stored. If a single S is transmitted to the deriving information process it is unlikely that information can be successfully obtained. Process 2.3 therefore waits until an informative message is received – say the S is stored until an O and another S are received, followed by a period of silence. The semantic contents "SOS" is transmitted (process 2.3) to the derive information process.

8.3.3 Information and Knowledge

Although the sign has been related to the concept (or interpretant) – that is, in some sense the meaning of the message has been understood – the system has yet to deal with that meaning. The ability to derive (semantic) information from the semantic contents of the message depends on:

- The ability of the system to interpret the semantic contents of the message.
- The ability to integrate the semantics of the message so interpreted with existing knowledge.

In the Morse code example, I must be capable of interpreting the semantics of "SOS" in terms of it being a distress call. I may have correctly derived the semantics from the code, but I may not have the required previous knowledge to be able to interpret it as a distress call. If I can interpret

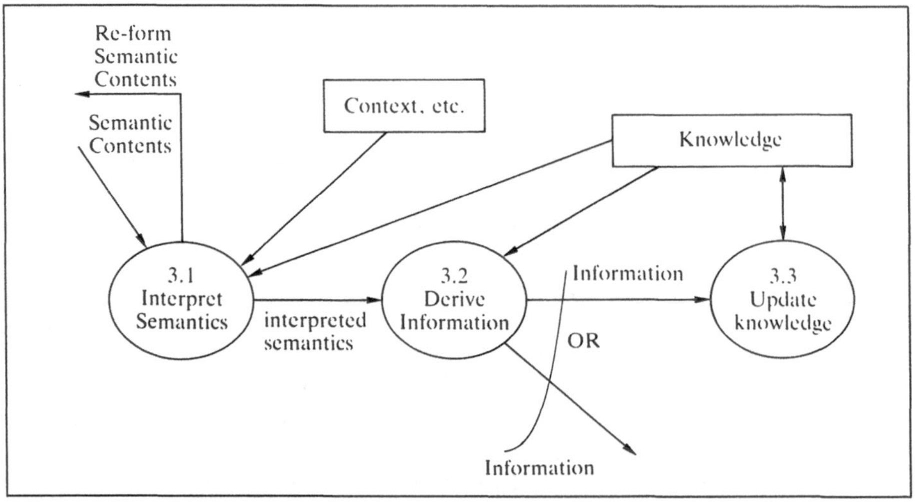

Fig. 8.5. Deriving information. Semantic contents, the content of the sign (the result of applying the semantic system structure to the message); re-form semantic contents, semantic contents along with contents indicating why they could not be interpreted; interpreted semantics, the result of associating the semantic contents with current context and stored knowledge; information, new knowledge (the result of associating the interpreted semantics with existing stored knowledge).

the semantics as a distress call, what information can I derive from this? It may be that I already knew that the other system was issuing a distress call. In such cases the message provides no information – there is no "surprise value". It may be that I didn't know this and so I am able to update my knowledge accordingly. It may be that such information will directly trigger some other function of the system.

The process of deriving information from the semantic contents of a message is illustrated by a sign-flow diagram in Fig. 8.5. Process 3.1 interprets the semantics in relation to the system's current state of knowledge and the context of the interaction. The interpreted semantics are passed to process 3.2. If it is not possible to interpret the semantics, the semantic contents, along with some indication of the problem, are passed back to process 2 (Fig. 8.2). Information is derived though process 3.2 in relation to existing knowledge. Some systems will have the ability to update the content and/or structure of their knowledge store in the light of this information (process 3.3). Other systems will not have this capability and the information will flow directly to the transmission processes.

8.3.4 Transmission

Receiving signals and deriving semantics and information from them is only half the story of interaction. The other half is the transmission of signals. To a large extent, this can be seen as the reverse of the receiving processes. However, we need to recognize that there are three ways to trigger the process of transmission of signals.

Process 3.2 (Fig. 8.5) shows that the information derived may be used either to update a knowledge store (process 3.3) or to act as a trigger mechanism for the transmission of signals. In this case it flows directly to process 5.1 (Fig. 8.6). This process formulates the semantics of the message, considering the range of semantic systems that are available, that is to be issued. These semantic contents are used by process 5.2 (Fig. 8.6) to select an appropriate system of signification. It is in these processes that the many issues concerned with the pragmatics of sign production must be considered (Eco 1976; Stamper 1973). A semantic system that is appropriate for the intended recipient, the context of the interaction and the semantic contents of the message must be chosen. Process 5.3 brings the semantic system and the output semantics together, and creates the structured set of signals to be transmitted (T-message).

For example, an automatic monitoring station may be designed to call the coast guard if it receives a distress call. Once process 3.2 has derived the information "distress call received" it passes this to process 5.1. This process exploits the system's knowledge of what to do when a distress call is received and hence formulates the output semantic contents. Process 5.2 is responsible for selecting the appropriate semantic system structure (the system of signification). Let us assume that the system only has a single semantic system for this purpose – an automatic telephoning facility.

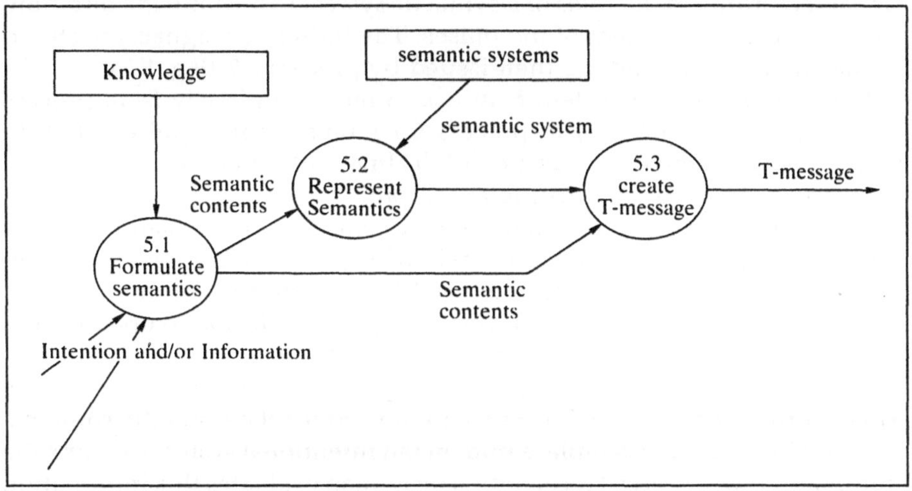

Fig. 8.6. Create T-message. Information, new knowledge (the result of associating the interpreted semantics with existing stored knowledge); intention, the intention to transmit a message; T-message, a structured set of signals (called T-message to distinguish it from message); semantic system, description of the semantic system selected; knowledge, representation of possible semantic systems plus general knowledge.

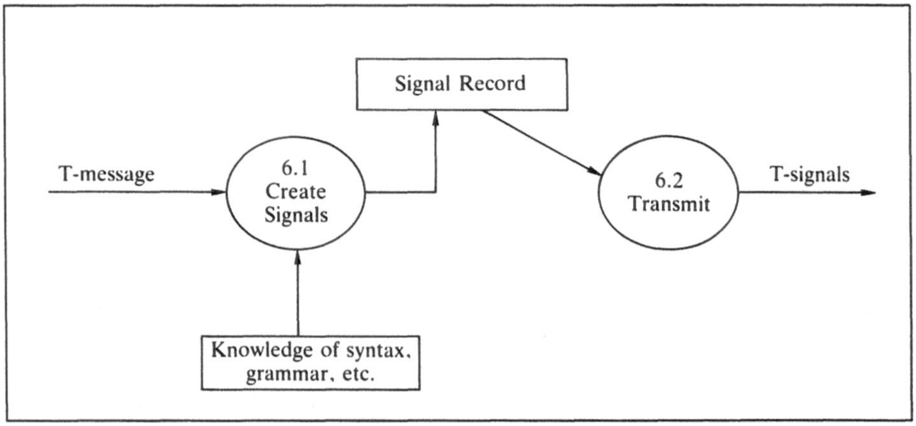

Fig. 8.7. Transmission. T-message, a structured set of signals (called T-message to distinguish it from message); T-signals, the elementary particles of communication (called T-signals to distinguish them from signals).

Process 5.1 formulates the appropriate semantics, given the fact that it has received a distress call and formulates the semantic contents, "dial 999" (say). The structure of the telephone system (e.g. a pulse telephone system) is retrieved from the system's knowledge base The semantics – "dial 999" – are brought together with this structure (process 5.3) and represented as a T-message consisting of some sequence of electrical pulses. This is passed to process 6.1 (Fig. 8.7), which creates and stores the individual signals according to the rules of a syntactic system describing the duration, strength and arrangement of the pulses. The individual signals are stored in the signal record and are then issued by process 6.2 (Fig. 8.7).

A less sophisticated system may pass a message directly from process 1.3 ("blip, blip, blip" etc.) to process 6.1 ("pulse, pulse, pulse" etc.). In such a system, there is no question of dealing with semantics. The system responds to an input by creating an output.

Finally, one can recognize that some systems store information and use this to formulate output on the basis of explicit goals (desired system states). In this case information is used to evaluate the current situation with respect to the system's goals (process 4.1, Fig. 8.8) and to update goals in the light of new knowledge (process 4.2). The system's goals and the latest information are used to create an intention to transmit a message. This is processed (process 5.1, Fig. 8.6) to produce the semantic contents.

Following the SOS example, a human (an intentional system) obtains the information "distress call received". The human evaluates this information and creates a goal of notifying the coast guard. This goal can be achieved if the human creates an intention to inform the coast guard. Process 5.1 for the human will offer several alternatives for formulating appropriate semantics. For example, the human could dial 999, wave and shout or

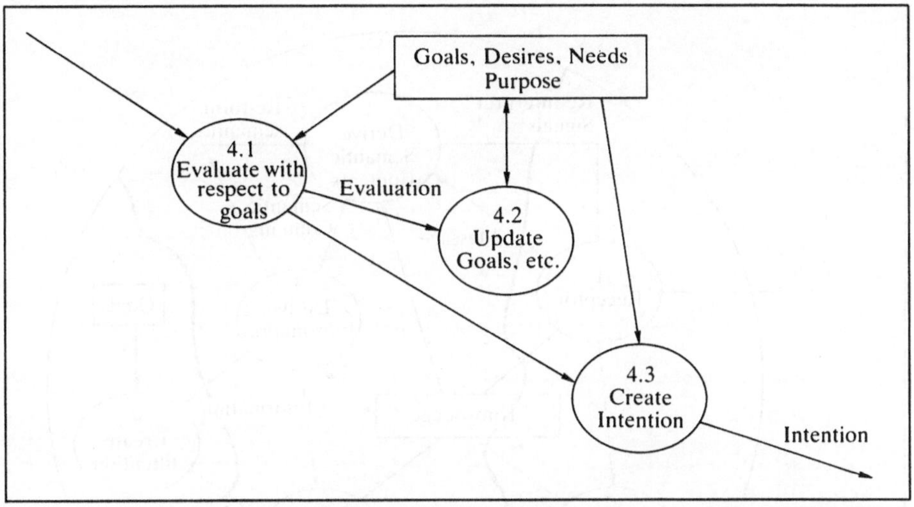

Fig. 8.8. Create intention. Information, new knowledge (the result of associating the interpreted semantics with existing stored knowledge); evaluation, a measure of how well current goals are being achieved; intention, the intention to transmit a message.

send a fax. In general, intentional systems will have access to more methods of formulating semantic contents than other systems. Once the semantic contents has been formulated, processing then continues as for the automatic monitoring system. Notice that process 5.1 is concerned with evaluating alternative semantic systems – considering the advantages and disadvantages of each – for formulating appropriate semantics. Process 5.2 selects the appropriate semantic *structure*, allowing the semantics to be encoded.

It is important to remember that the focus of this model is on the mechanisms of the receipt and production of signals. There are many considerations involved in the processes of sign production to do with selecting appropriate semantic systems, formulating the content of signs, choosing a medium for transmission, how the pragmatics of the signs are considered and so on. These are vital considerations, but have been left out of the current discussions since they do not affect the functional architecture. They do, however, affect what types of knowledge a system must possess. For example, for transmission, an agent should ideally have a model of the agents with which it is communicating, for without this knowledge it may select to transmit signals that the intended system is incapable of receiving. Eco (1976) devotes a substantial part of his book to sign production. In our model this knowledge has to be available to processes 5.1 and 5.2. Fig. 8.6, dealing with the create T-message process concerns all things semantic and pragmatic. Fig. 8.7, the transmit process, deals only with syntactic aspects.

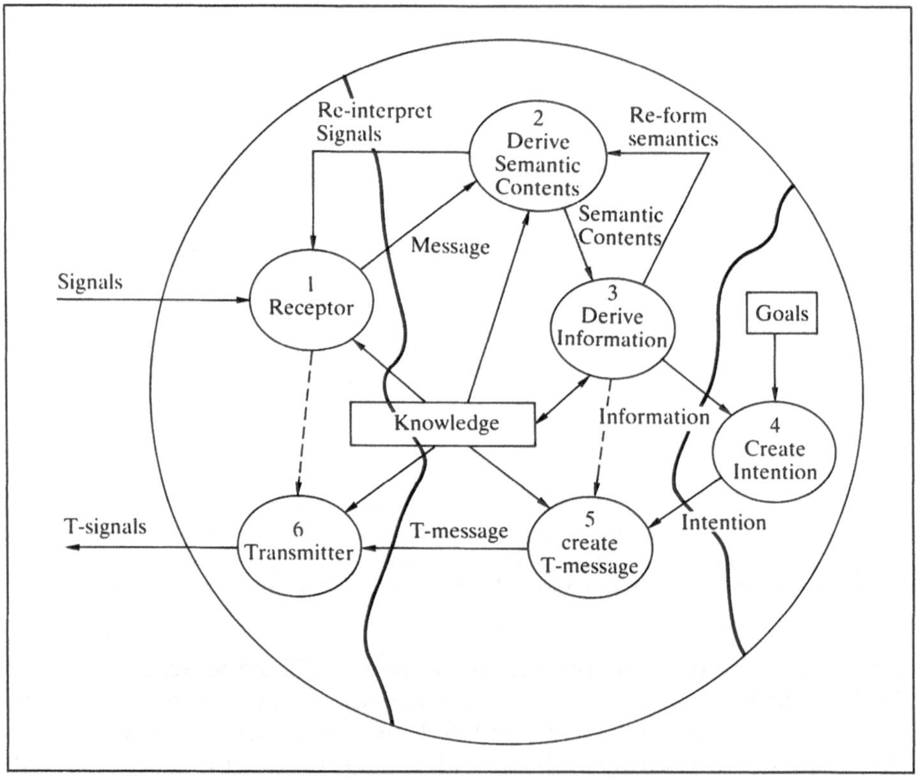

Fig. 8.9. General architecture of an interacting system.

8.3.5 Summary

We can now put the various processes together and represent the receipt and transmission of signals for interacting systems. This is shown in Fig. 8.9. The dotted lines illustrate two alternative paths from receipt to transmission for less sophisticated systems. In a "syntactic system" the receptor is linked directly to the transmitter. In an "information processing system" process 3 links directly to process 5.

8.4 Discussion

The touchstone of any architecture, or model, is its explanatory power. How useful is this semiotic analysis in understanding agent-based HCI, CSCW or DAI? The answer to this question is that it forces designers and users to be explicit about the scope and subtlety of the representations employed in their systems.

For any agent we can ask:

- What signals are detectable?
- What is the size and decay rate of the signal record?
- What knowledge does it possess of sign grammar, syntax and signalling conventions?
- What is the system's ability to create messages from signals?
- What semantic systems does the system have access to and what semantic systems does it know it has access to?
- What abilities does it have to derive and represent semantic contents?
- What ability does it have to represent the context of the interaction?
- Can it update its knowledge store?
- Can it derive information?
- What goals, motivations and purpose are represented in the system and to what extent can these be used in the system's reasoning?
- Can the system update its goals?

If agents are described in terms of the model presented here, these questions are opened up for examination. Moreover, the agent can be interrogated if tools are provided that enable the representations to be displayed. The agent can explain its actions in terms of these representations.

The literature on agent-based systems, CSCW and DAI rarely presents systems in sufficient detail so that they can be criticized from the point of view expressed in this chapter. However, some applications can be used to highlight the type of analysis that our semiotic view of interacting systems offers.

Payton's description of an Autonomous Land Vehicle (ALV) (Payton 1991) illustrates a system that could perform function 4.1 of the architecture, but was limited because it did not have a function 4.2. Although not explicitly stated by Payton (1991), the ALV presumably could receive only visual signals and could transmit only electrical signals sufficient to propel and steer the drive mechanism.

Kearney et al. (1991) describe a system of agents to help in organizing meetings, and six types of signal that the agents can send and receive. Each type of input (e.g. "message(tma(vin), inform, general–availability. . . . [etc.])") is associated with a semantic system that allows the system to derive the semantic contents of the message (such as "what is your current status?") and is associated with a well-specified set of outputs (such as "busy", "negotiation pending", "free"). These agents are thus information processing systems in terms of the model presented here as there is no explicit representation of the system's goals. A single interpretation of a message is possible and the system possesses knowledge of its status. The information derived from the message and the current knowledge (by process 3.2) is passed directly to process 5.1.

As a final example, we may consider an experimental adaptive system with which the author was involved (Benyon and Murray 1993; Jennings et al. 1991) as an "interface selection agent". The purpose of this system was to offer a menu interface to users of a database system who were having trouble using the command language interface. In terms of the architecture presented here, the main part of the system would be described as follows:

- Signals: the system could receive numeric signals.
- Signal record: the record could contain two numbers (X and Y).
- Process 1.3: the system produced a message consisting of two numbers (X and Y).
- Semantic systems: the system had a single semantic system, namely {Number of Tasks completed, Number of errors made}.
- Process 2.2: the system derived the semantic contents of the message {Number of Tasks completed = X and Number of errors made = Y}.

The system's knowledge base consisted of:

- A representation of all users (the user models) in terms of their spatial ability (values {high, low}), their computer experience (values {high, low, none}) and their frequency of computer use (values {frequent, occasional}).
- An inference rule: if interface = command and errors > 1 and tasks = 12 then spatial ability = low and command experience = low.
- Adaptation rules, the most relevant of which was: if spatial ability = low and command experience = none and frequency of computer use = occasional then interface = menu.

Process 3.1 exploited the system's knowledge of the context (whether the user was using the command interface or the menu interface) to interpret the semantic contents.

Process 3.2 used the knowledge base (the existing status of the user and the inference rule) in association with the interpreted semantics (number of tasks completed and number of errors made) to derive information concerning the user's spatial ability (if a user made more than one error in twelve tasks the user was considered to have a spatial ability of "low").

Process 3.3 updated the system's knowledge base (the user model part) accordingly (based on the result of applying the inference rule).

Process 4 was not available in the working system, but a suggested enhancement (Benyon 1993) is to include the explicit goal of maintaining a specified average task completion time. Then, if the system is developed so that it can receive a sign for the time taken to complete a task, information concerning the actual average task completion time can be evaluated against the specified goal in order to produce an intention to offer the appropriate interface.

Process 5.1 formulated the semantics of a T-message on the basis of the adaptation rules, creating the T-message "interface=menu" if appropriate.

Process 6 produced relevant signals that were sent to the interface control component of the system, which actually altered the interface if required.

8.5 Conclusion

Many architectures have been proposed for DAI and agent-based systems (see, for example, Alvey 1988; compare also Chapters 6 and 9). The approach proposed here is orthogonal to many of these because it focuses on the processes and structures necessary for communication between systems. It is a general architecture, which can be applied equally well to humans, to simple devices and to computer systems. I cannot understand my computer when it displays "Error = ID 2036" because I do not have the appropriate semantic system to interpret the message. My computer does not understand me when I shout at it because it cannot receive the signals. Certain abilities are necessary for communication and certain are desirable for improved communication.

The model presented here can be applied at many different levels of abstraction and in so doing it seems to avoid the dichotomy of "classical" versus "nouvelle" AI (Brooks 1991a). The model accepts that all interaction is "physically grounded", as emphasized in the nouvelle AI, yet also shows that signals can only be understood in terms of symbols (as produced by the interaction of signals and the semantic systems available to that system). Moreover, describing systems from this semiotic, interacting systems viewpoint makes explicit the signals that a system can receive and transmit, the abilities of that system to interpret and generate meaning and the degree to which the system is autonomous.

Appendix A: Examples of the Model in Action

In order to illustrate the model of interacting systems developed in Section 8.3, we will consider two examples. Although the first has overtones of a natural language processing problem, the reader should consider it from the semiotic perspective. Language has, of course, been a central concern of semiotics since its earliest days, but the purpose of presenting this example is to focus on the various processes and knowledge structures that were necessary for the interpretation of the signals. In the second example, a typical instance of human–computer interaction is used to emphasize the three different types of system (syntactic systems, information processing systems and intentional systems) that were mentioned briefly in Section 8.3.5. Process numbers refer to the architecture presented in Figs 8.2–8.9.

A.1 The Broadway Example

In this example, the functional architecture developed in Section 8.3 is applied to a recent experience I had in Sydney, Australia. If the supposed semantic structures and misunderstandings appear trivial, then perhaps the reader has more knowledge than I had at the time. The example describes the transmission and receipt of a message concerned with how I could get a bus from the train station to the University of Sydney.

1. Form Intention (process 4)
   Ask the attendant how to get a bus to the university
2. Create T-message (process 5)
   Where can I get a bus to the University? (including decisions on using the spoken medium and expressing it through the audio channel, etc.)
3. Transmit (process 6)
   Utter the sentence "Where can I get a bus to the University?"
4. Receive and store signals (processes 1.1 and 1.2)
   Phonemes preceded and succeeded by longer gaps
5. Create message (process 1.3)
   "Broadway"
6. Derive semantic contents (process 2)
   The semantic structure may be conceptualized as shown in Fig. A.1. This illustrates the current state of my knowledge. The sign-vehicle "Broadway" is associated with only two concepts (which are themselves complex concepts) – "Musical shows" and "New York". This structure is transmitted (through process 2.3) to step 7.
7. Derive Information (process 3)
   Interpreting the semantics (process 3.1) is difficult. The context informs me that the received message is unlikely to be a joke about musicals and

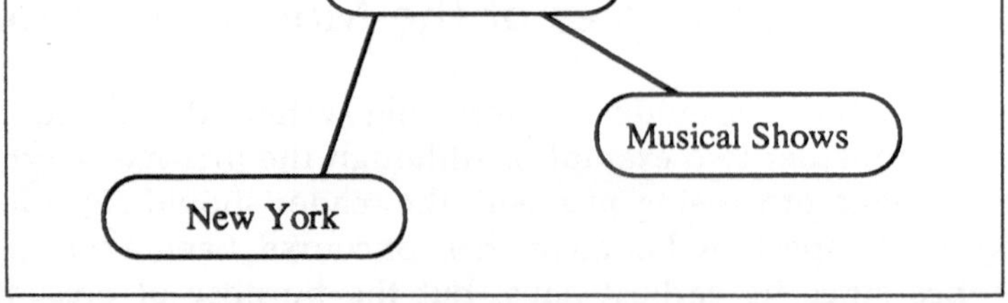

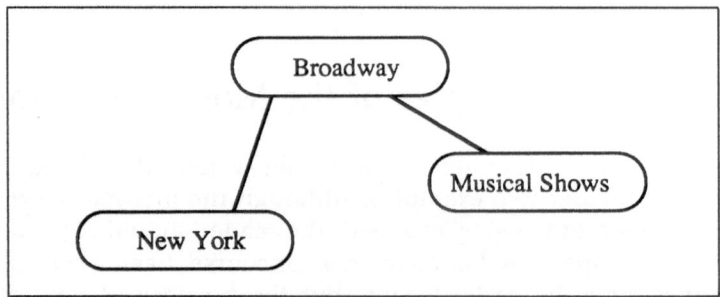

Fig. A.1. Conceptual view of semantic contents of message "Broadway".

the New York connection seems tenuous, to say the least. Re-forming the semantics (process 2) provides no further enlightenment since there are no other semantic systems that can be associated with "Broadway".

8. Re-interpret signals (process 1.3)
   Since the semantics cannot be used to derive useful information, the signals are re-interpreted: did he say "The Broad Way"? "The broad way"? "broad way"? Try the message "broad way" (i.e. recognize that the signals may have had a gap between "broad" and "way").
9. Derive semantic contents (process 2)
   A conceptual view of the semantic contents associated with this wider interpretation of the signals is shown in Fig. A.2. From this structure a number of semantic contents can be obtained, which are transmitted to the derive information process.
10. Derive information (process 3)

A number of interpretations of the semantics (process 3.1) are available:

- Broadway = street name (e.g. he would tell me about a street wouldn't he?).
- Broadway = a broad way, = a wide street/path.
- Broadway = "A broad way" and a broad way is a particular Australian concept (cultural unit). (We are in Australia and they may have different meanings for expressions).

The knowledge store is tentatively updated with a variety of these options and information is derived. Using the context that there's a wide street somewhere:

11. Form Intention (process 4)
    "Go and see if there's a wide street"
12. Receive signals (process 1)

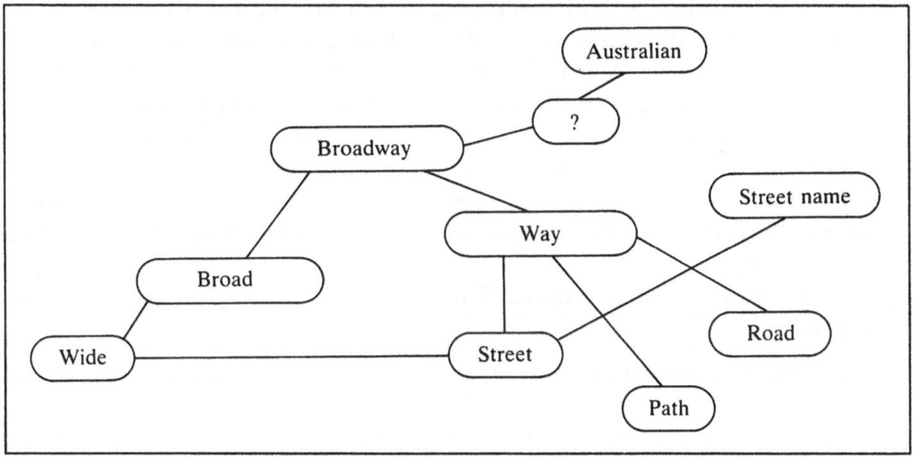

Fig. A.2. Conceptual representation of semantic structure associated with "broad way" message.

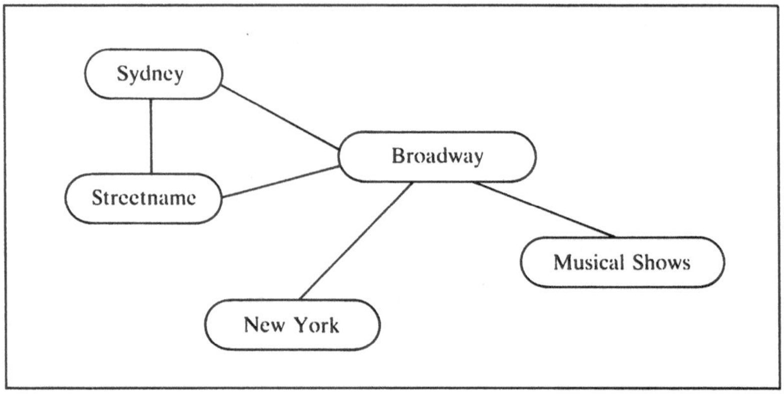

Fig. A.3. Portion of the assumed conceptual structure of knowledge after inferring that Broadway is a street name in Sydney.

Perceive sign on wall with the letters "Broadway" inscribed on it. Hence, create message (process 1.3) "sign which says 'Broadway'"

13. Derive semantic contents (process 2)
    The conceptual view of the appropriate semantic structure of signs on walls may be a proposition along the lines of "IF there's a sign on a wall THEN that's the name of the street, hence Broadway = street name"
14. Derive information (process 3)
    Broadway is the name of a street in Sydney. Hence, update the knowledge structure giving the conceptual representation of Fig. A.3.

A.2 Insert New Line Example

This example concerns the interaction of four systems (a human, a keyboard, a computer and a screen), which are required to perform the action of inserting a new line using a text processor. The arrangement is illustrated in Fig. A.4 and described in the ten steps below. Notice that the first system (a human) is an intentional system (steps 1–3), in which the output of signals is driven by the system's goals. The second (the keyboard) is a syntactic system (step 4), in which output is a purely mechanical response to input. There are no semantics. The computer's processing unit is an information processing system (steps 6–9), in which the meaning of signs is derived, but output is produced directly from the derivation of information. The screen is another syntactic system (step 10).

1. I form the intention of inserting a new line into a piece of text (process 4).
2. Selecting an appropriate semantic system, I create the semantic contents "Press <return>" and form a T-message with a content "press the return key" (process 5).

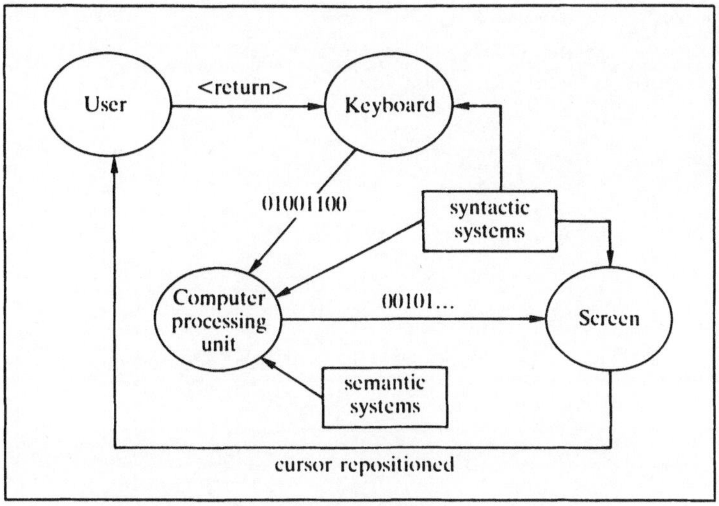

Fig. A.4. Systems interacting to insert a new line.

3. This is translated into the T-signals of physically pressing the <ret-urn> key on the keyboard.
4. The keyboard receives the signals that a particular key has been pressed (process 1) and issues the signals "01001100" (say) to the computer's processing unit (process 6).
5. The computer receives the bits "0,1,0,0,1,1,0,0", which it stores in its signal record. Applying the syntactic system, it passes the message "01001100" to process 2.
6. The semantic system is selected which allows the semantic contents <return> (was pressed) to be derived (process 2) and transmitted to process 3.
7. Process 3 uses the current contents (i.e. a particular software package is being used) to interpret the semantics of <return> as "new line is required". The information derived from this is something along the lines of "position cursor 1 centimetre below current position at the left-hand side of the screen".
8. This information is transmitted to process 5, which formulates the semantics of an appropriate T-message according to a semantic system relevant to the screen display. This describes where to position the cursor, details of spacing, etc. as a structured set of signals 00101001, 00011100, 10111000 (say).
9. The syntactic system is used to translate this message into an appropriate string of signals, which are transmitted to the screen (process 6).
10. The screen receives the signals and displays some appropriate signals by lighting certain pixels on the screen (processes 1 and 6).

Chapter 9

Supporting Human Experts' Collaborative Work: Modelling Organizational Context Knowledge in Cooperative Information Systems

S. Kirn

9.1 Introduction

Future information systems need to support human experts' collaborative work effectively. In general, human experts work in complex and heterogeneous domains, using different types of intelligent aids. Their work is geographically distributed and they apply a flexible, task-dependent collaboration style (Schmidt 1991). Malone and Crowston (1990) suggested that human experts address a significant portion of their work to coordinating themselves. At the same time, their (software) aids are mutually unrelated, being unaware of any context sensitivity of a user's work. This limits their utility much more than is necessary.

It is really not a new idea that effective assistance of human experts requires knowledge about their tasks and responsibilities as well as about their intentions, goals, plans, problem solving strategies and methods, etc. In so far as these issues are determined by the organizations the experts work for, we call this knowledge *organizational context knowledge*. In most cases, much of this knowledge is explicitly represented already in organization arrangements and organizational charts. However, it is not yet (explicitly) represented in today's information systems. This makes it extremely difficult to make effective use of such systems whenever an expert applies them to varying tasks (such as different project teams, organization committees, task forces, etc.). In addition, today's information systems are unable to support the human users' collaborative work at all. To support collaborative work effectively also requires the information systems to be able to cooperate. Furthermore, cooperative information systems must remember that their own problem solving work is part of their human users' work. Thus, Kirn and Schlageter (1992) pointed out that the agents' (stand-alone or cooperative) problem solving is dependent on (and thus embedded in) the process of the human experts' (stand-alone or cooperative) work.

Organizational context knowledge serves also to make information systems cooperative in the above sense. This stimulates us to investigate that kind of knowledge further. The modelling of organizational context knowledge is founded on organization theory, and (in accordance with our aim here) is to be enhanced by recent research in Distributed Artificial Intelligence (DAI). It results in a reference coordination architecture that supports the development of cooperative information systems in so-called sociotechnical environments.

The work described in this chapter forms part of the project FRESCO (*F*ede*R*ative *E*xpert *S*ystems *CO*operation). FRESCO aims at the support of human experts' collaborative work at the level of problem solving. The expert systems of FRESCO do not provide their human users with local domain knowledge only. Instead, they cooperate to improve the completeness and reliability of their local solutions as well. First results of FRESCO – still at a rather technical level – refer to cooperative ability as part of each expert system's problem solving capability (see Kirn 1991). Our current work aims to improve the expert systems' cooperative abilities further by letting them know about application-specific requirements of a task on hand. This includes model knowledge about the organizational context of human experts' problem solving, which is to be presented here. (On the subject of expert systems, see also Chapters 7 and 10.)

After a discussion of related work (Section 9.2), FRESCO, a DAI system in banking (Section 9.3.1), is introduced, after which the organizational implications that arise if a decision process is supported by a cooperative software system are considered (Sections 9.3.2 and 9.3.3). Next, a framework of organizational context knowledge modelling is presented in Section 9.4. Organizational context knowledge refers to all issues that are imposed by the organization an expert works for, and that are significant with respect to the expert system's cooperative problem solving. Finally, we discuss how organizational context knowledge applies when developing cooperative decision support systems. To this purpose, a seven-layer reference coordination architecture is presented (Section 9.5).

9.2 Related Work

Much work has been conducted in system science, management science and organization theory in order to improve the performance (effectiveness and efficiency) of organizational activities. Among the most interesting issues are: investigation of organizational structures, implementation and control of (cooperative) activities, task decomposition and result synthesis, coordination mechanisms, control of information flow, reporting and commitment procedures, etc. This also includes all those issues that relate to the use of computer technology by an organization. These elements are to be applied to the organization as a whole, to establish predefined problem solving strategies, to take effective use of the organization's capabilities and resources, and to ensure some kind of "organizational consistency". Thus, anyone applying to an organization must be aware of (or adapted to) those definitions and procedures that are currently established within the organization.

On the other hand, a lot of stimulating research has also been carried out in computer science. Its main focus is on the organization of distributed computing systems. Primarily, early work dealt with the implementation and evaluation of (hierarchical to decentralized) organizational structures. More recently, researchers in the field of (distributed) AI considered how social and sociological insights into the behaviour of human beings may also be applied to model autonomous intelligent agents. (The term "agent" is used within this chapter to denote any type of software module that is able to contribute to collaborative problem solving.) Fox (1981) proposed an organizational view of distributed systems. Malone (1987) presented a model of coordination in organizations and markets. Coordinating the activities of an organization requires an understanding of the behaviour of the groups that are part of that organization. To that purpose, Singh (1990) developed a formal theory of group intentions. This relates to the work of Parunak (1990), who applies social power to explicate how agents can control and dominate each other. Bond (1990) provided a normative model of collaboration in organizations which is founded on PROJECTS. Coordinating autonomous agents requires also the modelling of communication and conversation issues (e.g. see Numaoka 1990; Numaoka and Tokoro 1990). This includes developing strategies of conflict resolution that are required whenever independent agents are to act together (Klein et al. 1989; Klein 1990). This, in turn, extends our notion of intelligence: any autonomous cooperative software system is required to control (in a knowledge-based way) its involvement in cooperative processes, too. Thus, any cooperative agent has at its disposal the local domain capability as well as some amount of coordination capability (Klein 1990; Kirn 1991). The TOVE (TOronto Virtual Enterprise) project develops a common-sense model of a virtual enterprise in order to provide deep knowledge about all issues that stand behind the activities performed by an organization or a part of it (see Fox 1992). However, there is no work to date on the consequences that must be expected when cooperative software agents are applied in an organization.

9.3 FRESCO: Cooperating Expert Systems in Banking

9.3.1 Overview

Mostly, today's cooperative systems are designed top-down. However, it is much more interesting in practice to build them up from pre-existing agents; i.e. the aim should be to provide conventional intelligent stand-alone systems with the ability to cooperate rather than to follow the top-down approach. Such an approach promises some very useful advantages:

- Knowledge sharing (as an extension of the well-known concept of information sharing) will further improve the competitiveness of organizations.
- Complex intelligent systems are very expensive to implement and to maintain. Instead of applying them to local tasks only, their productivity will be substantially improved by integrating them into a cooperative environment.
- Cooperative systems allowing users to add new agents or to remove already existing ones dynamically are much more reliable than most of today's distributed problem solvers.

9.3.1.1 The FRESCO Architecture

FRESCO is a federative expert system that applies to a large financial application. It has been built up from several pre-existing conventional (i.e. stand-alone) expert systems. All of them are supporting human experts' work on complex domains in banking. As an example, the FRESCO system supports the collaborative work of banking experts who have to decide a large credit application of a medium-sized enterprise. In such a case, a number of different and interdependent tasks (e.g. evaluation of the client's reliability, its market position, the expected return on investment, the qualification of the client's management, etc.) are to be processed. Each human expert is responsible for (at least) one task. He or she uses a knowledge-based system which has, at the software level, cooperative abilities in order to support the collaborative work on the human users' level. FRESCO serves as a testbed and as a basis for further research, primarily concerned with those issues that relate to the cooperation and collaboration between complex intelligent systems. (We use the term *collaboration* in a more general sense than the term *cooperation*, to which, at least in the field of DAI, authors have given a very special (and restricted) semantics. For details, see Bond and Gasser (1988).)

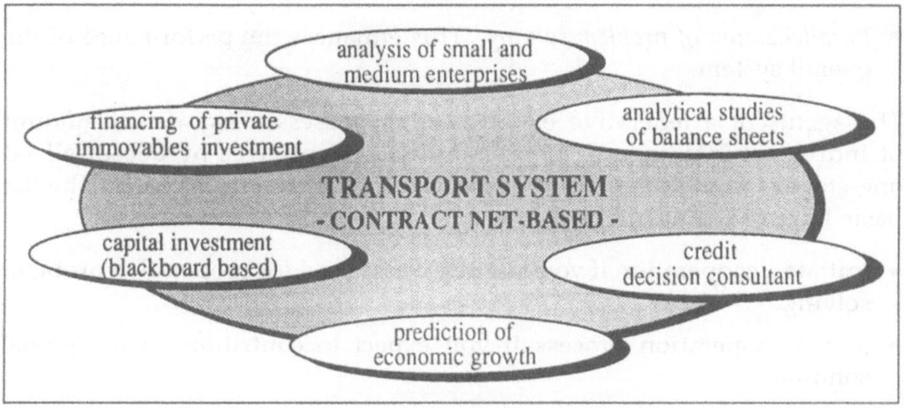

Fig. 9.1. The FRESCO system.

Figure 9.1 depicts the FRESCO system, disregarding those parts that are not of interest here (e.g. databases, system administration, etc.). The implementation of FRESCO is based on Prolog, Oracle and C.

The agents of FRESCO are completely autonomous, but their domain knowledge partially overlaps. As in real banking applications, each agent interacts with databases and with other software systems.

9.3.1.2 What Federative Expert Systems Are

FRESCO is called a *federative expert system.* On the one hand, the federative approach has its roots in the characteristics of the overall system (bottom-up design, completely decentralized, while at the same time tolerating different types of intelligent agents, no central control, no shared knowledge resources, no global schema). On the other hand, it is based on the attributes of the individual agents (intelligent, independent, autonomous). Federative expert systems provide a highly flexible environment for cooperation. According to Wiederhold (1989) and Kirn and Schlageter (1991) they promise some interesting advantages:

- *Extending the complexity barrier.* While it is difficult to administrate and evaluate large knowledge bases effectively, cooperation allows knowledge base modularization without losing the links between different pieces of knowledge.
- *Extensibility of the overall system.* Federative expert systems provide the system administration with facilities to include new agents easily and dynamically.
- *Knowledge base modularization.* Modularization improves system maintenance.

- *Parallelization of problem solving.* This enhances the performance of the overall system.

The agents of a federative expert system possess a significant amount of individual intelligence. They coordinate themselves by decentralized one-stage or multi-stage negotiations. Two simple meta-rules describe the basic lines of the agents' behaviour:

- Initiate a cooperation if you identify a real need for cooperative problem solving.
- Join a cooperation process if you expect to contribute to the global solution.

Based on these meta-rules, the agents of a federative expert system are benevolent and cooperative, but not destructive. (For further discussion of cooperation, see Chapters 1, 2, 5, 6, 10 and 11. On the subject of DAI, see Chapters 6, 8, 10 and 11.)

9.3.2 The Cooperative Problem Solving Scenario

FRESCO has been designed as an open system. Thus, its problem solving capability changes over time. Sometimes, new agents are added to the system, and others are removed from it. Each of the agents is able to collaborate with several users at any one time. These may process different tasks, follow different goals and objectives, and have to consider different restrictions. The agents participate in or initiate a cooperation only if they expect to benefit from the cooperative activity (see Kirn 1991). A cooperative style of problem solving is expected to be useful for an agent if it:

- Contributes to its local problem solving capabilities.
- Contributes to the agents' (task related) knowledge.
- Provides resources that are needed to solve the task at hand.
- Helps to allocate portions of a large task to some other agent etc.

Based upon the work of Smith (1980), the current implementation applies a contract net protocol to coordinate collaborative activities among the FRESCO agents. Thus, a manager agent decomposes complex tasks into sets of subtasks, which are then allocated to the most competent of the (competing) bidders. The agents process the subtasks independently of each other, and they return the subresults at the end of (local) problem solving. The manager synthesizes the subresults into an overall result, which is then given back to the user.

9.3.3 Shortcomings: An Organizational Perspective

Suppose FRESCO is being used in a bank. This requires restricting its behaviour to the bank's own style of problem solving, to its (intra-organizational) coordination requirements and mechanisms, to its (formal and informal) communication procedures, to the bank's internal quality control and to all the other issues that are imposed to guarantee "organizational consistency". In such a case, the following situations may arise (the terminology follows the contract net definitions):

- The manager of a task T allocates subtask T_j to agent$_i$, who has provided the most promising capability description. However, the organizational rules may definitely intervene to keep agent$_i$ apart from any knowledge that relates to T and its processing.
- A human expert applies to agent$_i$. However, he or she may not be allowed to benefit from the knowledge of that agent. Now, if the expert addresses a complex task to agent$_{j \ \ i}$ in FRESCO there is no means to prevent agent$_i$ from being involved. Exactly the same holds when a database is to be accessed.
- In general, a human expert has at his or her disposal a (more or less) detailed description of how to work on complex problems that may arise within his or her field of expertise. Based on such descriptions, the final solution can be interpreted and evaluated. Also, such "cookbooks" can make an important contribution to effective quality control. If the human expert is now to be supported by a system like FRESCO these guidelines (or even the formal rules) no longer apply to problem solving. Thus, it becomes difficult to understand how and why a certain solution has been derived. In such cases, it is also impossible to guarantee that exactly those agents are to be involved from which expertise is required.
- Also, conventional DAI systems do not deal with notification procedures. Thus, they do not guarantee to inform exactly those members of an organization who must know about a certain issue. This is a really important issue as far as it affects the organizational allocation of tasks, capabilities, resources and responsibilities. This makes it difficult or even impossible to control the behaviour of an organization, or at least parts of it.

Many similar issues can be identified easily. Common to all of them is that the definitions, rules and conventions being represented in organization arrangements and organizational charts are not fully considered when an expert applies a cooperative decision support tool.

9.4 Modelling Organizational Context Knowledge

As the agents of FRESCO are intelligent at the domain level as well as at the cooperation level, they understand (the relevant part of) the organization for which they work. Thus, they have a model of the organization which includes (at least):

- The organizational structure: components of the organization and the relationships that are imposed between them.
- The organizational activities, including the behaviour of the whole system, its goals and constraints.
- Descriptions of the resources, tools etc. that are available.
- The information systems infrastructure.

These basic elements can be used to build up an organization model providing a data dictionary of concepts (such as products, organizational units, negotiation procedures, etc.) that are common across a variety of organizations. However, in trying to construct models of organizations we have to consider the following modelling issues (based on Fox 1992):

- Are there any means to develop a generic model of the organization?
- Can the terminology be precisely defined? If so, what kind of use could it be?
- How detailed should an organization model be?
- How can we determine which is a better organization model?
- Can an organization model be consistent?
- Can an organization model be created and kept consistent over time?

According to Fox (1992) the following evaluation criteria might be useful when we are to decide on the most appropriate modelling concept:

- *Generality*. To what degree is the representation shared between diverse activities such as design and troubleshooting, or even design and marketing? What concepts does it span?
- *Competence*. How well does it support problem solving? That is, to what questions can the representation answer or what tasks can it support?
- *Efficiency*. Space and inference: does the representation support efficient reasoning, or does it require some type of transformation?
- *Perspicuity*. Is the representation easily understood by the users? Does the representation "document itself"?
- *Transformability*. Can the representation be easily transformed into another more appropriate one for a particular decision problem?
- *Extensibility*. Is there a core set of ontological primitives that are

partitionable or do they overlap in denotation? Can the representation be extended to encompass new concepts?

- *Granularity*. Does it support reasoning at various levels of abstraction and detail?
- *Scalability*. Does the representation scale support the modelling of large applications?
- *Integration*. Can the representation be used directly or be transformed so that its content can be used by existing analysis and support tools of the enterprise?

A system model of organizations (see Pattison et al. 1987) is built up from functional components (such as organizational units, different types of machines, etc.). Each functional component includes a definition, a microtheory, and a basic set of relations that are defined between the components of the microtheory. (Microtheories have been used extensively in the CYC project at MCC; see Lenat and Guha (1990).) Functional components perform tasks such as planning activities, negotiating conflicts, quality control, etc. They relate to organizational units, which are responsible for performing the task according to the constraints that are to be considered (such as time and quality requirements, consumption of resources, etc.).

Space limitations prevent an in-depth discussion of all those issues relating to the modelling of knowledge about organizations. Recently, Pattison et al. (1987) and Fox (1992) have provided good introductions to that topic, which can be used as a starting point.

Finally, we state that there is a modelling paradox. The goal of creating an organization model may be a good idea, but the result may be that nobody will use it: if it is large, then it may be too large to understand; if it is small, it may be irrelevant to the problem at hand.

9.5 A Multi-Layered Reference Coordination Architecture

This section discusses how the organizational context knowledge model is to be integrated into a cooperative human–computer problem solving environment. As the full details have been presented by Kirn (1992) we present only a brief overview.

The reference coordination architecture includes the following seven layers:

1. *Internal Self Model*. This refers to the agent's own self model represented by the agent's native knowledge representation language. Different Internal Self Models are mostly represented by different representation languages. Among others, the Internal Self Model of an agent includes its intentions, goals, plans and strategies, and its knowledge of its own

capabilities, resources, etc. It also includes the control knowledge that is used to control local problem solving. In the case of databases, the conceptual model of the database is part of the Internal Self Model. On the other hand, when considering Knowledge Acquisition and Documentation System (KADS)-based agents, the conceptual model of the agent (that has to be specified during system modelling) is also part of the agent's self model.

2. *External Self Model.* The External Self Model of an agent is derived by translating the Internal Self Model from the agents' native representation language to a Common Representation Language (CRL). The use of External Self Models covers two aspects: firstly, it enables cooperative problem solvers to communicate self-knowledge and to deal with (i.e. to evaluate, to reason about) the capability of each other; secondly, it provides a means to add knowledge that is not available within the domain knowledge base of an agent, but that is needed on the cooperation level. As an example, consider the knowledge that is needed to deal with the issue of heterogeneity.
3. *Export Services Model.* These describe which part of an agent's individual capability can be used by a certain collaborative process. An agent may possess different Export Services Models, each of which refers to another Coordination Model. The main function of an Export Services Model is to preserve the agent's *autonomy* and to control the use that other software agents, users or applications make of its local capabilities.
4. *Coordination Model.* This refers to a class of collaborative processes. Hence, within a collaborative problem solving environment, different Coordination Models may exist. Coordination Models integrate a set of Export Services Models. When performing a collaborative action among the agents, the Coordination Model provides the context of each local agent's problem solving. Coordination Models include knowledge about the distribution of capabilities over the whole system, and they may also describe how certain instances of collaborative processes are to be performed. This also enables a global system to learn about collaborative processes. Construction processors associate Coordination Models with the Export Services Models of the different agents. The Coordination Model contributes to two important features of collaborative systems: firstly, it supports the *distribution* feature of a system; secondly, it supports the *coordination* feature of the system, in that it models all the knowledge that is needed to coordinate cooperative (and even joint) actions among different agents.
5. *Application Model.* This refers to a certain class of applications that are to be performed by a set of cooperative agents. In general, each collaborative system possesses a set of different Application Models. Each Application Model may contain a set of application instances. An Application Model (and the application instances as well) provides all

the knowledge that is needed to perform collaborative actions among the agents in order to meet the goals and requirements of the application at hand. Whenever introducing an Application Model, it is compared against the Coordination Models that are currently available. This matching process determines whether the collaborative system is able to contribute to this (new) application. If not, the system can try to build a new Coordination Model by applying the construction processors to the External Self Models. If successful, the new Coordination Model is added to the overall system, and the new application can now be adopted. Application Models introduce the *application context* of collaborative problem solving.

6. *User Models.* These refer to a class of users or to a well-defined individual user of the collaborative system. They are needed for two purposes: firstly, they model those portions of the problem solving context that refer to the human user (expert); secondly, they make the agents knowledgeable about their human users' collaborative problem solving style. The first function relates to the external schema as it has been defined by Sheth and Larson (1990). The same application may be performed by different users. Within a certain application the users may perform the same task or different tasks. They may be responsible for the same or for a different portion of the whole application. They may be qualified to different degrees to fulfil the requirements of their tasks. Often, they aim at different goals. This kind of knowledge enables cooperative agents to be aware explicitly of the current state (and dynamics) of their users' (collaborative) problem solving. User Models introduce knowledge about the *human experts* into the system.
7. *Organizational Context Model.* Each application is embedded in a larger organization. Each application depends more or less on its organizational context. Thus, to understand fully a certain application it is necessary to know about the relevant organizational issues. This motivated the development of an Organizational Context Model. It describes the aims and objectives that are to be considered during problem solving, the allocation of resources, the intra-organizational relationships and dependencies, the reporting procedures, etc. It also includes which parts of an organization apply to the application, together with their (derived) organizational subgoals, capabilities, responsibilities, etc. The Organizational Context Model introduces *organizational issues* into human–computer collaborative systems.

Figure 9.2 shows how the seven layers of the reference architecture relate to each other. First of all, each agent has exactly one Internal Self Model and one External Self Model. An agent may possess different Export Services Models at the same time, which describe how it likes to contribute to a (set of) collaborative processes. Each Export Services Model can be connected to one or more Coordination Models. In contrast to the first three types of models, Coordination Models represent knowledge about the overall system. Each Coordination Model refers to exactly one Application Model. Each Application Model represents a set of application instances. In general, different User Models apply to each Application Model (and to each application instance as well). Finally, any User Model may be linked to one or more Organizational Context Models. The organization itself (which is shown in Fig. 9.2 purely for completeness) is not part of the reference coordination architecture.

9.6 Conclusions

This chapter considers the support of human experts' cooperative work by an intelligent and collaborative environment. The basic hypothesis is that the working context of human experts changes over time. It may even be

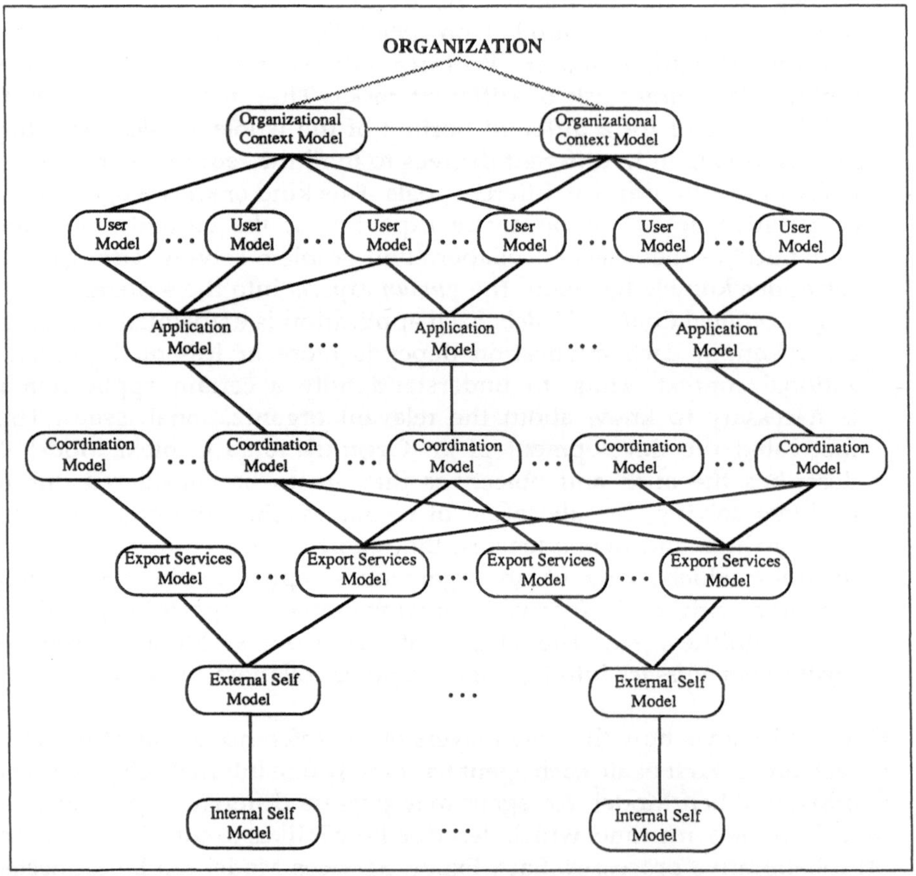

Fig. 9.2. A typical coordination architecture for a human–computer collaborative system.

different if an expert undertakes different tasks (committees, projects, etc.) at the same time. In the case of stand-alone support systems this may not be a problem, in that the different contexts can be represented as part of the user interface. However, cooperative systems solve problems by task communication. This supposes that an agent knows about the current working context of its human user. Furthermore, the agent must be able to reason about this context and to communicate it to other agents of the system. These considerations stimulated an investigation into how such contextual knowledge (which is slightly different from the current notion of problem solving context) can be introduced into a cooperative software environment.

The chapter focused on the organizational context of cooperative problem solving. After a brief overview of related work, it introduced FRESCO, a cooperative expert system application in banking. The FRESCO cooperative problem solving scenario shows that there is a strong need to represent organizational context knowledge to support and control cooperative activities. This introduced the discussion of the modelling issues, where we dealt with organizational context knowledge. One of the most important criticisms of the representation of organizations is the sheer amount of knowledge that has to be managed. However, most of this knowledge is already available as written text. Moreover, organizations possess a well-defined formal structure. Thus, the knowledge to be represented is easily decomposable. In the case of very large organizations, only part of the overall enterprise model is going to be used by an application anyway. This is why we strongly believe that such a model can be developed and used in an environment of cooperating problem solvers. An essential part of our future work will be the development of a modelling framework that helps to represent such organizational context knowledge.

The chapter concluded with an overview of a possible reference coordination architecture that integrates the organizational context model as its highest layer of coordination. One of the promises of this approach is that it provides us with a means to adapt cooperative problem solving environments to the current problem solving environment in a flexible way.

In conclusion, we state that it has been shown that cooperating intelligent agents are required to know about the current (organizational) context of local and global activities. This may be done by developing an appropriate representational model based upon the organizational information that is already available within the enterprise. This model can be integrated into a multi-layer coordination architecture, and thereby be introduced into the agents' cooperative activities. This, in turn, contributes to the coordination of local and global activities with respect to the specific requirements of a particular task at hand.

Chapter 10
Artificial Intelligence and Computer Supported Cooperative Working in International Contexts

J.H. Connolly

10.1 Introduction

Many opportunities exist or can be foreseen for Computer Supported Cooperative Work (CSCW) involving people working in different countries. This chapter is concerned with some of the problems that arise out of international CSCW and with the ways in which these may be tackled with the help of Artificial Intelligence (AI) technology.

The problems on which attention will be focused are all connected with the communication that needs to occur between the cooperating partners. The chapter therefore begins with a discussion of pertinent communication-related issues: firstly, the means of communication that may be open to the participants; secondly, the internationalization of the human–computer interface, through which users communicate with and via the system; and thirdly the social dimension of person-to-person communication. Next, an outline of relevant aspects of AI technology is presented; this encompasses natural language processing (including automatic translation), other aspects of intelligent user interface management, and expert systems. The final part of the chapter deals with the role of AI in addressing the communication problems mentioned above, and suggests that AI can be of service both by intervening in the communication process during CSCW task performance and by providing support for users and designers of CSCW systems.

10.2 Communication Issues

Computer networks have now advanced to the point where they provide a viable means of interaction between users on a truly worldwide scale. Among the benefits that accrue from this situation are the many opportunities that arise for carrying out CSCW in which participants from more than one country are involved. When such work is attempted there is naturally a high probability that the participants will come from different cultural backgrounds, and they may well have different native languages. Of course, even when all the cooperating partners in a CSCW task are situated in the same country, it is possible that such differences may be present, but plainly the likelihood is all the greater when genuinely international CSCW is in operation.

An indispensable prerequisite for successful cooperative working, as Smyth and Clarke (1990, pp. 113–114) point out, is *communication* among the participants (see also Chapter 1). However, when the cooperating partners have different cultural backgrounds, and especially when they do not share the same native language, there exists greater scope for communication difficulties and misunderstandings between the participants, *ceteris paribus*, than would otherwise be the case. The aim of this chapter is to consider ways in which AI may help in alleviating such communication problems.

In view of the importance of communication in international CSCW, we shall begin by considering various relevant issues in the communication field. We shall then present an outline of those aspects of AI technology that are of relevance to the matters on which this chapter is focused, drawing particular attention to issues that are especially related to Human–Computer Interaction (HCI) and/or distributed systems. In the light of this, we shall address the question of how AI may contribute towards successful international CSCW, with particular reference to:

- The role of AI as an active element within the process of computer mediated communication (CMC).
- The role of AI as a supporting technology in relation to CSCW.

The discussion of these matters will lead to a conclusion which will offer pointers to future research.

10.2.1 Methods of Communication

The methods of CMC that may be available to CSCW participants can be classified in at least two basic ways:

1. In respect of the means by which they are perceived by the human recipient: (i) visual and (ii) auditory.
2. According to whether the system of communication is based on linguistic symbols: (i) linguistic and (ii) nonlinguistic.

Given such a classification scheme, we may identify four basic media of communicative interaction:

1. Written text (= visual + linguistic). This may take one of two forms: (i) printed or typewritten text and (ii) handwritten text. Written text is intended to include not only natural language but also other products of alphanumeric symbols such as numbers, program code and so on. After all, numerals and other symbols such as "%" or "$" do represent words in English and other languages.
2. Speech (= auditory + linguistic). Again, this is intended to include spoken numerals and so on.
3. Images (= visual + nonlinguistic). This category includes pictures, diagrams, icons and so on. Images may be still or moving, and they may be monochrome or colour.
4. Sound (= auditory + nonlinguistic). Under this heading come auditory signals based on bleepers, bells, buzzers and such like, and auditory symbols (for example, a siren sound denoting a warning).

Combinations of more than one medium in a single message are, of course, possible (for instance, the annotation of diagrams by means of written text or voice), and indeed such combinations are the norm in multimedia communication systems.

Precisely what communication facilities are available to the user depends, naturally, on the system concerned. Multimedia communication over a telecommunications network requires a very wide bandwidth, and if such messages need to be transmitted quickly, then the capacity of the link may impose a limitation (Black 1987, pp. 15–30). In addition, the need for multimedia systems that can cope with a variety of languages, as is bound to arise in many applications of international CSCW, gives rise to further problems. One of these is the inadequacy of the conventional seven-bit ASCII codes to support the world's languages. However, a standard sixteen-bit system known as "Unicode" (short for "unique coding") has now been developed to alleviate this particular problem (Sprung 1990, p. 75). Moreover, multilingual software systems have been produced which support a variety of languages. Notable examples are Xerox's Viewpoint text processing facility and the multilingual version of BBN/Slate, which provides for document creation (including both text and graphics), electronic mail and teleconferencing (Sprung 1990, pp. 74–77). Thus, the technological basis for multimedia CMC is becoming increasingly solid.

Communication via computer networks is often classified as belonging to one or other of the following categories:

1. Synchronous
2. Asynchronous.

In synchronous communication, the participants are involved in the interaction at the same time. This is the case, for example, in normal telephone conversations. In asynchronous communication, on the other hand, the participants are involved in the interaction at different times. For instance, in an exchange of messages by electronic mail, the two participants need not be using the mail system simultaneously for the interaction to be successful, and if they are not, then the communication is asynchronous (Rapaport 1991, p. 2; Wilson 1991, pp. 98,103). Both the synchronous and the asynchronous types of communication fall within the purview of this chapter.

10.2.2 The Internationalization of the Human–Computer Interface

Since CMC necessarily entails the use of human–computer interfaces by the individuals involved, an issue of some importance concerns the design of those interfaces. Many guidelines for good interface design have been proposed in the past; see Sutcliffe (1988) or Barker (1989) for useful summaries. It is taken for granted that these apply in the present context just as they do elsewhere. However, the design of what Nielsen (1990a, p. v) terms "international user interfaces" (i.e. those intended for use in more than one country) raises a number of particular problems. These include the following, which are drawn mainly from del Galdo (1990), Taylor (1990) and Zobel-Pocock (1990):

1. *Numeric format.* Different conventions exist in different countries for the representation of numbers. For example, in the UK a decimal point is represented either as a full-stop or as a centred dot, whereas in France it is represented as a comma.
2. *Currency format.* Different countries not only use different currencies but employ different formats for the expression of monetary sums. For example, in the UK the "£" sign precedes the amount, whereas in Belgium the abbreviation for the Franc follows the numerical value.
3. *Telephone and fax numbers.* These differ in length from one country to another, and can contain various kinds of separator, such as spaces, hyphens or plus signs.
4. *Time-of-day format.* Twelve or twenty-four hour clock notations can be used. Moreover, time zones may be different for users in different countries.
5. *Date format.* The conventions for representing calendar dates vary from one country to another; the sequences "day–month–year", "month–day–year" and "year–month–day" are all possible. Alternatively, in some countries such as China and Japan, an entirely different calendar is used.
6. *Character sets.* As implied above, the character sets required to represent the written forms of the world's diverse languages are widely varied. To begin with, several different alphabets are in use, for example

the Roman, the Cyrillic (employed by a group of languages including Russian) and the Arabic. In addition, various non-alphabetic systems also exist, for instance the Chinese script and the Japanese Kanji script. (To represent the required range of Chinese characters, a twenty-four bit code is necessary; see Zobel-Pocock 1990, p. 220.) Even languages that employ the same basic system, for example those that utilize the Roman alphabet, may still differ in the precise character set used. For instance, French employs the "ç" symbol, which is absent from English. A further point is that scripts are not all read in the same direction. For example, whereas English is read from left to right, Arabic is read from right to left.

7. *Collating sequences.* A collating sequence constitutes the basis upon which characters and strings are sorted, the usual sequence being alphabetic order. This, however, varies from language to language. For example, in German "ö" precedes "o" in the conventional collating sequence, but in Swedish the reverse is true.
8. *Hyphenation.* The conventions associated with hyphenation vary from one language to another. For example, in German if the letter sequence "ck" is broken across two lines, then not only is a hyphen inserted but the "c" is also changed to a "k", so that for instance "decken" ("to cover") becomes "dek-ken".
9. *Punctuation.* Here again, different languages have different conventions. This is seen, for example, in relation to the use of capital letters and in relation to the form of quotation marks in English, French and German.

The internationalization of the human–computer interface is a subject that has received less attention to date them might have been expected. Nevertheless, as Taylor (1990, p. 158) remarks, it is assuming increasing importance within HCI, and indeed, as Nielsen (1990a, p. v) observes, the day will come when over half of computer users throughout the world will be employing interfaces that were designed in another country. The advent of international CSCW represents an important aspect of this trend.

10.2.3 The Social Dimension

The cultural differences that are found between one country and another (and, indeed, within individual countries) constitute a clear source of possible problems with regard to the social aspects of CMC in international contexts. This is particularly the case with communication via linguistic media. Consequently, we shall here focus our attention upon the social dimension of verbal rather than non-verbal communication.

It is important to realize that verbal communication is generally, and correctly, regarded as a multifaceted activity, in which several different types of information are conveyed simultaneously. In particular, Halliday (1970) suggests that language fulfils three distinguishable functions, and that each of these is in some way reflected within each act of linguistic communication. The functions in question are:

1. The *ideational* function, whereby language serves to express content.
2. The *interpersonal* function, whereby language serves to establish and maintain social relationships.
3. The *textual* function, whereby language serves to present information in a coherent manner within its context of utterance.

For example, in a sentence like:

You may like to familiarize yourself with the controls

the ideational meaning relates to (i) the activity described (i.e. the process of familiarization), (ii) who is to carry it out (i.e. the person addressed), and (iii) upon what object (i.e. the controls). The interpersonal function of this sentence, however, lies in conveying to the addressee information such as (i) the fact that the speaker is making a statement rather than, for instance, posing a question, (ii) the fact that an invitation (rather than, for example, a threat) is being made, and (iii) the fact that a choice is courteously being offered to the addressee, who is free to decline the offer if preferred. As for the textual function, the sentence is lent coherence by, for instance, the cross-reference of the two pronouns "you" and "yourself" (contrast, for example, the rather less coherent "You may like to familiarize myself . . ."), and it is related to its context through the reference to a set of entities in the external situation (the addressee and the controls of the relevant device).

The social meanings and implications conveyed through the interpersonal function of language are various. However, we may identify the following aspects as being particularly noteworthy in the present context, since they represent particular sources of possible misunderstandings or other undesired reactions in international and/or intercultural communication:

1. Group relationships: (i) identity and (ii) solidarity.
2. Attitude: (i) politeness and (ii) sufficiency.

When people communicate by means of language, and especially when they speak rather than write, they almost inevitably convey some information as to their identity, not only as individuals but also as members of specific social and/or national groups. To some extent this is due to speakers' deliberate choices – for example, when teenagers employ the latest slang expression in order to associate themselves with the fashionable trends of youth culture – but more generally the information in question is communicated by aspects of language behaviour that are difficult or impossible consciously to control. For example, the language that one speaks, and the accent with which one speaks it, will more often than not reveal one's nationality and, furthermore, the social grouping to which one belongs. This social grouping may be based on regional provenance (for instance the South-West of England) or on social stratum (for example the middle class of the relevant society) or on a mixture of both. There is, of course, nothing at all wrong or regrettable about this; on the contrary, it is an element in the fascination and richness of human languages. Nevertheless, it can cause problems, for example where two participants, A and B, are trying to converse in B's language, which is not A's mother tongue, and B has a strong regional accent which A finds difficult to understand. There is also the possibility that A will in any case resent conducting a dialogue in B's language, though people of different nationalities may vary as to how they feel about this kind of situation, and speakers of English are reputed to be less tolerant of it than, for instance, Dutch, Turkish or Chinese speakers; see Saville-Troike (1989, pp. 193–194).

Another problem stems from the widespread human tendency to construct stereotypes of other people. For example, Giles (1971) reports on an experiment in which the subjects heard a passage of prose read out by speakers with the Southern British Standard accent (known as Received Pronunciation, or RP) and two regional accents (South Welsh and Somerset). Purely on the basis of the voices heard, the subjects rated the RP speakers as more intelligent and industrious than the speakers with regional accents, but having less integrity and social attractiveness. In fact, the passage had been read out by the same speakers in three different accents! Nevertheless, the experiment bears out the fact that stereotyping is carried out, and there must be a danger that it could exert an influence of a less than desirable kind within CMC.

On the other hand, one of the roles that verbal communication can fulfil is the establishment and maintenance of social *rapport* or "solidarity" between speakers, including those of different national and cultural backgrounds, provided that they have a language in common. This is generally referred to as the "phatic" use of language (Jakobson 1960). English speakers have the reputation of talking about the weather for that purpose. However, different nations and cultures have quite different conventions here. For instance, members of certain peoples, such as the Athabaskan Indians of Arctic Canada, can happily be silent in each other's company, whereas English speakers tend to find silence embarrassing and uncomfortable in social situations other than with close friends or relatives (Loveday 1983, pp. 172–173). The Japanese, too, are disinclined to talk simply for the sake of avoiding silence (Loveday 1983, p. 173). These different cultural characteristics again lead to stereotyping, with the Athabaskans and Japanese being seen by English speakers as socially distant, while

English speakers are themselves seen as incorrigible chatterboxes, who are superficial and lacking in sincerity.

A further role that language may fulfil is that of a vehicle for the expression of attitudes, both towards the addressee and towards the subject matter of the conversation. One of the most obvious markers of attitude towards the addressee is the degree of politeness employed, and the normal expectation is, of course, that reasonable courtesy will be accorded. However, not all cultures share the same idea of what is and is not polite. For example, to refuse a request is regarded as less than courteous in Middle Eastern societies, and can result in the person who anticipates the unwelcome request steering the conversation off the point, so that the occasion for the refusal is obviated. Similarly, in Japanese society, saying "no" is tantamount to offering abuse, and its avoidance can lead a person to equivocate or even to walk away from the conversation (Loveday 1983, pp. 173–174). Westerners can easily misinterpret such tactics as displays of evasiveness and prevarication.

Speakers' attitudes can also be conveyed by the "prosody" of an utterance, i.e. characteristics such as its pitch, intonation (or melody), loudness and rhythm (see Crystal 1969, 1975; Cruttenden 1986). Here, again, however, there is scope for misunderstandings when people from different cultural backgrounds are involved. For instance, Gumperz and Cook-Gumperz (1982) document a situation in which a West Indian speaker unintentionally sounded rude and aggressive to the ears of a group of native English people simply because he used prosodic phenomena, such as loudness and frequent changes in voice pitch, in a different manner from that which is normal in British society.

Discourse structure, too, though in the first instance a matter of the textual function of language, can play a part in the signalling of attitude. Interactive discourse (or dialogue) in traditional English-speaking societies is based on a convention that the participants take turns to make their contribution. It is thus regarded as impolite to interrupt, except in an emergency. In West Indian society, however, it is acceptable for two people to be talking at once, and therefore unnecessary to wait one's turn when the current speaker reaches a suitable point (Reisman 1989, p. 113). This, however, is not generally appreciated by those who are not accustomed to the West Indian conventions, and can provoke an adverse reaction. To take another, rather different, example, we may turn to a paper by Danièle Godard (1977), a French person who moved to the USA. Godard tells us that in France, it is considered very rude, when telephoning, not to identify oneself to the person answering the phone before asking to speak to some other individual. In the USA, however, this convention does not apply, and so the structure of the opening of telephone conversations is different. Godard, though, arrived in the USA quite unaware of this, and was rather shocked on the first occasion when she encountered it.

As for speakers' attitudes to their subject matter, this can be made manifest in a variety of ways, but here we shall mention just one, which again revolves around discourse structure. The concept on which we shall focus our attention is that of "sufficiency", which concerns the question of how much explicit verbal content it is appropriate to include within a discourse (Loveday 1983, p. 180). In some cultures, such as in Japan, it is considered proper to talk around a point rather than moving quickly to the crux of the issue, as is expected in British or American society. For English listeners, the temptation is to become impatient while waiting for the Japanese speaker to come to the point, whereas the Western procedure strikes the Japanese as offensively assertive (Loveday 1983, p. 181).

It may well be that the international Information Technology (IT) user community is less varied in its social expectations of linguistic communication than the world's societies at large. Nevertheless, it is clearly possible for misunderstandings to arise as a result of the cultural differences outlined above, and it would be most imprudent to suppose that they could not occur in the context of CMC during international CSCW.

10.3 Relevant Branches of AI

As for the relevance of AI technology in the present context, there are several branches of AI that are applicable. These include the following:

1. Natural Language Processing (NLP). This encompasses a number of topics: (i) analysis of natural language input, (ii) generation of natural language output, (iii) speech recognition, (iv) handwriting recognition, (v) speech synthesis, and (vi) interlingual translation.
2. Other aspects of intelligent user interface management: (i) cooperative interaction handling, and (ii) multimedia interface management.
3. Expert systems.

Plainly, to describe all these areas in detail would require several books. Here, therefore, we must confine ourselves to a concise overview, together with some reference to fuller treatments to which the interested reader may refer. Our purpose in the present section is simply to survey in broad outline the existing field. The applications to international CSCW will be discussed subsequently.

Natural language analysis systems are generally designed to accept input entered via a keyboard, and to parse this input so as to produce an interpretation of the latter in terms of a representation of its meaningful elements and their interrelationships. This process, if it is to be carried out fully, requires access to all types of linguistic knowledge with reference to the language concerned. These include:

1. The vocabulary (or lexicon) of the language.
2. The grammar of the language, comprising: (i) morphology (which deals with word-internal patterning, such as plural formation in nouns), and (ii) syntax (which relates to the patterns whereby words are formed into larger groupings, such as phrases and sentences).
3. The semantics of the language (which deals with the meanings of words and of the larger groupings just mentioned).
4. The pragmatics of the language (which relates to the interpretation of elements with reference to their context, for example determining the reference of pronouns like *he* or *she* in a particular sentence within a text).

Natural language generation systems employ the same kinds of linguistic knowledge to carry out the reverse of the analysis process. That is, they begin with a representation of the content or meaning to be expressed, and convert this into the actual sentence or sequence of sentences which convey that meaning. A useful overview of natural language analysis and generation systems may be found in Allen (1987).

Speech recognition systems accept spoken utterances as input and attempt to identify the words of which they consist. For this to be done adequately, however, a knowledge-based system is necessary. Suppose, for example, that the input utterance happens to be "lead is poisonous". In that case, even if there are no recognition errors, the systems cannot decide whether the first word was "lead" or "led", unless either its vocabulary is restricted so as to exclude "led" (hardly a satisfying solution) or it has access to grammatical knowledge which will rule out "led" as being impermissible in the context concerned. For a good account of speech recognition technology, see Ainsworth (1988).

In order to recognize handwritten words (be they hand-printed or written in cursive script), it is necessary to employ a character recognition system. Such systems fall into one of two categories: "on-line", where the input is entered by means of a stylus and pressure-sensitive tablet, and "off-line", where the contents of a document are input via a scanner. Systems of the latter type are known as Optical Character Recognition (OCR) systems, and they are also applicable in the case of typewritten or printed data that are entered into the computer from a scanned document rather than via the keyboard. Because of the inherent variability in handwriting, character recognition by computer is error-prone. For example, if the input is the sentence "Substitute X for Y", the system may be unable to determine whether the middle letter in "for" is an "o" or an "a". In cases such as this, it once again requires access to linguistic knowledge in order to reach the correct decision. (In the example just given the hypothesis that the dubious letter was "a" would be rejected on the grounds that the resulting word, "far", would not fit the syntactic context.) As for the recognition of printed or typewritten words in scanned documents, differences in fonts, for instance, can give rise to variability and consequent uncertainty in recognition. A survey of work in on-line character recognition is found in Tappert et al. (1990), while a recent paper on off-line OCR was written by Bozinovic and Srihari (1989).

Speech synthesis systems produce output in the form of spoken utterances. These may be generated on the basis of text input or on the basis of a semantic representation which has first to be converted into a sentence and then into spoken form. The former option is termed "text-to-speech synthesis", while the latter is known as "speech synthesis from concept". Both types of system require the exploitation of linguistic knowledge if they are to be successful. Speech synthesis from concept can be regarded as an extended form of natural language generation, while text-to-speech systems involve some analysis of the input, followed by synthesis of the output. The analysis phase is necessary in order to make it possible to provide an appropriate prosody for the synthesized speech. The analysis in question again requires access to linguistic knowledge. A useful overview of speech synthesis is found in Witten (1982, 1986), while a detailed account of a leading text-to-speech system is provided by Allen et al. (1987).

With regard to Machine Translation (MT), the two main approaches that are currently favoured are the "transfer" strategy and the "interlingua" strategy. The transfer approach involves (i) parsing the input in the source language into an abstract representation which contains information on the vocabulary, grammatical structure and semantic properties of the sentence concerned; (ii) converting (or "transferring") this representation into a representation pertaining to the target language, with the aim of achieving as close a match between the two representations as possible; and (iii) expressing the content of the second representation in the form of an actual sentence in the target language. Clearly, this three-stage procedure again requires access to linguistic knowledge, in respect of not only both source and target language but also the process of translating from one to the other. As for the interlingua approach, this is not a three-stage but a two-stage procedure, which involves parsing the input into a much more abstract representation, which can be taken as an underlying representation both of the input and of the nearest equivalent sentence in any other language. The second stage then consists of converting the abstract representation into the appropriate sentence in the desired target language. Whatever strategy is adopted, whether transfer, interlingua or some alternative less sophisticated (and less adequate) approach based on look-up and adjustment, it is possible to add speech input and/or output facilities. A useful entry point to the literature on MT is provided by Tucker (1987) and other contributions to Nirenburg (1987).

AI may be employed in other ways, too, in connection with the intelligent management of the user interface. To begin with, it may be applied to the handling of HCI in a manner that is appreciated by the user as being cooperative. Bolc and Jarke (1986, pp. vii–viii) identify five ways in which a user interface may display cooperative behaviour; namely, in relation to:

1. The formulation and acceptance of requests submitted by the user to the computing system. For example, suppose that a person is using a natural language interface to query a database containing information on events at the local concert hall, and types in the question "When is the Mozart concert?", to which the system replies "6 March at 7.30 p.m.". If the user then wants to find out when a different concert, featuring works by Beethoven, is to take place, then a fairly natural course of action would be to type in the query "The Beethoven concert?". This input constitutes, of course, a fragmentary (or "elliptical") piece of text, and not a well-formed sentence of English. Nevertheless, a cooperative system will interpret it as equivalent to "When is the Beethoven concert?" and respond accordingly. For further discussion, see Hendrix et al. (1978, pp. 125–126) and Allen (1987, pp. 357–362).
2. The presentation of responses by the computing system to the user. The central issue here is that a literal answer to a question may be unhelpful. For example, if the user types in the question "Can you tell me the date of the Beethoven concert", then it is not much good if the system simply replies "Yes"! A more cooperative response would be "19 July at 8.00 p.m.". The problem of designing a system capable of displaying this type of cooperation is discussed in Chin (1991), who shows that in order to be able to operate effectively, such a system requires a knowledge base with a considerable number of different components, relating both to NLP and to the user's apparent intentions as inferred by the system from the interaction. (For further discussion of cooperation, see Chapters 1, 2, 3, 5, 6, 9 and 11.)
3. The reaction of the system to exceptional situations. For example, it is common for users to make typing errors when entering commands into a computer system, and the mistyped words constitute exceptions to what the system has been programmed to expect as input. Typically, the result will be an error message to the user, but a more cooperative response would be for the system to attempt to correct the error and merely ask the user to confirm the correction. For further relevant discussion of this kind of error-tolerant handling of input, see Carbonell and Hayes (1987).
4. Support of the user faced with the task of navigating through complex dialogues. In a complex interaction, it may well happen, for instance, that the human–computer dialogue shifts from one topic (such as the programme of concerts at an auditorium) to another (such as the location of the auditorium) and then back to the first. A cooperative system will

keep track of the exchange and will facilitate a smooth resumption of interrupted topics of dialogue. For further information, see Grosz and Sidner (1986, pp. 192–199).

5. Adaptation by the system to changes in respect of users, tasks and interactional roles (cf. Morik 1989, p. 366). Users may range from outright novices to highly knowledgeable and experienced experts; they may be engaged in any of a vast range of possible tasks; and they may adopt various roles in the human–computer dialogue, such as the supplier of data, the requester of information or the issuer of commands. A system that can be adapted to these different circumstances may be seen as more cooperative than one that offers the same user interface in all situations. Certain systems of this kind can make the requisite adjustments automatically and dynamically; these are described as "self-adaptive" (see Edmonds 1981, pp. 420–421; 1982, p. 235; Mason and Thomas 1984, p. 163). For further discussion of adaptivity in the user interface, see Edmonds (1987), Browne et al. (1990). Adaptivity is also among the topics addressed by Dix, Finlay and Hassell in Chapter 3 and by Jones and Edmonds in Chapter 2.

As will be evident, a user interface that is cooperative in all of these different ways will require a large and wide-ranging knowledge base. Norcio and Stanley (1989, p. 401) point out that an adaptive user interface needs to be able to draw on an internal representation of knowledge relating to:

1. *The user*. The system needs to construct and maintain a model of each user, including his or her objective circumstances, cognitive and perceptual abilities and preferences, relevant background knowledge, beliefs, goals and plans (Kobsa 1988, p. 91; Wahlster and Kobsa 1989, p. 5; see also Chapters 1 and 11).
2. *The interaction*. The system requires a general knowledge of how dialogue is structured and how it functions, together with a specific knowledge of the history of the current dialogue, incorporating a representation of the entities and states-of-affairs mentioned therein, their attributes and the relationships between them. Such knowledge is often described in terms of a "discourse model"; see, for example, Schuster (1988). Some writers, including Schuster, consider the discourse model to be part of the user model, while others, for example, Cohen and Levesque (1988), do not.
3. *The task*. The goals of a user interacting with a computer system generally relate to the accomplishment of some task. For the system to adapt in such a way as to enhance the efficiency with which this task can be carried out, it needs to construct and maintain a model of the task concerned. Some work relating to this problem is described by Greenberg and Witten (1985). A model of the task is also one of the requirements for an intelligent on-line help system; see further

Rissland (1984, pp. 381–384), Fisher et al. (1985, p. 165) and Kearsley (1988, p. 56–59).

4. *The system.* Adaptation is, of course, constrained by the capabilities of the system itself. For example, it can happen that the amount of information to be presented as output to the user is more than will fit on to the screen. However, if the system has knowledge of its own limitations and of how to react to the problems to which they give rise, then it may be able to adapt accordingly, for example by restructuring its output in such a way as to overcome constraints on screen size.

Moreover, a knowledge base containing these components would also be useful in relation to the achievement of other forms of cooperative behaviour in the user interface apart from adaptation, including those listed by Bolc and Jarke (1986) (see pp. 152–153). A knowledge of dialogue structure and function is needed in coping with the entry of elliptical text by the user, the formulation of cooperative responses on the part of the system, the toleration of errors in the input and the handling of interruptions in the discourse. Error tolerance can also be enhanced through the exploitation of user and task models, and in addition requires the use of robust parsing techniques; see further Carbonell and Hayes (1983).

It is appropriate at this juncture to mention the concept of "autonomous user agents". An "agent" in this sense is characterized by Waterman (1978, p. 696) as a program that is interposed between the user and the system with which he or she is interacting. It may have any of a variety of purposes, for example (i) helping the user to learn and utilize complex remote systems; (ii) acting as an electronic mail filter; (iii) providing clerical support (e.g. reminding the user of appointments or filling in routine forms); or (iv) detecting and correcting user errors. In short, it may provide the kind of services that are associated with cooperative computing systems. Consequently, in particular, user agents offer a possible basis around which to design cooperative user interfaces; cf. Smyth (Chapter 1). An "autonomous" user agent (AUA) is one that is capable of taking its own initiatives; cf. Chin (1991, p. 181). An example of such behaviour might occur when the AUA volunteers some information to help the user, having perhaps noticed evidence of some misconception on the part of the person concerned. AUAs have other possible uses in relation to CSCW as well, as is apparent from the other chapters in this book.

The other aspect of intelligent user interface management identified above relates to multimedia interaction. Enabling a system to cope with the potentially simultaneous input or output of information in different media poses various problems to the designer of the user interface. For example, on the input side, a user might enter verbal information while pointing at some object on a graphics display, and the system would need to integrate the input from the two different channels in such a way that the interpretation of the linguistic information was related to the pointing gesture. On the output side, the system might be faced with the question of choosing the most appropriate medium, or combination of media, in which to present the results of its processing to the user. In order to perform such tasks successfully, the system needs to have access to a knowledge base which includes suitably enhanced dialogue and user models, as well as a component concerned with multimedia output planning strategies; see Neal and Shapiro (1991), Wahlster (1991).

A further major branch of AI that is of potential relevance to CSCW is the technology of expert systems (cf. Chapters 7 and 9). These systems can be self-contained and potentially stand-alone units, which typically contain:

1. A knowledge base relating to some specialist subject domain.
2. An inference engine capable of drawing conclusions on the basis of this knowledge base.
3. A knowledge acquisition component.
4. A user interface that includes a facility for the system to explain its reasoning.

For a fuller description, see Forsyth (1984), Jackson (1990). Alternatively, they may take the form of modules (often referred to simply as "experts") within larger systems, such as automatic speech recognizers (see, for example, de Mori et al. 1987) or adaptive systems (see, for example, Browne et al. 1990, who incorporate an "application expert" into an adaptive front-end to an electronic mail system). Such "experts" generally contain a knowledge base and an inference engine, but not a knowledge acquisition component or a user interface of their own. Expert systems are particularly useful in contexts where human expertise is scarce and/or the relevant knowledge is difficult to formulate in algorithmic terms.

The survey undertaken in this section has encompassed a variety of AI systems. For each type of system there are, of course, questions that arise as to the details of their design and implementation. These questions pertain to such matters as the internal functional architecture of the systems, and whether they should be based on conventional symbolic AI, on neural networks (see, for instance, Rumelhart and McClelland 1986; Beale and Jackson 1990), or on a hybrid combination of the two. Space does not permit a discussion of these issues. However, there is one matter relating to design and implementation which must be mentioned briefly, as it is particularly relevant to CSCW over networks. The topic in question is that of Distributed Artificial Intelligence (DAI).

The field of DAI is surveyed by Bond and Gasser (1988), who point out that both knowledge bases and the processes that draw upon their resources may be distributed in various ways, including spatially and temporally. The possibility of knowledge bases being distributed around more than one geographical location is one which arises naturally in remote CSCW, while the fact that knowledge may become available or unavailable at some point in time is a consideration that particularly affects asynchronous collaboration. Both these potentialities give rise to problems such as the coordination of the interaction among processes, the division of tasks and the synthesis of the results. Bond and Gasser (1988, p. 10) see self-adaptation as a promising avenue towards the solution of such problems. DAI is further discussed in relation to CSCW in Chapters 6, 8, 9 and 11.

Finally, although the above survey has concentrated upon applications in which AI is involved at run-time, it should be remembered that knowledge-based technology can also be used in the design, implementation and evaluation of intelligent systems. For further discussion of these possibilities, see Foley et al. (1991).

10.4 Communication Problems and the Role of AI

Having conducted a brief survey of the relevant branches of AI, we may now move on to consider the ways in which AI technology may help to solve or alleviate the various CMC problems that might be expected to arise in connection with international CSCW. Of course, we cannot hope to cover all the possible applications of AI in this field, but we can certainly point out some promising avenues for investigation. We shall divide our discussion into two sections, concerned with the role of AI in relation to:

1. Intervention in the communication process.
2. Support for system users and designers.

10.4.1 Intervention in the Communication Process

There are several ways in which AI technology may usefully be employed to intervene in the actual process of communication between the participants in international CSCW. First of all, it may be exploited at the input stage, where the material to be communicated via the network is entered into the system. An example is seen in user interfaces designed to accept Japanese text input, which employ AI techniques to arrive at the correct sequence of Kanji characters; see Zobel-Pocock (1990, p. 224). Kanji are Chinese-style characters, each of which represents a whole word rather than an individual speech sound (or phoneme). The number of Kanji characters in common use runs into thousands, with the result that the entry of Kanji into a computer via a keyboard is far from straightforward. The alternative is to use a character set based on the individual phonemes of Japanese. Two such sets are available, known as Katakana and Hiragana. However, even if Japanese text is input in the form of Katakana and/or Hiragana, the user may still wish it to be displayed on the screen in the form of Kanji. This means that it has to be converted inside the computer. The problem here, though, is that there is a many-to-many relationship between the Kanji and their pronunciations, so that it is not simple to carry out the conversion process. The choice of the correct Kanji must be inferred from the context, and it is for this purpose that AI techniques are employed.

AI can also be put to use in the output of communicated information to the recipient. Two examples may be given here. Firstly, the format of numerals, currencies, times of day, dates, and such like, may be automatically adapted for the benefit of a recipient who is accustomed to different conventions from the originator of the message. Machine intelligence is called for here when, for example, the computer needs to infer from the context whether an expression like "1/2" is supposed to mean "one half" or "the first of February", before deciding to put it through a date-format conversion procedure. Secondly, it can happen that a message which fits on to the sender's screen does not fit on to the recipient's, in which case there may be a choice of how to cope with the situation: split the message into two screens, scale down the size of the original so that it fits the recipient's screen, or some other strategy. The choice of an appropriate action will depend on such factors as whether the message is textual or pictorial, but if the adaptation is to be carried out automatically, then again some machine intelligence is demanded.

Other, more radical, forms of intervention in the CMC process are also possible through the use of AI. To begin with, incoming information can be filtered in such a way that a participant receives only what he or she wishes to see, provided of course that the filtering criteria can be adequately defined and that material which satisfies those criteria can be recognized and distinguished from material which does not. A filtering facility of this kind might be particularly useful in systems used by more than two participants engaged in tasks where some of the communication activity is relevant only to certain members of the group. As filtering takes time, it may be more appropriate within an asynchronous than a synchronous communication environment.

A further possibility for intervention in the communication process lies in the translation of material from one medium or form into another, for example text-to-speech, speech-to-text or handwritten-to-printed text. Even more ambitious is the conversion of multimedia material into a single-medium message or vice versa, or from one combination of media to another. These various translation processes would clearly require the use of the relevant aspects of AI technology. Again, they would involve a time delay, and may thus be particularly suitable for application in asynchronous communication contexts.

Situations where the participants do not share a common language represent a formidable problem for CMC. Obviously, MT (both written and spoken) has a major role to play here, though the current state of spoken MT is not particularly advanced, with the result that once again the AI technology is better suited to the asynchronous than to the synchronous type of communication.

Speakers with no common language may well try to rely more on pictorial and/or gestural forms of communication than on natural language. Multimedia systems are thus potentially of particular use in such circumstances. On the other hand, non-verbal symbols have certain drawbacks. They are limited in what they can convey, they are often ambiguous even in context, and one symbol or gesture can have one meaning in one culture and either another meaning or no meaning at all in a different culture; see further del Galdo (1990), Sukaviriya and Moran (1990). Consequently, there is no real substitute for natural language communication, with the attendant requirement for MT, in CMC where the participants have no common tongue. However, the natural language may well be supplemented by pictures or diagrams, forming multimedia messages, the translation of which presents a further challenge to MT technology.

10.4.2 Support for System Users and Designers

AI may be of help to participants in international CSCW in other ways besides those mentioned so far, by providing support which either assists in accomplishing the cooperative task or makes available information that can improve the chances of successful communication. For example, certain cooperative tasks may involve one or more participants in accessing databases and/or knowledge-based systems (KBS). Not only is AI inherently involved in KBS, but intelligent access facilities to databases and knowledge bases can also be provided, for example a natural language front-end. Multimedia databases with intelligent front-ends which allow for either single-medium or for multimedia queries offer further scope for the application of AI, as does the provision of cooperative access facilities to databases or knowledge bases whose contents are in foreign languages, thus creating the need for a translation capability within the query system.

The contents of the databases and knowledge bases in question may relate to any subject with a bearing on the cooperative task. In particular, there is the possibility of producing a database or expert system pertaining to the communication conventions of specific nations and cultures, which could be consulted prior to engaging in CSCW, with a view to minimizing the risk of misunderstandings arising out of the intercultural differences mentioned earlier.

As for the use of AI in the design of systems to support international CSCW, this could be applied to various aspects of the problem, but the design of the user interface suggests itself as a particularly likely beneficiary here. If participants in CSCW are to collaborate effectively, then it seems plausible to presume that the computer systems they utilize will need to display comparable functionality with one another. If this is so, then these systems will require user interfaces with reasonably similar facilities. However, it is not at all straightforward to transpose an interface designed for one culture into another. There may be problems in such matters as the choice of icons, the translation of command words from one language to another, or the specification of command-language syntax so as to accord with local preferences; see further Nielsen (1990b), Ossner (1990) and Sukaviriya and Moran (1990). These are issues in relation to which a suitable expert system might be developed and play a helpful role. Thus, AI would find useful applications in both the design and the running of CSCW systems.

10.5 Conclusion

In conclusion, it may be seen that there is plenty of scope for employing AI in connection with international CSCW. However, a great deal more research and development is called for before the full potential of AI in this field can be realized. Experimental scientific research is required in order to discover more about international and intercultural differences relating to both human–human communication and human–computer interaction, while considerable technological advances are needed in each and every one of the branches of AI mentioned earlier. On the other hand, the field of enquiry with which the present chapter has been concerned is so rich in fascinating questions to address that researchers are likely to find it attractive. If this proves to be the case, then the prospects for future progress are excellent.

Chapter 11

On the Definition and Desirability of Autonomous User Agents in CSCW

D. Jennings

It has been said by Alan Kay that user interfaces of the 1990s will not be tool-based as in the 1980s, but will instead be agent-based. How intelligent will these agents be? How will they be displayed? How will they support group working? (from the announcement for the UK CSCW SIG seminar on "AI, Autonomous User Agents and CSCW")

11.1 Introduction

This chapter is principally concerned with user agents as they might appear to users of Computer Supported Cooperative Work (CSCW) systems: that is, with interface agents rather than software agents. I gives examples to show the difficulty of establishing a clear perspective on interface agents from the user-centred point of view. This difficulty is related to the differing conceptions of agents held within computer sciences and social sciences, and it is argued that this makes user agents a poor starting point for the design of CSCW systems. As an alternative, I suggest that CSCW design should start from the task domains, stages and functions of groupwork, and that the role of agents should then be situated within this framework. I sketch some initial steps towards developing this approach.

In what follows I address issues of how Autonomous User Agents (AUAs) might be displayed to users of CSCW systems. Thus, I am more interested in interface agents than in software agents. Also, my perspective is mainly taken from the social sciences, rather than the computer and cognitive sciences (which are the domains of the designers of software agents). At the risk of opening myself to criticism of armchair philosophizing and possibly of trouble making, I want to look at some conceptual and terminological issues to do with what might count as

AUAs. My aim in doing this is to clarify some of the domains where AUAs might and might not be a suitable basis for CSCW. I am also interested in adding a reflexive twist to this debate by looking at how computer/cognitive scientists can cooperate with social scientists on the definition and development of technologies like AUAs for CSCW. (Readers are also referred to Chapters 1 and 8 for discussion relevant to the present chapter.)

For the software designers of CSCW systems, the question of what constitutes an agent is usually fairly clear. An agent is part of the architecture of the system, with certain lines of code embodying it. (Having said that, however, the definition of an agent can apparently sometimes be unclear, even to software designers. When a computer scientist was asked, at the end of presenting a paper to a recent CSCW conference, why he used the term "agents" to refer to parts of his architecture, he replied that, "'agents' *sounds* sexier – they are autonomous processes"!) For users the question is not so cut and dried, however, for outside the world of code, users perceive many beings functioning as agents of some sort, including humans as well as other animate and inanimate entities. I illustrate this with three examples of interfaces and agents that are not specific to CSCW.

Consider first the common example of a software application reminding or advising users that they are about to make an irreversible step, such as quitting without saving. This reminding function is the sort of task an interface agent could do: a little face could pop-up and say, "If you quit now, you'll lose any changes you made – do you want to ignore the changes, or would you like me to save them for you?". This is not a style that many applications have chosen. But it would be functionally equivalent, and either way the system appears to have some agency, whether or not there is an interface agent *per se*. The interface agent could be no more than a graphical representation (as in a video game), so it might not be a "proper" software agent. My point is that the use of *interface* agents is primarily a stylistic one that we can separate from the use of software agents in the system architecture. While a software agent might be used to parse dates, for example (see Chapter 4), it is unlikely that this function would be presented on the interface as an agent.

A typical expert system exhibits the features of agency and autonomy to varying degrees (in the sense that the users' inputs do not fully determine its outputs). However, if it is used in circumstances where users have discretion over whether to use the system, and whether or not to accept its "opinion" when they do use it, then that system is being treated by its users more as a tool than as an agent.

The final example is from an advertisement for IRMA Workstation for Windows from Digital Communications Associates (*PC Magazine* 1991), which caught my eye. In part it runs, "The new 1.1 version virtually installs itself. ... The new Intelligent User Assist automatically senses the communications adapter in your PC ... [and then] pre-configures the software to suit". This reminded me of Norman's discussion of the installation of film in a projector in *The Design of Everyday Things* (1988). His argument there was that the task of working out which part of the projector to feed the film through placed too much strain on users, and that the solution to this was to *internalize* the function of film feeding in the design of the artefact, as has been done in the case of the video cassette. As far as users are concerned, this is an analogous solution to that achieved by the Intelligent User Assist. But we don't think of the housing of a video cassette as an intelligent assistant! The solution only breaks down when the tape winds itself round the internal mechanism, or the software fails to install correctly. If this happens, users may be in a worse situation when the function is internalized than when it has to be done manually!

The point of this comparison is to demonstrate that agency as a quality or entity does not necessarily inhere in an artefact or system, but may be attributed by sociocultural convention or individual choice. Woolgar (1985, 1989) has offered some suggestive accounts of the ways in which this attribution can take place. He has proposed, on the basis of some ethnographic work, that representation technologies may undergo similar routines of socialization as people so that they may become trusted "agents of representation". In the CSCW context, this raises the question of whether AUAs are born or made. In other words, is the degree to which any interface is agent-based primarily a designers' issue or a users' issue?

11.2 Incorporating the Differing Viewpoints of Social Scientists and Computer Scientists

By now it may seem that once-simple terms have been clouded over with obfuscation and slippery usage! I have suggested that this confusion is more acute when we look at *using* agent-based systems than when we are *designing* them. Nevertheless, the existence of any confusion has implications for design practice. I shall characterize this confusion as being drawn up along the lines of social versus computer science. I shall then use some ideas developed by a social scientist (Leigh Star) in the context of Distributed Artificial Intelligence (DAI) development. These ideas are pertinent because they address the questions:

> How can two entities (or objects or nodes) with two different and irreconcilable epistemologies cooperate? If understanding is necessary for cooperation, as is widely stated in the DAI literature, what is the nature of an understanding that can cooperate across viewpoints? (Star 1989, p. 42)

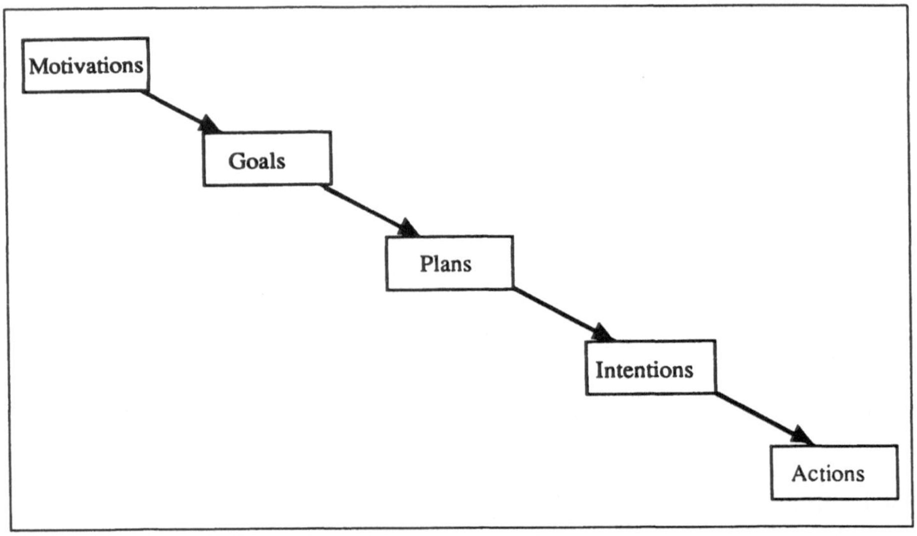

Fig. 11.1. Waterfall model: goals and action.

I want to characterize the computer/cognitive science model of autonomy and agency in terms of two main features. The first, which I call the "waterfall model" of intention and action, is encapsulated in the following passage and in Fig. 11.1:

> The autonomy assumption is important because I want to characterize actions as being "caused" in the following sense. . . . Motivations give rise to goals. Goals give rise to plans. Plans give rise to (among other things) intentions. Intentions give rise to actions. Some actions lead to effects in the physical world. It is the embodiment of the causal chain, particularly from goals to physical actions, which I will use as my definition of *agency*. (Storrs 1989, p. 324)

The second I call the "object-oriented model" of subjectivity and communication. This holds that agents are pre-given or pre-defined entities, and that the passing of messages between them may draw on or change their features in some way but leaves their fundamental nature unaltered and unquestioned. This model is represented in Fig. 11.2.

These models are clearly applicable to software agents. By contrast, there is a school of thought in the social sciences – from Vygotsky and Heidegger through to Lacan and Foucault – that suggests that language, or "message passing", is the very fabric out of which our human subjectivity, our agency and our relative autonomy are woven. Our intentions and actions do not have meaning in and of themselves, but only through their reception and interpretation in the social, intersubjective realm (for attempts to work through some of the implications of this school for Artificial Intelligence (AI) and Human–Computer Interaction (HCI) see Bateman 1985; Jennings 1991). This makes the problem of user modelling (cf. Chapters 1 and 10), on which the intelligent interface approach is based, considerably less tractable.

This account sketches briefly what is in fact a wide and rich variety of models. But if it gives an indication of the range of approaches, how can we reconcile such apparently incongruent perspectives? On the basis of studies of scientists from different backgrounds, Star (1989) suggests that successful cooperation *can* take place between parties who have different goals, employ different units of analysis, and who have poor models of each other's work:

> They do so by creating objects that serve much the same function as a blackboard in a DAI system. I call these *boundary objects*, and they are a major method of solving heterogeneous problems. Boundary objects are objects that are both plastic enough to adapt to the local needs and constraints of the several parties employing them, yet robust enough to maintain a common identity across sites. They are weakly structured in common use, and become strongly structured in individual-site use. (Star 1989, p. 46)

Star clearly hopes that the boundary object concept will itself become a boundary object to help social scientists and DAI developers cooperate successfully, and I share this hope. But what other boundary objects can we find to assist cooperation in the definition and development of CSCW and perhaps AUAs?

Unfortunately I do *not* think that the agent concept can fulfil the criteria for a useful boundary object and become part of the exchange currency between social and computer scientists. The discussion above shows

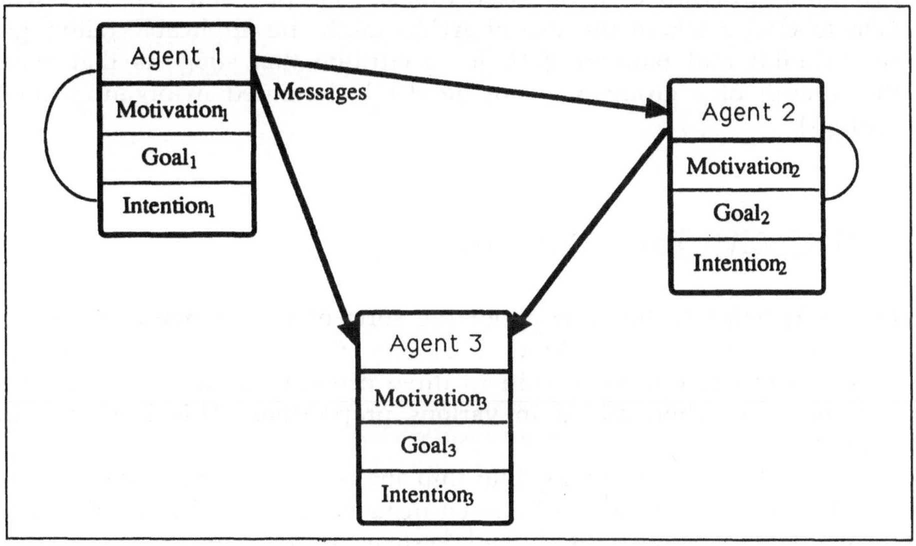

Fig. 11.2. Object-oriented model of agency/subjectivity.

Table 11.1. CSCW task domains

Applications	A person or group of people approach the system as a tool to achieve a particular goal in a task domain with which they are already familiar. They already know what type of output they want, and they use the system as a means of achieving this.
Communications medium/environment	A person or group of people approach the system as a means of sending, moderating, editing or receiving information, to, with and from other people. They may or may not know exactly what output they want, but they know that the means of achieving it is primarily through relationships and interactions with other people, rather than with the system *per se*.
Exploratory learning environment	A person or group of people approach the system with a limited knowledge of a particular topic or task domain. They do not have a specific output in mind from the interaction.

that the concept of an agent is too plastic and not robust enough. And I think the same can probably be said of terms like "intelligent" and "autonomous".

Instead, I would like to add my support to the position, common among social scientists in CSCW (e.g. Norman 1991), that we should start from the patterns and requirements of cooperative work, and then move on to discuss appropriate computer support – including perhaps the use of interface agents. In the next sections, I start from groups, their task domains, and their stages and functions in a project. I hope that these will prove to be more robust concepts, and that they will help to clarify where the use of AUAs might be applicable (although see Schmidt and Bannon 1992, for a critique that suggests that even the concept of a group may not be clearly bounded in organizational settings).

11.3 CSCW Task Domains

Firstly, it helps to be clear about the sorts of task domain in CSCW. I propose a basic threefold classification, which is not a set of discrete categories, but more akin to three primary colours making up a full spectrum when mixed in various proportions. This is shown in Table 11.1.

These definitions inevitably blur into one another to some extent. There may be family relationships between instances of each classification, but the family trees are also interlinked. Systems for real-time process control, shared information storage and so on can be seen as related to one or more of the families.

One particular thing to bear in mind about the classification is how the distinction between design and use cuts across it. For example, a system could be designed as an application to meet specific requirements, but could admit possibilities of use in other ways, as a communications medium or an exploratory environment (cf. the "task–artefact" framework, Carroll et al. 1991; see also Nardi and Miller (1991) for an account of how spreadsheets can mediate collaborative work). So, the classifications are clearly not mutually exclusive as far as use goes, and may not be for design either.

How does this classification help us think about agent-based interfaces in CSCW? Laurel (1990) describes interface agents as software entities which act on behalf of the user. They should display the features of:

- responsiveness
- competence
- accessibility

(Note that the features of acting on behalf of the user and being responsive would seem to imply a relative *lack* of autonomy – I return to this point later.)

She further identifies the types of task that an agent might be suited to carrying out as:

- Information: for example, to aid navigation and browsing, information retrieval, sorting and organizing, filtering.
- Learning: giving help, coaching, tutoring.
- Work: reminding, advising, programming, scheduling.
- Entertainment: playing with or against, performing.

It is important here to reiterate the distinction between Laurel's interface agents and other types of software agent. An interface agent is visible to users as an "independent" entity, and may engage them in dialogue or appear to manipulate the interface itself. The representation of the interface agent may or may not be driven by a software agent. Other types of software agent need not be visible to users (although, of course, users may still attribute the actions performed by such agents to the system's *agency*).

On the basis of Laurel's work, I suggest that interface agents are probably most suited for systems intended to be used primarily as *exploratory learning environments*. This is the situation where information and learning are likely to be most useful. And entertainment is a good way of seducing users into further exploration. Examples of effective uses of interface agents in learning environments are given by Oren et al. (1990) – a system that offers tutorials on various perspectives on

American history – and by Adelson (1992) – a French language learning application.

However, I would take issue with the use of interface agents for reminding and advising users in the course of their work in some contexts. In the case of *applications*, where in my definition users are already familiar with the task domain in which they are operating, the use of agents that might appear to break into the flow of a task is questionable. This approach may be helpful when the user is about to take an irreversible step (e.g. quitting without saving, deleting a file). It can also be used when users' tasks can be relied on to follow a simple, invariant sequence. But such circumstances are rare, for, as Suchman (1987) showed, users' plans may be subject to constant revision, even for apparently simple tasks. So it may *not* be helpful to have an agent try to "second guess" a user, because more often than not the user will want to override, or at least check, the agent's decisions and actions. And this problem will increase dramatically if there are more than a small number of agents.

This reveals what I think is a fundamental tension in HCI and CSCW. On the one hand there is the aim of subjugating the system to users' wills and their goals. On the other there is the aim of giving the system (or its agents) the intelligence to be able to anticipate users' goals and behaviour, and the autonomy to act on this (see Jennings 1991 for a fuller discussion of this tension). The optimum trade-off point between these conflicting aims will depend on the specifics of local context.

For *communications media/environments* the use of interface agents would on the face of it seem even less desirable than for applications. The common view is that communication should be as "im-*media*-te" as possible, with the features of face-to-face communication being the asymptote towards which development and progress should lead. Working from this assumption, the use of an agent (software or human) to mediate communication should be avoided wherever possible.

Actually, I would argue, along with Hollan and Stornetta (1992), that even the face-to-face scenario is a medium of sorts, with particular features which mean that it is not best suited to all types of communication and cooperation. There are a number of ways in which (human) agents mediate interaction between people. Let us consider a few of these:

- Policing or security agent
- Moderator or chairperson
- Gatekeeper, secretary or personal assistant
- Expert consultant
- Facilitator.

Where there are clear security rules that have been decided organizationally or politically, these could possibly be embedded in an interface agent. But in the case of a group chairperson the skills required are much fuzzier, making it less desirable to put an AUA in such a position of power where the users of the system are subjugated to it. Systems should entrust floor control to informal social regulation wherever possible, and we should minimize the degree to which these systems force particular styles of coordination. (For further discussion relevant to the subject of floor control, see Chapters 2 and 5.)

The gatekeeper role is traditionally seen as being of relatively low status, but this often masks the power associated with such positions. This power is by its nature informal: its rules are nowhere clearly specified. *Wherever a system exerts any power over its users, the legitimacy and source of that power must be subject to careful scrutiny.* I suggest that in cases where a system's power is not clearly an embodiment of agreed statutes, it will be more socially acceptable for that power to be meted out by human agents. This is on the grounds that they can be held more directly accountable.

But can we imagine instances where an interface agent had little or no direct power over its cooperating users? Perhaps an interface agent could be part of an on-line discussion team, which could call on it (as a responsive, competent and accessible member) to help with a particular issue. One way to ensure the acceptability of such an agent would be to make its actions very simple and transparent.

My own favourite "agent" is a sort of personal facilitator for tackling creative dilemmas. It is based on a simple pack of cards, so it is not very "intelligent". In 1975, Brian Eno and Peter Schmidt developed 125 "Oblique Strategies", a set of lateral thinking prompts designed to help unfreeze the creative process, each of which is written on a card. You pick a card at random and then you adopt the strategy written on it. Some examples of the strategies are: "Retrace your steps", "Remove specifics and convert to ambiguities", "Honour thy error as a hidden intention" and "Cascades". Why not apply this sort of facilitating principle to group dynamics? One of the groups that I participate in has experimented with de Bono's (1985) "Thinking Hats" approach, in which six notional hats, each with a colour assigned to it, represent six interactional roles or strategies. For example: one role is a sort of "devil's advocate"; one gives emotive, gut reactions (positive or negative); while another is charged with seeding new ideas or growth. When group members put on one of the hats, they accept a discipline in the type of contribution they will make to the ensuing discussion. But they have first collectively assented to this discipline. Perhaps an AUA could (randomly?) assign hats to group members using a CSCW system? In some group contexts, this could, I think, represent an intelligent usage of a relatively unintelligent technology.

11.4 Group Stages and Group Functions

McGrath's (1990) framework of the stages and functions of group projects is useful for highlighting the factors that technologies to support groupwork must take into account. McGrath suggests that a group's project activity can be divided into up to four stages:

- Stage I: Inception and acceptance of a project (goal choice)
- Stage II: Solution of technical issues (means choice)
- Stage III: Resolution of conflict, political issues (policy issues)
- Stage IV: Execution of performance requirements of project (goal attainment)

While Stages I and IV are by definition necessary parts of any successful group project, Stages II and III may be bypassed in some (simple) cases. The proportion of resources taken by each stage may thus vary considerably.

McGrath elaborates his framework by classifying three types of function carried out within a group. As well as the *production* function, which contributes directly to the project goal, there is a *member-support* function, which is the group's contribution to its component parts, and a *well-being* function, which is the group's contribution to its own system viability. These functions are further clarified in Table 11.2.

How can we use this framework to ascertain what sort of computer support would be useful for group project activities? If we take the contents of each cell in the table, can we establish where the use of AUAs would be (i) possible and (ii) desirable?

Firstly, I make the human-centred assumption that the group comprises only human members; AUAs would not count as group members. Woolgar

Table 11.2. Group stages and functions (from McGrath 1990, p. 30)

	Group contribution functions		
Stages	*Production*	*Member support*	*Group well-being*
Inception (goal choices)	Production opportunity demand	Inclusion opportunity demand	Interaction opportunity demand
Problem solving (means choices)	Technical problem solving	Position status attainments	Role net definition
Conflict resolution (political choices)	Policy conflict resolution	Payoff allocation	Power distribution
Execution (goal attainment)	Performance	Participation	Interaction

(1985) demonstrates the possibility of questioning this assumption, so we should be clear that it is backed up by a value judgement (that is, that it is not desirable to give the technology the same status as its users). From this assumption there appears to be minimal opportunity for AUAs to support any of the member-support functions in the middle column, as these seem to be essentially social in nature.

At the inception stage, computer support clearly has a contribution to make. More potential stakeholders or group members can be given the opportunity to interact in making the goal choice. But in many cases, electronic mail or conferencing systems will provide adequate support to this process, and it is not clear what added value AUAs could provide in this area.

Moving to the second row of the table, the Thinking Hats example discussed earlier provides an example of a particularly self-conscious form of role net definition. This sort of strategy could be usefully deployed for technical problem solving as well. Other types of computer support for this stage would include shared databases, possibly with some intelligence built into the front-end, and computerized domain expertise, which could take either tool-based or agent-based form.

The conflict resolution stage is more problematic, particularly when we take into account what I have already argued about the "interference" of systems in power relations. Such interference is normally perceived when the system reifies a power relationship which, in the normal flow of human discourse, would be subject to constant renegotiation. It could be argued against this that AUAs could be used to *facilitate the process* of group interaction leading to political choices. But anyone who has tried to facilitate a debate of a hot political issue would tell you that, even with the most neutral of intentions and strategies, it is very hard to convince opposing factions that you are being impartial. The ease with which any "losing" party could use the system as a scapegoat for reaching the "wrong" decision could outweigh any advantage from the system being perceived initially as neutral.

In fact, the situation is complicated by the possibility (not acknowledged in the table) that the distinction between technical and policy choices may sometimes be blurred and may itself be negotiated within the group. One of the best ways to win policy arguments is to present the issue as a technical one for which you possess the relevant expertise (consider the example of this chapter, which aims to construe social science as the appropriate discipline to tackle questions about AUAs!).

Finally, at the execution stage, groupware applications and communication media could be useful both for task performance and for supporting interaction between group members.

What this discussion shows is that, among the group activities that computers could support, there are few – if any – that intrinsically call out for AUAs as a design solution. That is not to say that AUAs will not be a part of some useful CSCW designs in particular contexts (though I have indicated that there are some areas of group activity where the use of AUAs might be contentious or deleterious). What it does mean is that to focus on AUAs as an interface style to drive CSCW design would be to put the cart in front of the horse.

11.5 Conclusions

Let me summarize my key points:

1. There is a distinction between software agents and interface agents – it is possible to have one without the other.
2. Users' attribution of agent qualities to any type of technology is affected by many factors, not just by designers' intentions.
3. The use of agent-based interfaces is primarily a choice of style rather than function.
4. The agent-based style may be most appropriate for attracting and interesting users in exploratory learning environments, and possibly for supporting innovative approaches to group dynamics.
5. Intelligent user agents *per se* are not a good starting point for cross-fertilization of ideas between social and computer scientists, or for CSCW design decisions.
6. Instead, we should start from task domains, group project activities and group circumstances, and leave decisions about interface agents to later in the design process.
7. There is a broad range of group project activities, and computer support should be directed to only those activities where it is appropriate and non-controversial.

To conclude, I will answer the questions that I quoted at the head of this chapter in an admittedly glib, but hopefully provocative, manner.

11.5.1 How Intelligent Will Agents Be?

I am tempted to say that their intelligence will be inversely proportional to that of their designers. That is, a good designer would produce a design of sufficient elegance that no one element in it would need to be programmed with complex rules. However, AI may be the best design solution when a system has to deal with a wide range of needs and uses. Also, because such questions are often affected by issues of standardization and the like, it is partly the intelligence of the design community as a whole that will decide the matter.

11.5.2 How Will They Be Displayed?

Generally, they won't be – except in some systems designed to provide learning environments. Intelligent agents may represent an effective basis for the architecture of DAI systems (I do not have the expertise to comment on this), but, largely, users want tools that they can use, not agents that appear to have ambitions to use them.

11.5.3 How Will They Support Group Working?

Software agents may support a range of simple operations that are naturally routine, or that the user community has previously agreed to routinize. Interface agents will be less common. They may support group performance activities and some aspects of technical problem solving. They may be used to draw group members into exploring learning environments. They could possibly be used to support lateral thinking and creativity in novel forms of group interaction. Computer support could also be useful as a means of making the group's progress towards its goals visible to all members, but it is unclear whether agents would be necessary or appropriate for this.

11.5.4 A Case Example

I believe that my position as outlined above is consistent with a consideration of the role of agents in the Information Lens and Object Lens systems (Crowston and Malone 1988). These represent one of the best established approaches to software agents in CSCW. In the Information Lens, semi-structured messages are analysed in terms of "frames" – again, a well-established AI concept that requires less sophistication than some more recent AI ideas. The agent that performs this analysis is not displayed on the system's user interface. The design is elegant (i.e. quite simple), but nevertheless requires that users agree to adopt common frameworks for their messages if its full power is to be used. Its most common uses are as an aid to performance and problem solving tasks like sifting large amounts of information (which is, in fact, essentially a single-user application) and scheduling meetings.

Acknowledgements I would like to thank my colleague Ian Franklin for contributing ideas which helped to develop this chapter.

References

Adelson B (1992) Evocative agents and multi-media interface design. In: Proceedings of the Human Factors in Computing Systems Conference, CHI-92. ACM, New York, pp 351–356

Ainsworth WA (1988) Speech Recognition by Machine. Peregrinus, London

Allen J (1987) Natural Language Understanding. Benjamin Cummings, Menlo Park, CA

Allen J, Hunnicutt MS and Klatt D (1987) From Text to Speech: The MITALK System. Cambridge University Press, Cambridge

Al-Merri J and McGregor DR (1992) Document retrieval using signature files. Technical Report KBS-6-92, Computer Science Department, University of Strathclyde, Glasgow

Alvey (1988) Workshop on intelligent agents. Philips Research Laboratories, Redhill, Surrey

Apple Computer Inc. (1987) Apple Macintosh HyperCard User's Guide. Cupertino, CA

Axelrod R (1984) The Evolution of Cooperation. Basic Books, New York

Barker P (1989) Basic Principles of Human–Computer Interface Design. Hutchinson, London

Barlow J and Dunne PES (1991) Applying a model of concurrency to computer supported cooperative work. In: Proceedings of Computers in Writing, IV, University of Sussex, pp 175–183

Bateman J (1985) The role of language in the maintenance of intersubjectivity: A computational approach. In: Gilbert GN and Heath C (ed) Social Action and Artificial Intelligence. Gower, Aldershot, pp 40–81

Battle SA (1990) A partial orders semantics for constraint based systems. In: Golumbic MC (ed) Advances in Artificial Intelligence: Natural Language and Knowledge Based Systems. Springer-Verlag, New York, pp 219–226

Beale R and Jackson T (1990) Neural Computing: An Introduction. Hilger, Bristol

Bench-Capon TJM and Dunne PES (1989) Some computational properties of a model for electronic documents. Electronic Publishing – Origination, Dissemination and Design 2(4): 231–256

Bench-Capon TJM, Dunne PES and Staniford G (1991) RAPPORTEUR: From dialogue to document. In: Proceedings of Computers in Writing, IV, University of Sussex, pp 175–183

Benyon DR (1993) Adaptive systems: A solution to usability problems. User Modeling and User Adapted Interaction 3: 65–87

Benyon DR and Murray DM (1993) Applying user modelling to human–computer interaction design. AI Review 6: 43–69

Black UD (1987) Data Communications and Distributed Networks, 2nd edn. Prentice-Hall, Englewood Cliffs, New Jersey

Blake RR and Mouton JS (1962) The inter group dynamics of win–lose conflict and problem solving collaboration in union management relations. In: Sherif M (ed) Intergroup Relations and Leadership. Wiley, New York, pp 94–140

Blake RR, Shepard HA and Mouton JS (1964) Managing Inter Group Conflict in Industry. Gulf, Houston, TX

Bolc L and Jarke M (ed) (1986) Cooperative Interfaces to Information Systems. Springer-Verlag, Berlin

Bond AH (1990) PROJECTS: A normative model of collaboration in organizations. In: Huhns M (ed) Proceedings of the 10th International Workshop on Distributed AI, Bandera, Texas, 23–27 October. MCC Technical Report ACT-AI-355-90, Austin, Texas, Chapter 14
Bond AH and Gasser L (ed) (1988) Readings in Distributed Artificial Intelligence. Morgan Kaufmann, San Mateo, CA
Bozinovic RM and Srihari SN (1989) Off-line cursive script word recognition. IEEE Transactions on Pattern Analysis and Machine Intelligence 11: 68–83
Branki NE, Edmonds EA and Jones RM (1993) A study of socially shared cognition in design. Environment and Planning B: Planning and Design 20: 295–306
Branki NE, Jones RM and Edmonds EA (1994) An analysis of media integration for spatial planning environments. Environment and Planning B: Planning and Design 21
Broadbent G (1973) Design in Architecture. Wiley, Chichester
Brooks RA (1991a) Elephants don't play chess. In: Maes P (ed) Designing Autonomous Agents. MIT Press, Cambridge, MA, pp 3–16
Brooks RA (1991b) Intelligence without representation. Artificial Intelligence 47: 139–159
Browne D, Norman M and Adhami E (1990) Methods for building adaptive systems. In: Browne D, Totterdell P and Norman M (ed) Adaptive User Interfaces. Academic Press, London, pp 85–130
Carbonell JG and Hayes PJ (1983) Recovery strategies for parsing extragrammatical language. American Journal of Computational Linguistics 9: 123–146
Carbonell JG and Hayes PJ (1987) Robust parsing using multiple construction-specific strategies. In: Bolc L (ed) Natural Language Parsing Systems. Springer-Verlag, Berlin, pp 1–32
Carroll JM and Carrithers C (1984) Training Wheels in a user interface. Communications of the ACM 27(8): 800–806
Carroll JM, Kellogg WA and Rosson MB (1991) The task–artifact cycle. In: Carroll JM (ed) Designing Interaction: Psychology at the Human–Computer Interface. Cambridge University Press, Cambridge
Cherry C (1966) On Human Communication, 2nd edn. MIT press, Cambridge, MA
Chin DN (1991) Intelligent interfaces as agents. In: Sullivan JW and Tyler SW (ed) Intelligent User Interfaces. ACM Press, New York, pp 177–206
Clarke AA and Smyth M (1993) A cooperative computer based on the principles of human cooperation. International Journal of Man–Machine Studies 38: 3–22
Cohen PR (1988) On the relationship between user models and discourse models. Computational Linguistics 14: 88–90
Cohen PR and Levesque HJ (1988) On acting together: Joint intentions for collective actions. In: Collected Draft Papers from the 1988 Distributed AI Workshop, Technical Report CRI-88-41, Computer Research Institute, University of Southern California, Los Angeles, CA
Cook S and Birch G (1991) Modelling groupware in the electronic office. International Journal of Man–Machine Studies 34(3): 369–394
Cox BJ (1986) Object Oriented Programming: An Evolutionary Approach. Addison-Wesley, Reading, MA
Crowston K and Malone TW (1988) Intelligent software agents. Byte 13(13): 267–274
Cruttenden A (1986) Intonation. Cambridge University Press, Cambridge
Crystal D (1969) Prosodic Systems and Intonation in English. Cambridge University Press, Cambridge
Crystal D (1975) The English Tone of Voice: Essays in Intonation, Prosody and Paralanguage. Edward Arnold, London
Cypher A (1991) EAGER: Programming repetitive tasks by example. In: Robertson SP, Olson GM and Olson JS (ed) Proceedings of the Human Factors in Computing Systems Conference, CHI-91, Reaching through Technology, New Orleans. ACM, New York, pp 33–39
de Bono E (1985) Six Thinking Hats. Penguin, Harmondsworth
del Galdo E (1990) A European evaluation of three document formats for hardware installation guides. In: Nielsen J (ed) Designing User Interfaces for International Use. Elsevier, Amsterdam, pp 45–69
DeMarco T (1979) Structured Systems Analysis and Design. Prentice-Hall, Englewood Cliffs, New Jersey
Demazeau Y and Muller J-P (1990) Decentralized artificial intelligence. In: Demazeau Y and Muller J-P (ed) Decentralized AI. North Holland, Amsterdam, pp 3–13

de Mori R, Lam L and Probst D (1987) Rule-based detection of speech features for automatic speech recognition. In: Haton JP (ed) Fundamentals in Computer Understanding: Speech and Vision. Cambridge University Press, Cambridge, pp 155–179

Deutsch M (1949a) A theory of cooperation and competition. Human Relations 2: 129–152

Deutsch M (1949b) An experimental study of the effects of cooperation and competition upon group processes. Human Relations 2: 199–231

Deutsch M (1968) The effects of cooperation and competition upon group processes. In: Cartwright D and Zander A (ed) Group Dynamics, 3rd edn. Harper and Row, New York, pp 461–482

Deutsch M and Krauss RM (ed) (1960) The effect of threat on interpersonal bargaining. Journal of Abnormal and Social Psychology 61: 181–189

Dijkstra EW (1968) A constructive approach to the problem of program correctness. BIT 8: 174–186

Dix A (1990) Non-determinism as a paradigm for understanding the user interface. In: Thimbleby H and Harrison MD (ed) Formal Methods in Human–Computer Interaction. Cambridge University Press, Cambridge, pp 97–127

Dix A (1991) Formal Methods for Interactive Systems. Academic Press, London

Dix A and Finlay J (1989) AMO – The interface as medium. In: Smith MJ and Salvendy G (ed) Proceedings of HCI International '89 – Third International Conference on Human Computer Interaction (Abridged Proceedings – Poster Sessions), p 22 (available from the authors)

Dunne PES and Staniford G (1991) A formal language basis for studying computational properties of graph-theoretic models. Bulletin of the EATCS 44: 292

Dunne PES and Staniford G (1992) CASS: A cooperative authorship support system. In: Ouaili M (ed) Proceedings of Journées Internationales des Sciences Informatiques (JISI'92), Tunis, 20–22 May. Ecole Nationale des Sciences de l'Informatique, Université de Tunis II, pp 129–140

Durfee EW, Lesser VR and Corkill DD (1987) Coherent cooperation among communicating problem solvers. IEEE Transactions on Computers 36: 1275–1291

Dykstra EA and Carasik RP (1991) Structure and support in cooperative environments – the Amsterdam conversation environment. International Journal of Man–Machine Studies 34(3): 419–434

Eco U (1976) A Theory of Semiotics. Indiana University Press, Bloomington

Eco U (1984) Semiotics and the Philosophy of Language. Indiana University Press, Bloomington

Edmonds EA (1981) Adaptive man–computer interfaces. In: Coombs MJ and Alty JL (ed) Computing Skills and the User Interface. Academic Press, London, pp 389–426

Edmonds EA (1982) The man–computer interface: a note on concepts and design. International Journal of Man–Machine Studies 16: 231–236

Edmonds EA (1987) Adaptation, response and knowledge. Knowledge-Based Systems 1: 3–10

Edmonds EA and Ghazikhanian J (1991) Cooperation between distributed knowledge-bases and the user. In: Weir G and Alty JL (ed) HCI and Complex Systems. Academic Press, London, pp 245–253

Edmonds EA and McDaid E (1990) An architecture for knowledge-based front-ends. Knowledge Based Systems 3(4): 221–224

Edmonds EA, Murray BS, Ghazikhanian J and Heggie SP (1992) The re-use and integration of existing software: a central role for the intelligent user interface. In: Monk AF, Diaper D and Harrison MD (ed) People and Computers VII. Proceedings of the HCI '92 Conference. Cambridge University Press, Cambridge, pp 415–427

Faloutsos C and Christodoulakis S (1984) Signature files: an access method for documents and its analytical performance evaluation. ACM Transactions on Office Information Systems 1(4): 267–288

Fisher G, Lemke A and Schwab T (1985) Knowledge-based help systems. In: Borman L and Curtis W (ed) Proceedings of the Human Factors in Computing Systems Conference, CHI-85, 14–18 April, San Francisco, CA. North Holland, Amsterdam, vol II, pp 161–167

Flores F, Graves M, Hartfield B and Winograd T (1988) Computer systems and the design of organisational information. ACM Transactions on Office Information Systems 6(2): 153–172

Foley J, Kim WC, Kovakevic S and Murray K (1991) UIDE: an intelligent user interface design environment. In: Sullivan JW and Tyler SW (ed) Intelligent User Interfaces. ACM Press, New York, pp 339–384

Forsyth R (ed) (1984) Expert Systems: Principles and Case Studies. Chapman and Hall, London

Fox MS (1981) An organizational view of distributed systems. IEEE Transactions on Systems, Man and Cybernetics 11: 70–80

Fox MS (1992) The TOVE project: towards a common sense model of the enterprise. In: Belli F and Radermacher FJ (ed) Proceedings of the 5th International Conference on Industrial and Engineering Applications of Artificial Intelligence and Expert Systems, IEA/AIE-92, Paderborn. Springer-Verlag, Berlin, pp 25–34

Furuta R (1989) An object based taxonomy for abstract structure in document models. Internal Report, Computer Science Department, University of Maryland, College Park, Maryland

Gabriel RP, White JL and Bobrow DG (1991) CLOS: integrating object-oriented and functional programming. Communications of the ACM 34(9): 28–38

Gammack JG, Battle SA and Stephens RA (1989) A knowledge acquisition and representation scheme for constraint-based and parallel systems. In: Kleinman DL (ed) Proceedings of the IEEE International Conference on Systems, Man and Cybernetics, vol III, Cambridge, MA, November. IEEE, New York, pp 1030–1035

Gammack JG, Fogarty TC, Battle SA and Miles RG (1991) Management decision support from large databases: the IDIOMS project. In: Mesward G (ed) Proceedings of the AMSE International Conference on Signals and Systems, Warsaw. AMSE Press, Tassin-la-Demi-Lune, pp 213–219

Gane C and Sarson T (1979) Structured Systems. Prentice-Hall, Englewood Cliffs, New Jersey

Genesereth MR and Nilsson NJ (1987) Logical Foundations of Artificial Intelligence. Morgan Kaufmann, Los Altos, CA, pp 307–327

Georgeff MP (1987) Planning. Annual Reviews of Computer Science 2: 166–178

Giles H (1971) Patterns of evaluation to RP, South Welsh and Somerset accented speech. British Journal of Social Clinical Psychology 10: 280–281

Godard D (1977) Same setting: different norms: phone call beginnings in France and the United States. Language in Society 6: 209–219

Gray WD, Hedley WE and Murray D (ed) (1993) Proceedings of the 1993 International Workshop on Intelligent User Interfaces. ACM Press, New York

Greenberg S (1991) Personalisable groupware: accommodating individual roles and group differences. In: Bannon L, Robinson M and Schmidt K (ed) Proceedings of the Second European Conference on Computer-Supported Cooperative Work (EC-CSCW '91), Amsterdam, September. Kluwer, Dordrecht, pp 17–31

Greenberg S and Witten IH (1985) Adaptive personalized interfaces: a question of viability. Behaviour and Information Technology 4: 31–45

Greif I and Sarin S (1988) Data sharing in group work. In: Greif I (ed) Computer-Supported Cooperative Work: A Book of Readings. Morgan Kaufmann, San Mateo, CA, pp 477–508

Grice HP (1975) Logic and conversation. In: Cole P and Morgan JL (ed) Syntax and Semantics, vol 3, Speech Acts. Academic Press, London, pp 41–58

Grosz B and Sidner C (1986) Attention, intentions, and the structure of discourse. Computational Linguistics 12: 175–204

Grudin J (1990) Groupware and cooperative work: problems and prospects. In: Laurel B (ed) The Art of Human–Computer Interface Design. Addison-Wesley, Reading, MA, pp 171–185

Gumperz JJ and Cook-Gumperz J (1982) Interethnic communication in committee negotiations. In: Gumperz JJ (ed) Language and Social Identity. Cambridge University Press, Cambridge, pp 145–162

Halliday MAK (1970) Language structure and language function. In: Lyons J (ed) New Horizons in Linguistics. Penguin, Harmondsworth, pp 140–165

Henderson DA and Card S (1986) Rooms: the use of multiple virtual workspaces to reduce space contention in a windows-based graphical user interface. ACM Transactions on Graphics 5(3): 211–243

Hendrix GG, Sacerdoti ED, Sagalowicz D and Slocum J (1978) Developing a natural language interface to complex data. ACM Transactions on Database Systems 3: 105–147

Hjelmslev L (1961) Prolegomena to a Theory of Language. University of Wisconsin, Madison
Hoare CAR (1985) Communicating Sequential Processes. Prentice-Hall, Englewood Cliffs, New Jersey
Hollan J and Stornetta S (1992) Beyond being there. In: Proceedings of the Human Factors in Computing Systems Conference, CHI-92. ACM, New York, pp 119–125
Husband RW (1940) Cooperation versus solitary problem solution. Journal of Social Psychology 11: 405–409
Jackson P (1990) Introduction to Expert Systems, 2nd edn. Addison-Wesley, Wokingham
Jakobson R (1960) Linguistics and poetics. In: Sebeok T (ed) Style in Language. MIT Press, Cambridge, MA, pp 350–377
Jennings D (1991) Subjectivity and Intersubjectivity in Human–Computer Interaction. PAVIC Publications, Sheffield Hallam University, Sheffield
Jennings F, Benyon DR and Murray DM (1991) Adapting systems to individual differences in cognitive style. Acta Psychologica 78(1–3): 243–256
Kass R and Finin T (1988) Modeling the user in natural language systems. Computational Linguistics 14(3): 3–22
Kay A (1984) Computer software. Scientific American 251(3): 41–47
Kay A (1990) User interface: a personal view. In: Laurel B (ed) The Art of Human–Computer Interface Design. Addison-Wesley, Reading, MA, pp 191–207
Kearney PJ, Sehmi A and Smith RM (1991) Support for multi-agent systems. Sharp Laboratories, Oxford
Kearsley G (1988) Online Help Systems: Design and Implementation. Ablex, Norwood, NJ
Kirn S (1991) Cooperation ability of intelligent agents in federative environments. PhD thesis, University of Hagen, Germany
Kirn S (1992) Cooperative systems in open environments – what do they know and what are they able to do? International Journal of Intelligent and Cooperative Information Systems 1(3)
Kirn S and Schlageter G (1991) Competence evaluation in federative problem solving – how to make expert systems cooperative. In: Proceedings of the 11th International Workshop on Expert Systems and their Applications, Specialized Conference on 2nd Generation Expert Systems, Avignon, France, 28–31 May, EC2, Nanterre, pp 95–108
Kirn S and Schlageter G (1992) Coordinating autonomous problem solvers: the two dimensions of nested negotiations. In: Vogt F (ed) Information Processing 92. Proceedings of the 12th World Computer Congress, Madrid, Spain, 7–11 September, vol III: Intelligent Systems and Personal Computers. North-Holland, Amsterdam, pp 150–156
Klein M (1990) Towards conflict resolution in cooperative design systems. In: Proceedings of the 10th International Workshop on Distributed AI, Bandera, Texas, 23–27 October. MCC Technical Report ACT-AI-355-90, Austin, Texas
Klein M, Lu SC-Y, Baskin AB and Stepp RE (1989) Towards a theory of conflict resolution in cooperative design. In: Proceedings of the 9th International Workshop on Distributed AI, Rosario Resort, Eastsound, Washington, pp 329–350
Kobsa A (1988) User models and discourse models: united they stand. . . . Computational Linguistics 14: 91–94
Koo R (1989) A model for electronic documents. ACM SIGOIS Bulletin 10(1): 23–33
Laszlo E (1969) System, Structure and Experience. Gordon and Breach, London
Laughlin PR, McGlynn RP, Anderson JA and Jacobson ES (1968) Concept attainment by individuals versus cooperative pairs as a function of memory, sex and concept rule. Journal of Personality and Social Psychology 8: 410–417
Laurel B (1990) Interface agents: metaphors with character. In: Laurel B (ed) The Art of Human–Computer Interface Design. Addison-Wesley, Reading, MA, pp 355–365
Laurel B (1991) Computer as Theatre: A Dramatic Theory of Interactive Experience. Addison-Wesley, Reading, MA
Laurel B, Oren T and Don A (1990) Issues in multimedia interface design: media integration and interface agents. In: Chew JC and Whiteside J (ed) Proceedings of the Human Factors in Computing Systems Conference, CHI-90, Empowering People. ACM, New York, pp 133–139
Lenat D and Guha RV (1990) Building Large Knowledge Based Systems: Representation and Inference in the CYC project. Addison-Wesley, Reading, MA
Linderholm O (1992) HP's desktop and application integration solution for Windows. Byte 17: 62

Loveday L (1983) Rhetoric patterns in conflict: the sociocultural relativity of discourse-organising processes. Journal of Pragmatics 7: 169–190
Lyons J (1977) Semantics. Cambridge University Press, Cambridge
Lyytinen KJ and Ngwenyama OK (1994) What does computer support for cooperative work mean? A structurational analysis of computer supported cooperative work. Accounting, Management and Information Technology, in press
MacKay DM (1969) Information, Mechanism and Meaning. MIT Press, Cambridge, MA
MacLean A, Carter K, Moran T and Lovstrand L (1990) User-tailorable systems: pressing the issue with buttons. In: Chew JC and Whiteside J (ed) Proceedings of the Human Factors in Computing Systems Conference, CHI-90, Empowering People. ACM, New York, pp 175–182
Malone TW (1987) Modeling coordination in organizations and markets. Management Science 33(10): 1317–1332
Malone TW and Crowston K (1990) What is coordination theory and how can it help design cooperative work systems? In: Tatar DG (ed) Proceedings of the 3rd Conference on Computer Supported Cooperative Work (CSCW-90), Los Angeles, CA, 7–10 October. ACM, New York, pp 357–370
Malone TW, Grant KR and Turbak FA (1986) The Information Lens: an intelligent system for information sharing in organisations. In: Mantei M and Orbeton P (ed) Proceedings of the Human Factors in Computing Systems Conference, CHI-86. ACM, New York, pp 1–8
Manheim ML (1989) Issues in the design of a symbiotic DSS. In: Blanning R and King D (ed) Proceedings of the 22nd Hawaiian International Conference on Systems Sciences, vol III. IEEE Computer Science Press, Washington, DC, pp 14–23
Manheim ML, Srivastava S, Vlahos N and Tseng C (1991) Working with an intelligent assistant: experiments with a symbiotic DSS for production planning and scheduling. In: Milner R (ed) Communication and Concurrency. Prentice-Hall, London, pp 386–395
Mantei M (1988) Capturing the Capture Lab concepts: a case study in the design of computer supported meeting environments. In: Proceedings of the Conference on Computer Supported Cooperative Work (CSCW-88), Portland, OR, September. ACM, New York, pp 257–270
Marwell G and Schmitt DR (1975) Cooperation: An Experimental Analysis. Academic Press, London
Mason MV and Thomas RC (1984) Experimental adaptive interface. Information Technology, Research, Design, Applications 3(3): 162–167
McCarthy J (1959) Programs with common sense. In: Sutherland GBBM (ed) Proceedings of the Teddington Conference on the Mechanisation of Thought Processes. HMSO, London, pp 77–84
McCarthy J (1990) Elephant 2000: a programming language based on speech acts (available from MIT)
McGrath JE (1984) Groups, Interaction and Performance. Prentice-Hall, Englewood Cliffs, New Jersey
McGrath JE (1990) Time matters in groups. In: Galegher J, Kraut RE and Egido C (ed) Intellectual Teamwork: The Social and Technological Foundations of Cooperative Work. Lawrence Erlbaum, Hillsdale, NJ
Milner R (1980) A Calculus of Communicating Systems. Springer-Verlag, New York (Lecture Notes in Computer Science)
Milner R (1991) Communication and Concurrency. Prentice-Hall, London
Minsky M (1987) The Society of Mind. Heinemann, London
Morik K (1989) User models and conversational settings: modelling the user's wants. In: Kobsa A and Wahlster W (ed) User Models in Dialog Systems. Springer-Verlag, Berlin, pp 364–385
Nagl M (1978) A Tutorial and Bibliographic Survey on Graph Grammars. Springer-Verlag, New York (Lecture Notes in Computer Science)
Nardi BA and Miller JR (1991) Twinkling lights and nested loops: distributed problem solving and spreadsheet development. International Journal of Man–Machine Studies 34: 161–184
Neal JG and Shapiro SC (1991) Intelligent multi-media interface technology. In: Sullivan JW and Tyler SW (ed) Intelligent User Interfaces. ACM Press, New York, pp 11–43
Nelson TH (1990) Literary Machines. Mindful Press, Sausalito

Nielsen J (ed) (1990a) Designing User Interfaces for International Use. Elsevier, Amsterdam

Nielsen J (1990b) Usability testing of international interfaces. In: Nielsen J (ed) Designing User Interfaces for International Use. Elsevier, Amsterdam, pp 39–44

Nirenburg S (ed) (1987) Machine Translation: Theoretical and Methodological Issues. Cambridge University Press, Cambridge

Norcio AF and Stanley J (1989) Adaptive human–computer interfaces: a literature survey and perspective. IEEE Transactions on Systems, Man and Cybernetics 19: 399–408

Norman DA (1988) The Design of Everyday Things. Basic Books, New York

Norman DA (1991) Collaborative computing: collaboration first, computing second. Communications of the ACM 34(12): 88–90

Numaoka C (1990) A conceptual framework for modeling conversation in open distributed systems. PhD thesis, Keio University

Numaoka C and Tokoro M (1990) Conversation among situated agents. In: Proceedings of the 10th International Workshop on Distributed AI, Bandera, Texas, 23–27 October. MCC Technical Report ACT-AI-355-90, Austin, Texas, Chapter 13

Nunamaker JF, Applegate LM and Konsyuski BR (1988) Computer aided deliberation: model management and group decision support. Operation Research 36(6): 826–847

Oosthuizen GD (1988) The use of a lattice in knowledge processing. PhD thesis, Department of Computer Science, University of Strathclyde

Oosthuizen GD and McGregor DR (1988) Induction through knowledge base normalisation. In: Kodratoff K (ed) Proceedings of European Conference on Artificial Intelligence, Munich. Pitman, London, pp 396–401

Oren T, Salomon G, Kreitman K and Don A (1990) Guides: characterizing the interface. In: Laurel B (ed) The Art of Human–Computer Interface Design. Addison-Wesley, Reading, MA, pp 367–381

Ossner J (1990) Transnational symbols: the rule of pictograms and models in the learning process. In: Nielsen J (ed) Designing User Interfaces for International Use. Elsevier, Amsterdam, pp 11–38

Pankoke-Babatz U (ed) (1989) Computer Based Group Communication – The AMIGO Activity Model. Ellis Horwood, Chichester

Parunak HvD (1990) Toward a formal model of interagent control. In: Proceedings of the 10th International Workshop on Distributed AI, Bandera, Texas, 23–27 October. MCC Technical Report ACT-AI-355-90, Austin, Texas, Chapter 11

Pattison HE, Corkill CG and Lesser VR (1987) Instantiating descriptions of organizational structures. In: Huhns M (ed) Distributed Artificial Intelligence. Pitman/Morgan Kaufmann, San Mateo, CA, pp 59–96

Payton DW (1991) Internalized plans: a representation for action resources. In: Maes P (ed) Designing Autonomous Agents. MIT Press, Cambridge, MA, pp 89–104

Peat HJ and Willet P (1991) The limitations of term co-occurrence data for query expansion in document retrieval systems. Journal of the American Society for Information Science 42(5): 378–383

Preston AM (1991) The "problem" in and of management information systems. Accounting, Management and Information Technology 1(1): 43–69

Rada R and Martin BK (1987) Augmenting thesauri for information systems. ACM Transactions on Office Information Systems 5(4): 378–392

Rapaport M (1991) Computer Mediated Communications. Wiley, New York

Rasmussen J (1986) Information Processing and Human–Machine Interaction. North-Holland, Amsterdam

Reisman K (1989) Contrapuntal conversations in an Antiguan village. In: Bauman R and Sherzer J (ed) Explorations in the Ethnography of Speaking, 2nd edn. Cambridge University Press, Cambridge, pp 110–124

Rissland EL (1984) Ingredients of intelligent user interfaces. International Journal of Man–Machine Studies 21: 377–388

Robinson M (1991) Double-level languages and cooperative working. AI and Society 5: 34–60

Rodden T (1990) Supporting cooperation in software engineering environments. PhD thesis, Department of Computing, Lancaster University

Rodden T and Sommerville I (1991) Building conversations using mailtrays. In: Bowers JM and Benford SD (ed) Studies in Computer Supported Cooperative Work. North-Holland, Amsterdam, pp 159–172

Rumelhart DE and McClelland JL (1986) Parallel Distributed Processing: Explorations in the Microstructure of Cognition, vol 1: Foundations. MIT Press, Cambridge, MA
Saville-Troike M (1989) The Ethnography of Communication: An Introduction, 2nd edn. Blackwell, Oxford
Schmidt K (1991) Analysis of cooperative work – a conceptual framework. Technical Report, Cognitive Systems Group, Roskilde, Denmark
Schmidt K and Bannon L (1992) Taking CSCW seriously: supporting articulation work. Computer Supported Cooperative Work 1(1–2): 7–40
Schuster E (1988) Establishing the relationship between discourse models and user models. Computational Linguistics 14: 82–85
Selfridge OG (1959) Pandemonium: a paradigm for learning. In: Proceedings of the Teddington Conference on the Mechanisation of Thought Processes. HMSO, London, pp 513–526
Shannon CE and Weaver W (1949) The Mathematical Theory of Communication. University of Illinois Press, Illinois
Shaw MJ, Harrow B and Herman S (1991) Distributed artificial intelligence for multi-agent problem solving and group learning. In: Nunamaker JF (ed) Proceedings of the 24th Hawaiian International Conference on Systems Sciences, vol III. IEEE Computer Society Press, Washington, DC, pp 13–26
Sherif M and Sherif CW (1953) Groups in Harmony and Tension. Harper and Row, New York
Sheth AP and Larson JA (1990) Federated database systems for managing distributed, heterogeneous and autonomous databases. ACM Computing Surveys 22(3): 183–236 (Bellcore Technical Report TM-STS-016302, Piscataway, NJ)
Shoham Y (1990) Agent-orientated programming. Stanford University Technical Report, STAN-CS-1335-90, Stanford University, CA
Shure GH, Meeker LJ and Hansford EA (1965) The effectiveness of pacifist strategies in bargaining games. Journal of Conflict Resolution 9: 106–117
Singh M (1990) Group Intentions. In: Proceedings of the 10th International Workshop on Distributed AI, Bandera, Texas, 23–27 October. MCC Technical Report ACT-AI-355-90, Austin, Texas, Chapter 12
Smith JB, Weiss SF, Ferguson GF, Bolter JD, Lansman M and Beard DV (1986) WE: a writing environment for professionals. Technical Report 86-025, Department of Computer Science, University of North Carolina at Chapel Hill (also published in Proceedings of the National Computer Conference, 1987. AFIPS Press, Reston, VA, pp 725–736)
Smith R (1980) The contract net protocol: high-level communication and control in a distributed problem solver. IEEE Transactions on Computers 29(12): 1104–1113
Smyth M and Clarke AA (1990) Human–human cooperation and the design of cooperative machines. ICL Technical Journal 7(1): 110–127
Sprung RC (1990) Two faces of America: polyglot and tongue-tied. In: Nielsen J (ed) Designing User Interfaces for International Use. Elsevier, Amsterdam, pp 71–102
Stamper R (1973) Information. Batsford, London
Star SL (1989) The structure of ill-structured solutions: boundary objects and heterogeneous distributed problem solving. In: Gasser L and Hughes MN (ed) Distributed Artificial Intelligence, vol 2. Pitman, London, pp 37–56
Stefik M, Foster G, Bobrow DG, Kahn K, Lanning S and Suchman LA (1987) Beyond the chalkboard: computer support for collaboration and problem solving in meetings. Communications of the ACM 30(1): 32–47
Storrs G (1989) A conceptual model of human–computer interaction? Behaviour and Information Technology 8: 323–334
Sturrock J (1986) Structuralism. Paladin, London
Suchman LA (1987) Plans and Situated Actions: The Problem of Human–Machine Communication. Cambridge University Press, Cambridge
Sukaviriya P and Moran L (1990) User Interfaces for Asia. In: Nielsen J (ed) Designing User Interfaces for International Use. Elsevier, Amsterdam, pp 189–218
Sullivan JW and Tyler SW (ed) (1991) Intelligent User Interfaces. ACM Press, New York
Sutcliffe A (1988) Human–Computer Interface Design. Macmillan, Basingstoke
Tappert CC, Suen CY and Wakahara T (1990) The state of the art in on-line handwriting recognition. IEEE Transactions on Pattern and Machine Intelligence 12: 787–808

Taylor A, Hardy V and Weaver J (1988) The DHSS Local Office Demonstrator: a systemic approach to organisational and human issues in knowledge based systems design. In: Joint ICL and Ergonomics Society Conference on Human and Organisational Issues of Expert Systems, May
Taylor D (1990) Creating international applications: a hands-on approach using the Hewlett-Packard NLS package. In: Nielsen J (ed) Designing User Interfaces for International Use. Elsevier, Amsterdam, pp 123–158
Thimbleby H (1986) The design of two innovative user interfaces. In: Harrison MD and Monk AF (ed) People and Computers: Designing for Usability. Proceedings of the HCI '86 Conference. Cambridge University Press, Cambridge, pp 336–351
Thimbleby H (1990) User Interface Design. ACM Press, New York
Thompson G, Frances J, Levacic R and Mitchell J (1991) Markets, Hierarchies and Networks. Sage, London
Took R (1990) Surface interaction: a paradigm and model for separating application and interface. In: Chew JC and Whiteside J (ed) Proceedings of the Human Factors in Computing Systems Conference, CHI-90, Empowering People. ACM, New York, pp 35–42
Toulmin SE (1958) The Uses of Argument. Cambridge University Press, Cambridge
Tsrichritzis DC and Lochovsky FH (1982) Data Models. Prentice-Hall, Englewood Cliffs, New Jersey
Tucker AB (1987) Current strategies in machine translation research and development. In: Nirenburg S (ed) Machine Translation: Theoretical and Methodological Issues. Cambridge University Press, Cambridge, pp 22–41
van Rijsbergen CJ (1979) Information Retrieval, 2nd edn. Butterworth, London
Vickers G (1981) The poverty of problem-solving. Journal of Applied Systems Analysis 8: 15–21
Viller S (1991) The Group Facilitator: a CSCW perspective. In: Bannon L, Robinson M and Schmidt K (ed) Proceedings of the Second European Conference on Computer-Supported Cooperative Work (EC-CSCW '91), Amsterdam, September. Kluwer, Dordrecht, pp 81–95
Wahlster W (1991) User and discourse models for multimodal communication. In: Sullivan JW and Tyler SW (ed) Intelligent User Interfaces. ACM Press, New York, pp 45–67
Wahlster W and Kobsa A (1989) User models in dialog systems. In: Kobsa A and Wahlster W (ed) User Models in Dialog Systems. Springer-Verlag, Berlin, pp 4–34
Waterman DA (1978) A rule-based approach to knowledge acquisition for man–machine interaction. International Journal of Man–Machine Studies 10: 693–711
Welch TA (1984) A technique for high performance data compression. Computer 17(6): 8–19
Wiederhold G (1989) Partitioning and composing of knowledge. Technical Report, Stanford University
Wilson P (1991) Computer Supported Cooperative Work. Intellect, Oxford
Winograd T and Flores F (1987) Understanding Computers and Cognition: A New Foundation for Design. Ablex, Norwood, NJ
Witten IH (1982) Principles of Computer Speech. Academic Press, London
Witten IH (1986) Making Computers Talk: An Introduction to Speech Synthesis. Prentice-Hall, Englewood Cliffs, New Jersey
Woolgar S (1985) Why not a sociology of machines? The case of sociology and artificial intelligence. Sociology 19: 557–572
Woolgar S (1989) Representation, cognition, self. In: Fuller S, de Mey M and Woolgar S (ed) The Cognitive Turn: Sociological and Psychological Perspectives in the Study of Science. Kluwer, Dordrecht, pp 201–223
Zobel-Pocock RA (1990) International user interfaces. In: Nielsen J (ed) Designing User Interfaces for International Use. Elsevier, Amsterdam, pp 219–227

Subject Index

Name Index